How acts of kindness can enrich our lives

The Hesed Boomerang

Bais Yaakov of Queens Anniversary Dinner
Celebrating 40 Years

Motzei Shabbos, March 13, 1999

לזכר נשמת
אסתר בת ר׳ יחיאל ע״ה

The Hesed

How acts of kindness
can enrich our lives

Boomerang

By Jack Doueck

YAGDIYL TORAH PUBLICATIONS, INC.

Edited by Rabbi Michael Haber
Design by Deenee Cohen
Typography by Meira Hochster
Permissions by Laurie Sheppard
Typing of Original Manuscript by Toni Siporin Drucker/Sara Sultan
Cover Photograph by Susan Menashe

Published by Yagdiyl Torah Publications, Inc.
P.O. Box 427
Deal, New Jersey 07723

PRINTED IN THE UNITED STATES OF AMERICA

In Honor of Our Parents

Shirley and Morris Sutton

who have truly exemplified
Hesed throughout their lives

By their children

Jessie and Lottie Sutton

Joseph and Laurie Sutton

Adam Sutton

Sarah Sutton

Table of Contents

Acknowledgments 11

Introduction: What is the Hesed Boomerang? 15

Prologue: What Difference Do I Make? 21

Part One: How Hesed Can Enrich Our Lives 27

Chapter 1: The Physical Impact of Hesed 29
The Mountain Climber / Hesed and the Immune System /
Hesed And Longevity / Hesed And Energy

Chapter 2: The Psychological Impact of Hesed 32
Hesed and Stress Reduction /Hesed and Depression / Skeptical?

Chapter 3: Hesed as a Healthy Response to Suffering 36
Kadima / "I Know Their Pain" / Arthur's Mom / M.A.D.D. /
The Waxmans / Summary

Chapter 4: The Liberating Effect of Giving 43
"Why am I Speaking?"/ Yearning to Give /Last Piece of Bread

Chapter 5: Hesed and Longevity 47
Hesed at One Hundred / Two Hundred Pints

Chapter 6: Hesed is Forever 49
A Good Man Can Never Die / In Our Daughter's Eyes

Chapter 7: Are We Giving – Or Receiving? 53
Camp Simcha / Our Lives - Their Lives / Look Up At The
Stars / The Strength Inside / Lessons / The Need To Give

Chapter 8: Two Visits 59
"Today I Have Hope" / "In Life, My Children, In Life"

Summary of Part One: The Natural Paradox 66

Part Two: Standing Up and Speaking Out 69

Chapter 9: When Will We Wake Up? 71

Chapter 10: The Power Not To See 74

Chapter 11: "I Went Back to Bed" 78

Chapter 12: The Cursed Earth 81

Chapter 13: Outrage 83

Chapter 14: Abraham's Response to the Suffering of Others 88
His "Brother" / "Shall The Judge of the Earth Not Act Justly?" / How Do We Respond? / The "Children of Abraham" / Learning From His Own Pain / "Wait Until I Unload My Mules" / "What Has Become of Our Humanity?"

Chapter 15: A Seasoned Hesed Professional 99

Chapter 16: Why Moshe? 101

Chapter 17: The Choice is Ours 105

Summary of Part Two 108

Part Three: Everyday Kindness 109

Chapter 18: Everyday Kindness 111
48 Hours / "I'm Just a Regular Guy" / Hesed in the Little Things / Five Kind Words / Three-Step Hesed Technique / 42 Ideas For Everyday Kindness / New York Cares / The Hesed Boomerang Principle / Dollar for Dollar / Flat Tire / "We'll Take Turns" / Hesed Goal-Setting / The Daily Hesed Practice Chart

Chapter 19: Taking Notice of Others 128
When Does the Day Begin? / The Chafetz Chayim and A Cold Child / Sugar Frosted Flakes / Birthday Girl / Joel's Day / Taking Notice and Taking Action / "If This Were My Mother"

Chapter 20: Smile and Watch the World Smile Back 139
From the Outside In / Smile When You Awake / Smile When You Greet Someone / The Value of a Smile / Good Morning. Herr Mueller / Smiling For Life / "I am Sure He is Still in There"

Chapter 21: Hesed With Our Speech 148
Helping the "Poor" / Teaching People / Calming People. Creat-

ing Peace and Love / Preventing Harm / Motivating to do Hesed is Hesed Too /Good Advice / Fundraising/ Praying for Others / Reassure the Poor with Words / Hesed and Persistence in Keeping Your Promises / The Hesed Boomerang Principle / A Kind Word Can Save A Life

Part Four: Dimensions Of Hesed **157**

Introduction to Part Four: The World is Built on Hesed ..159

Chapter 22: Charity **162**
Charity and the Hesed Boomerang Principle / "Test Me!"/ The Prayers of the Charitable / Whose Money is it? / The Power of Charity / The Charity of Doctors /The Money We Take With Us/ The Promises of Jewish Tradition / Indirect Hesed/ Charity with an Ulterior Motive/ The Effort of Charity/ Even the Poor Must Give / The Eight Levels of Charity / The Eternal Investment / The Hesed Trust Fund / "Real Estate" / The Curses of Apathy / A Good Name/ The Nobel Prize / A Higher Standard for Ourselves / She Opened the World for Others, and Now the World has Opened for Her

Chapter 23: Hospitality **178**
"And Abraham Ran..." / Amon and Moav / Hospitality? / The Antithesis / A Hospitality 'How–To' / Bloodshed / The Hesed Boomerang Principle / Abraham's Hospitality Boomangs Back To His Descendants

Chapter 24: Visiting the Sick **187**
A Visit / The Hesed Boomerang Principle / A Bikur Holim Primer / "I Am Not What You See" / Contract On His Life

Chapter 25: Feeding the Hungry........................**199**
Two Dreams / Why Rebecca? / Mazon / Feed the Children / Trevor's Gang / Leftovers / "Gleaners" / Donate. Don't Dump/ The Ten Dollar Fine/ "How Can I Not Sigh?"/The Hesed Boomerang Principle/ With Your Own Hands/The Antithesis/ Rabbi Yehezkel Landau: The Rewards of Feeding the Hungry

Chapter 26: And Hesed For All **215**
Hesed is Plural / The Stork / Hesed For the Elderly / Hesed To The Dead and Comfort To The Mourners / Hesed by Rejoicing With the Bride and Groom / "You Make a Difference to Me" / Lost At Sea / Should I Get Involved? / Just One Life

Chapter 27: Hesed by All People **228**
Hesed by Children / "Give" / Hesed by Prisoners

Epilogue **233**
Walking in His Ways / God's Image / God 'Cries' When We
Suffer / The Man Of Hesed / A God Who Cares

Appendix: Hesed and the Jewish Holidays **239**

Chapter 28: Hesed and the Jewish Holidays **241**

Chapter 29: Days of Awe **244**
"Is This the Fast that I have Chosen?" / Asking for Hesed –
Performing Hesed / "Forgive Me" / Hesed Opportunities on
the Days of Awe / "I Know How They Feel"

Chapter 30: Hesed and the Shalosh Regalim:
Passover, Shavuot and Succot **250**
The Book of Ruth: Going The Extra Mile / The Word Hesed
As A Hidden Structure For Ruth / The Book of Ruth and the
Hesed Boomerang / See How God's Hidden Providence Re-
wards Acts of Hesed / Ruth And Shavuot / Hesed Opportuni-
ties On The Shalosh Regalim

Chapter 31: Hesed and Tu Bishvat **259**
Readings / Sheheheyanu / Hesed Opportunities On Tu Bishvat

Chapter 32: Hesed and Purim **262**
The Book of Esther: Summary / Hesed Opportunities On Purim

Chapter 33: Hesed and Tisha Be-av **268**
History / My Beloved Knocks at the Door / Baseless Hatred /
Baseless Hatred in Action / The Letter of the Law / "Where
Are You?" / The Holy Temple / Two Brothers On The Hill /
Hesed is God's First Priority / Hesed Opportunities On Tisha
Be-av

Chapter 34: Hesed and Hanukah **279**
Judaism's Triumph and Contribution to Society / Our Mission /
Hesed Opportunities on Hanukah

Torah Publications Cited in this Book **291**
For Further Study **293**
About the Author **301**

Acknowledgments

It is with great humility and gratitude to God that I present this book to you. I thank God for giving me the strength and the courage to research and write this.

Mr. Morris Sutton and his wonderful son Jessie M. Sutton have undertaken the financial responsibility of publishing this book through their foundation. As would be expected with a book about *hesed*, this is a non-profit project and we have committed all proceeds to charity. The Sutton family's generous and unwavering commitment to kindness is a shining example of the principles described in this book.

I want to thank Mr. and Mrs. Abe M. Cohen and family. Without their encouragement and confidence in me, this book would never have come to fruition. The cost of most of the initial typing was absorbed by the Cohens. Thank you.

Special thanks goes to my Rabbi, Rabbi Dr. Raymond Harari. Your guidance and friendship for the past fifteen years helped mold my thinking, strengthen my commitment and focus my goals. Your help with this book was invaluable and just another example of your unselfish dedication to Torah and *hesed*. Thanks again and "tizkeh lemitzvot".

To Rabbi Michael Haber, it has been my good fortune to have you edit and publish this book. Without you, this book would not have been a reality. You embraced the project from the beginning. Your encouragement and dedication to its completion was an inspiration to me and will serve me well in other endeavors that I pursue. Thanks for the late nights spent poring over the sources. May you continue to write, edit and publish books that enrich the lives of others.

In publishing this book, Yagdiyl Torah Publications has provided us with expert individuals to fill our needs.

Deenee Cohen has greatly enhanced the appearance of the book by her exceptional design of the cover layout and book format.

Meira Hochster's word processing was not made easier by the seemingly endless revisions we made — but the end result was still superb.

Laurie Sheppard tackled copyright approvals and permissions in a very determined, professional manner.

Toni Siporin Drucker and Sara Sultan had the patience to type the manuscript of this book. Working with Toni and Sara was a blessing I'll never understand how I deserved.

The photograph on the cover of this book was taken by Susan Menashe. Susan is a professional, an artist, and a wonderful human being. Thank you Susan.

The woman in one of the cover photos of this book is Virginia Sultan, my grandmother. She is depicted as being helped by Robin Falack. This was obviously staged. In reality, my grandmother does not need help crossing the street. In fact, she is always the one to help others, and has always inspired me with the kindness that she practices. She has been my paradigm of the "Hesed Boomerang" theory. Her acts of *hesed* for others give her the energy and joy and passion for life. Grama, I thank you and will love you forever.

My students, who have attended my classes and seminars over the last ten years, have always shown so much interest and enthusiasm in this material. I have truly learned more from you, my students, than from anyone else.

A note of thanks to the following organizations that I am so proud to have been a part of. The members of these committees have inspired me to volunteer my time and speak publicly on their behalf. These include: Sephardic Bikur Holim, Magen David Yeshiva, Bnei Shaare Zion, Just One Life, Hatzoloh of Flatbush, The Jerusalem Center for Research, National Children's Lukemia Foundation, Ride for Freedom, Count Me In For Children With Down Syndrome, Tzivos Hashem, American Friends of Olom Hachesed, The Sephardic Educational Center, Ozar Hatorah, Amnesty International, CitiHarverst and Feed the Children.

To my parents, Haskell and Annette Doueck: Your never-ending love has sustained me. Your encouragement has given me hope. Your enthusiasm about my work and your confidence in my dreams have given me the strength and determination to persevere. You have always believed in me and you took pride in my accomplishments. I am (and always have been) very fortunate to have you as parents. Thank you.

To my children: Hal, Annette, Ezra and Roberta: May God bless you with a life full of love, peace, health and happiness. Most of what is written in this book is written for you. Our Friday night bedtime storytelling custom has blossomed into the book you are holding in your hands. I hope what you read here will be no surprise. You have heard this stuff from me over and over each and every week of your whole lives. This book would never exist without you and your unending love.

Finally, to my loving wife Jamie: Thank you for putting up with me for the past eleven years. While I was writing about *hesed*, you were busy taking care of our children, cooking food for poor people, hosting guests, organizing buses to take senior citizens shopping, visiting the sick, consoling the sad and helping and enriching the lives of everyone around you (including me, of course). This book was written in my "spare time." That means Jamie had to do the real work, the real *hesed*, while I wrote and taught about it. I will always love you and I thank you for your confidence in me, your incredible patience, your warm smile and your love.

If the writing of this book was an act of *hesed*, then this *hesed* has already "boomeranged back" to me in many, many ways.

This book is dedicated to the memory of my friend, Joseph D. Beyda. His passing has left a void in the lives of all who knew him and whose life he touched. He will be remembered for his abundant generosity with both money and time in the pursuit of helping the troubled and the needy. His ready ear and warm heart were a great solace to hundreds of people throughout the world. His wonderful children will remember him for his unconditional love for them and his total acceptance of their need and desire to have them reach their full potential. His faith and trust in people will be remembered forever and will fill their hearts with happiness, not sadness, as they remember his life. He leaves behind a legacy of laughter, good works, friends and family that will cherish his good works forever.

We miss you, Joe and we will never forget you.

Introduction

WHAT IS THE HESED BOOMERANG?

In April of 1995, I bought my first boomerang. It was manufactured in Australia. A boomerang is just a curved piece of wood that is hand-made. In ancient times it was used as a weapon. Today, people in Australia play with it just as Americans would play with a "Frisbee". A week later I took it to the park and tried it.

After a little practice, I was able to throw the boomerang into the air at a certain angle (about 2 o'clock, the wind blowing at 12 o'clock) and it took off about 200 feet, went completely around and came back to me! It was just amazing. This curved little piece of wood was designed with the aerodynamics to do a very cute trick. The more I practiced throwing and angling the boomerang, the further and further I was able to send it and have it return. This Australian-created toy really took skill, it took patience and practice. It was a lot of fun.

The next day I was giving a class in Lenox Hill Hospital to a group of volunteers. These volunteers would visit the sick in the hospital for about an hour and then they would attend a Torah class for another hour-and-a-half.

The topic of my class was The Power Of *Hesed*. I wanted to give an inspiring lecture on the importance of visiting the sick. I spoke about how to visit sick or elderly people. I talked about the sources and texts in Jewish tradition that emphasize *bikur holim* (visiting the sick) and how many of them promise rewards to the volunteer (or the *ba-al hesed*).

I told the group of about twenty-five adults a few true stories that I hoped would encourage them to continue their acts of *hesed*, of loving-kindness. Somewhere in the class, somehow, the idea expressed was that *hesed* doesn't only enrich the lives of the people we do it for. Acts of *hesed* enrich the lives of the "doers" as well. What surfaced was the old theory of "*what goes around comes around.*" The volunteers spoke about their *hesed* experiences and how these experiences changed them and helped them and gave them new perspectives, new contacts, new hobbies, new friends and more enriched and meaningful lives.

Then it hit me. Someone said: "It's just like a boomerang!" I told them that the day before, I spent some time in the park with my kids playing with this new handmade boomerang that I had bought from this Australian company. The idea hit *me* like a Boomerang. "*Hesed* boomerangs back to you! What you give is what you get!"

Now, for some reason, the word boomerang, when used as a verb, ("I'm afraid it will boomerang") today has a negative connotation. In this book, however, we are using the word positively. When we write, *hesed boomerangs back*, we mean that it comes back to repay you.

In any case, our hypothesis is by no means scientific. I do not know of anybody who has any statistics on the personal consequences of doing *hesed*. Can we say with any certainty that we always get rewarded (in this world) for altruism? To be sure, it is unscientific.

Some of the greatest *ba-alei hesed* (doers of loving-kindness) had suffered a great deal in their lives. Some of the greatest of our

Rabbis and Sages did incredible acts of charity and suffered severe illnesses and diseases.

So, is it always true that *hesed*, by definition, boomerangs back to us? Can it be proven? Of course, the answer is "no".

If we look deeper into our psyche, our spirit, the positive consequences of acts of altruism are as innumerable, as they are personal and subjective. Very often it does seem that in some perhaps magical, paradoxical way, the *hesed* we do returns to us — it boomerangs back.

As we will see, according to Jewish tradition, acts of *hesed* do not go unrewarded. As we will see, when we take notice of the details in our lives, we often find that our *hesed* boomerangs back in many different personal ways.

The purpose of this book is to provide encouragement and inspiration for all those looking to enrich their lives with acts of Hesed.

This book is divided into four parts.

Part One, entitled "How *Hesed* Can Enrich Our Lives", deals with the importance of *hesed*. It describes why loving-kindness is a basic component of our true purpose in life, and how compassionate behavior tends to "boomerang back" to us in many ways.

Part Two is called "Standing Up and Speaking Out". This part emphasizes the importance of fighting apathy. It warns us about the apathy that permeates our society. This part was written to inspire and encourage people to make a decision to not "stand idly by", but to help the world become a better place to live in.

Part Three, "Everyday Kindness," provides real-life examples of people who practice *hesed*.

Part Four, "Dimensions of *Hesed*" is divided into categories, such as hospitality, visiting the sick, feeding the hungry, etc.

These last two parts, three and four, provide the reader with a practical *Hesed* Manual. In these sections, we list types of *hesed* the reader can perform, and we provide inspiring case histories of people who have done so.

I have attempted to include very practical information that can be used on a daily basis, such as a list of 42 ideas for simple, "everyday kindness". I have compiled a list of what I have called "42 rules of *bikur holim*", which will help people in their visits to the sick. Also included is a sample "Daily *Hesed* Chart" to help in your "*Hesed* Training".

These parts are replete with sources in Jewish tradition that promise reward for acts of *hesed*. From the Torah, the prophets, the holy writings and through the oral tradition, there are important statements and inspiring anecdotes about the powerful effect of *hesed*.

The appendix to this book is "*Hesed* and the Jewish Holidays". Every Jewish holiday provides us with unique and exciting opportunities for *hesed*. This section reviews the Jewish holidays and describes their themes, special holiday prayers, customs, concepts, lessons, and opportunities for *hesed*. It is my hope that after reading the appendix, your holidays will be life-enriching experiences. You can refer to this section before each holiday to help you enjoy it and enrich it with *hesed*.

Ever since that first lecture in Lenox Hill Hospital, I have given many more classes on this topic. Over and over, people approach me to tell me their personal *hesed boomerang* stories. Most of these experiences are truly amazing. If I included half of these stories in this book it would probably be another two hundred pages. Instead, I included just a few of them. I hope these stories will jar your memory and allow you to say (as many have told me), "you know, come to think of it, I *have* got a personal *hesed boomerang* story as well!"

All of the stories in this book are true and verifiable. Many are my own personal experiences. The purpose of describing these stories and people is to instill hope and confidence that *hesed* can be created simply and it can grow enormously and enrich the lives of all those associated with it.

I would like to clarify two important points.

Firstly, I do not want to mislead the reader into thinking and expecting that every time one does an act of kindness, it automatically or instantaneously boomerangs back. Obviously, this is not the case.

Even when one knows how to look for the boomerang effect of the kindness, it sometimes feels as if it never comes.

Yet, whether or not the act of kindness boomerangs back to us, it enriches our lives, and the lives of those around us.

Secondly, nobody should practice acts of kindness *so that* one can have them boomerang back to him. The sages caution us not to do good deeds on the condition of receiving a reward.*

All in all, I have attempted to write a book that is as steeped in law, texts and tradition as it is in inspiring anecdotes, interesting descriptions of incredible personalities and practical calls for real action. *My wish is for the reader to experience this book, not merely read it and put it down.* It was written to make you laugh, to make you cry and to let you enjoy the message. Its goal is to educate through facts and informative discussion, to inspire through true stories, and to give you practical advice and How-To's to take the next steps and live its ideal.

Does *Hesed* really boomerang back? Only if you want it to.

You have already accomplished the first step: You have acquired this book and started to read it. The rest is up to you.

May it be God's will that this work will motivate people to live the true way of God, a way of *hesed* and of sincerity. May God give all its readers the strength to use its ideas, to practice its principles and to create a more loving, more sensitive, more peaceful and more compassionate world.

Prologue

What Difference Do I Make?

Prologue

WHAT DIFFERENCE DO I MAKE?

One day, as I was writing this book, I sat on the boardwalk in Long Branch, New Jersey. I watched the waves crack against the shore. I witnessed the beautiful sunset. The colors were just spectacular: pink, purple, gray, orange, blue, yellow. Just a beautiful, breathtaking sight.

Then, as I took all this beauty in, a cold chill went down my spine. This world that God created, I thought, is so powerful, so independent, so timeless. I was overwhelmed by it.

I began to think: *Eighty years from now, I won't be here. But, this sunset will. My body will be buried in the ground, but the waves will still be splashing against the shore with all of the power and vibrancy which they have today. God's nature is all around me. And, as I witness its eternal beauty, I think:*

What difference do I make?
The world will still turn without me.
Why do I exist?

What is my purpose, my role, my contribution?
How can my life possibly have meaning?
What impact can I have on the world, before I leave it?
I can't stand the thought of living a small, insignificant, mean-
ingless *life. I need to make an impact.*

Then, I remembered what I had been teaching all these years:

My acts of *hesed*, my love for others, the kindness that I show
to others can all make an impact.

If I can spend my life giving of myself to others, then I will
have made an impact. *Then, my life would have been worth living.*
Then, I would be ready to allow them to place my body beneath the
earth, and move on to another form of existence.

Right at that very moment, on the boardwalk, it all became so
simple to me: acts of loving-kindness, compassion and altruism make
my life meaningful and significant. The sun will still set with such
beauty eighty years from now, without me. But the world can be a
little more loving, a little more kind *because I lived in it.*

Many people go through life with fundamental questions reso-
nating in their minds:

How can we make our lives more meaningful?
How can we "feel good" about living?
How can we rid ourselves of our perpetual "restlessness," and
sleep easier?
How can we be certain that we live for a good reason?

The answer is one word: *hesed*. It is *loving-kindness*. It is
mercy — it is *compassion*. Hesed is *going the extra mile* for another human being. It is doing the right thing even when you don't
"have to".*

If my life is one entire statement of *compassion* and love, then
my life is worth living. To the extent, on the other hand, that I am
selfish, greedy, cruel, callous, cold, unfeeling, unconcerned or ignorant of the cruelties in the world, my life is *worthless*. In other
words, *the world could do without me.*

When does the world really need me? When do I make a real difference — alive and not dead? *When I am a contributor!* When I am a *player!* When I stand up and speak out against cruelty and intolerance. When I extend a helping hand to the needy.

Rabbi Akiva was born about 20 CE and lived for one hundred twenty years. He was a great leader of the Jewish people during a critical time in history.

Rabbi Akiva taught: the verse in the Torah (Leviticus 19:18), *You should love your friend as you love yourself* (generally known as *love thy neighbor)* is its greatest principle.

Among Rabbi Akiva's close friends and colleagues was another brilliant sage, Shimon ben Azzai.* Ben Azzai disagreed with Rabbi Akiva over what the most important principle of the Torah is. To Ben Azzai, the verse and principle was not *Love your friend as you love yourself,* it was (Genesis 5:1): *This is the book of the generations of man.*

Why? Because this verse says it all. All human beings are the children of one man – Adam. We are all related. We are all connected. What happens to one of us happens to us all. We are all one family.**

Actually, we learn from both opinions. We must treat others as we treat ourselves. And, our regard for humanity must transcend race, creed or gender. If we can truly imagine and believe that we are one big family, we might understand a little more about our purpose here in this world. Love and *hesed* are not options. They are our primary purpose for being.

The Midrash (Genesis Rabah 8:5) describes what was happening at the time God was about to create Adam. The angels, says the Midrash, lined up in groups. Many of them said: "Do not create man!" Just then, the angels representing *hesed* argued: "please, do create man, for he will practice acts of loving-kindness!" Then God immediately created Adam.

The message of this interesting Midrash is very clear. Man

was created to do good, to do *hesed*. This is a major component of our mission in life.

And so, that day on the boardwalk made me think to myself: Will my life be a statement of *compassion*, or will it be a statement of "honor" and materialism? Will I live a life which the world could do without — or will I make a difference?

Part One

How Hesed Can Enrich Our Lives

— *1* —

The Physical Impact of Hesed

THE MOUNTAIN CLIMBER

There is a story told about a traveler who was crossing mountain heights of untrodden snow. He was freezing as the fierce wind and ice blew against his face. He couldn't feel his fingers or his toes. Then the night came. He struggled bravely against the urge for sleep, which weighed down his frosty eyelids. He knew that if he fell asleep, he would freeze to death.

He lay down in the snow ready to die, not able to feel his limbs, for they were freezing. Then, he decided to fight. He stood up to give death one last bout. He decided he had to try harder. So, in pain, he started to walk against the night wind.

Just then, his foot struck against a heap lying under the snow, right in his path. He stooped down, pushed the snow aside, and found a man. This man had given up, half buried on the freezing mountain. He picked him up and started fiercely rubbing the frozen man's limbs. It was working. The man opened his eyes. So he kept up the work until the morning. He kept moving and rubbing until dawn. Then the sun rose and warmed the two men, who were now friends.

The effort to restore another to life brought back to the man warmth and energy. This *"hesed* energy" saved his own life as well. We call it the *hesed boomerang. Hesed* has a way of returning to us and enriching our lives. It warms us and keeps us from freezing to death.*

HESED AND THE IMMUNE SYSTEM

According to the research of Dr. Paul Pearsall, when a person helps other people, he experiences an immediate healthy biochemical response that enhances his immune system and strengthens him. In his words:

> *There is a real biochemical reaction in our bodies when we are altruistic. The immune system is strengthened and we actually become healthier when we reach out to assist other people. Research has shown that even the simple act of watching someone help someone else results in immediate and measurable enhancements of the immune system.*
>
> *Do something for someone today. Pay attention to how your body reacts when you help someone. You will feel actual positive changes taking place in the body. Helping someone is one of the best ways to get a super joy high.* **

HESED AND LONGEVITY

Scientists at the University of Michigan studied 2,754 people for twelve years. They interviewed them between 1967 and 1969 and followed them closely afterward.

What they found was startling (if it were a new drug it would have been hailed as a revolutionary advance in modern medicine). They discovered that men who did volunteer work at least once a week are *two-and-a-half times* as likely to remain alive during the study as men who did not do volunteer work.

The men who did less volunteer work had a 250% bett chance of dying during the twelve year period. These results we independent of the age, gender, or health status of the subjects at the time they first entered the study.*

HESED AND ENERGY

Dr. Dean Ornish has the only scientifically proven program to reverse heart disease without drugs or surgery. In his book, *Reversing Heart Disease*,** he makes a recommendation: *perform volunteer work*. He says that you not only enjoy how it makes you feel, but it "opens your heart"; it unclogs your arteries and gets the blood and oxygen flowing again.

Dr. Ornish says that acting selflessly is the most selfish way to behave, since it maintains our sense of inner peace and joy.

Furthermore, this heart surgeon tells us: "Altruism, compassion, and forgiveness — opening your heart — can be a powerful means of healing the isolation that leads to stress, suffering and illness.

"In other words, altruism, compassion and forgiveness are in our own best self-interest, for they help to free us from our limitations and to empower us".

Nowadays, many life insurance companies ask prospective clients not only if they smoke but if they do *volunteer work* on a steady basis!

— *2* —

The Psychological Impact of Hesed

HESED AND STRESS REDUCTION

Modern research has shown that doing acts of *hesed* actually affects your brain (and body) chemistry. There are hormones called endorphins that are released, which *improve your immune system*. *Hesed* helps fight depression, and anxiety. *Hesed* is an *antidote* for sadness and stress. By putting yourself out and focusing on other people, your own worries and fears are lessened. The next time you feel melancholic, sad or anxious, try doing an anonymous good deed and see how you feel.

Look at "the Biology of Stress and *Hesed*" chart. As you can see from the chart, *hesed* can create real physiological changes in your body. It can reduce your stress and help keep you healthy. *Hesed* enriches our lives in more ways than one!

THE BIOLOGY OF STRESS AND HESED	
WHEN ONE IS STRESSED	WHEN STRESS IS REDUCED BY ACTS OF HESED
SYMPATHETIC NERVOUS SYSTEM	PARASYMPATHETIC NERVOUS SYSTEM
Dilates pupils	Constricts pupils
Stimulates tear glands	Inhibits tear glands
Inhibits salivation	Increases salivation
Accelerates heart rate	Slows heart
Increases blood pressure	Decreases blood pressure
Dilates bronchi	Constricts bronchi
Decreases digestive functions of stomach, pancreas and intestines	Increases digestive functions of stomach, pancreas and intestines
Adrenaline secretion	No secretion of adrenaline
Inhibits bladder contraction	Bladder contraction
Pituitary gland secretes ACTH and TTH	No abnormal secretion of pituitary
Hormones increase cellular metabolic activity throughout the body, increase heart rate, conserve water, elevate body temperature, increase oxygen consumption	No abnormal hormonal activity
The body's immune response is inhibited.	The body's immune system is strong
The thymus and lymph nodes decrease in size.	No abnormal thymus activity

HESED AND DEPRESSION

Noted psychiatrist, Dr. Alfred Adler (author of *What Life Should Mean to You*) used to tell his patients suffering from melancholy or slight depression:

> *You can be cured in fourteen days if you follow this prescription: Try to think everyday how you can please someone.*
>
> *The most important task imposed by religion has always been 'Love thy neighbor...'.*
>
> *It is the individual who is not interested in his fellow man who has the greatest difficulties in life and provides the greatest injury to others.*
>
> *It is from among such individuals that all human failures spring...*

How many stories do you know of people who were stressed or sick or depressed and then "forgot themselves", focused on altruism, on helping others and were "rewarded" with health and happiness?

Carl Jung once said: "About one third of my patients are suffering from no clinically definable neurosis, but from the *senselessness and emptiness of their lives.*"

Albert Schweitzer wrote, "I don't know what your destiny will be, but one thing I do know: *The only ones among you who will be really happy are those who have sought and found out how to serve.*"

Benjamin Franklin used to say, "when you are *good* to others, you are *best* to yourself."

Henry C. Link was the Director of The Psychological Service Center in New York:

> "*No discovery of modern psychology,*" he wrote, "is, in my opinion, so important as its *scientific proof of the necessity of self-sacrifice* (or discipline) *to self-realization and happiness.*"

SKEPTICAL?

Can it be that focusing on others really creates peace and happiness? Can doing a good deed that puts a smile of joy on someone's face really make us feel fulfilled? Was Dr. Adler serious when he gave his patients a *prescription of hesed* that promised to cure them from depression in two weeks? Can *hesed* really have such a wonderful physical and psychological impact on our health and the quality of our lives? Can it truly enrich our lives?

There are two ways to answer these questions.

One way is to do research — reading the works of the great minds of medicine, psychology, and neurology. If we do so, we will see that many conclude similarly: that altruism helps cure sick people, and helps prevent sickness and depression.

The second way to answer these questions — to determine if *hesed* will have a real psychological impact on our lives — is *to try it.* Reading about it is one thing. Doing it is quite another.

Skeptical? Then — put the *hesed* boomerang theory to the test.

Go on a visit to Camp Simcha (for terminally ill children with cancer).

Get out and visit the poor. Share their grief or give out food in a shelter.

Walk outside and feed a homeless person.

Visit an old age home.

Visit patients in the hospital.

Just practice a few "random acts of *hesed*" and watch their rewards boomerang back to you! Watch how *hesed* enriches your life and the lives of the people around you.

We will discuss the above suggestions in depth. Keep reading!

— 3 —

Hesed as a Healthy Response to Suffering

D r. Hans Selye is an internationally celebrated physician and recipient of a Nobel Prize for his scientific research. Dr. Selye has recommended a scientific solution to people who are suffering, to people who are grieving, or in mourning. *He advised that they use their inner resources to step out beyond themselves and reach out to others.*

Dr. Selye calls this the *magnificent paradox*: When people strengthen others, they, in effect, strengthen themselves. When people help others, they help themselves. Dr. Hans Selye suggests that people who are in pain attempt to lose themselves in *the concern and love for others,* and through this "loss", they paradoxically "find" fulfillment and relief.*

The noted psychiatrist, Dr. Karl Menninger, advised his grieving patients to make the effort to go beyond themselves and "put themselves out" to achieve, what he calls, "the vital balance". Emotional and psychological health and healing begins when we ask not: *"Why is this happening to me?"* or *"Why did my loved one have to die?".* It starts when we ask: *"How can I change my focus*

from 'me and my grief' outward, to my family and friends."
There are many examples of people who understood how to turn their sadness into joy, their pain into fulfillment, through the practice of *hesed*. The following are just five cases of individuals who proved that the healthiest (and most constructive) response to suffering is practicing acts of *hesed*.

KADIMA

Rabbi Chaim Plato is a Brooklyn-born Rabbi who graduated Summa Cum Laude from Brooklyn College. He then worked in France and now is one of the leaders of Radin Yeshiva in Netanya, Israel.

His tenth child, Moshe, was born with Down Syndrome.

Rabbi Plato had a potential tragedy on his hands: He had a baby that was mentally retarded. His response was love. His response was action.

Rabbi Plato decided to open the *Kadima School for Special Children*. His mission was to establish a state-of-the-art program that would help children with Down Syndrome and show their parents (and the world around them) that "not only will they be no burden, but rather they will be their pride and joy!"

"Kadima" means step forward, move on! The school "mainstreams" the Down children with normal children and teaches both to focus on positive abilities and attitude rather than on disabilities and differences.

Fully one half of the children born with Down Syndrome are abandoned by their parents in the hospital. The vast majority of these children deteriorate rapidly and die. Rabbi Plato decided that "it is crucial to educate society to the true potential of these loving children. They can live normal lives and develop into self-sufficient adults. They are loving and lovable; They have feelings and emotions just like any other child."

Many Down Syndrome children today hold college degrees.

Rabbi Plato says that their success is a direct result of parental love, special care, and educational support. A Down Syndrome child need not be a victim of the family and society. He can be what God intended : "A special child!"

Today, Rabbi Plato helps hundreds of children and families build new, productive lives. He built a school where unconditional love and *hesed* are the foundation for success. He responded to his sad situation with powerful action, commitment, drive and positive thinking.

"Down Syndrome kids have an extra chromosome. I think in that chromosome is an extra bit of love and peace. If the rest of the world could get that from these kids, it would be a more loving, more tolerant and more peaceful world to live in."

Rabbi Chaim Plato certainly understood what it means to "put yourself out." He fought his sadness with *hesed* and turned it into joy.

"I KNOW THEIR PAIN"

On November 15, 1994, my friend, Steve Shor, told me about his son Meir. In 1990, Meir had been in a car accident. The hospital informed the family that, after testing his blood, they realized he had a severe case of leukemia. He was only fifteen.

Steve closed his successful contracting business and, for two years, searched for a bone marrow donor to save his son. Finally, he found a donor. The one-in-twenty-thousand odds of finding a match were overcome.

Just on the eve of the transfusion, for no apparent reason, the donor backed out. Meir died three months later at the age of seventeen.

How did Steve Shor respond to the death of his son? Was it with bitterness? With hatred and anger? No.

Steve decided to "put himself out" and dedicate the rest of his life to helping children who were stricken with Leukemia. He created the *National Children's Leukemia Foundation*. He won the support of famous actors and actresses, politicians, professional athletes, and even Presidents Ronald Reagan and Bill Clinton.

He has been written up in the papers as a man who has helped thousands of children.

He told me: "When I see other children with the deadly disease — I see my son Meir. When I visit with the families, be they black, Hispanic or whatever, I feel like they're a part of my family. I need to help them. I know their pain — first hand! I feel that their child is my Meir and it is happening all over again."

Steve discovered a way to prevent some of the more than forty-five thousand deaths of children with Leukemia each year, as well as the deaths of thousands of breast cancer patients. He found out that if the hospital was able to save the umbilical cord of newborn babies, and remove the blood stem cells and use these for Leukemia victims, almost countless lives can be saved each year. He is now raising the money to purchase freezers and computer systems for hospitals, so they can save the cords and help save lives.

Steve Shor has taught me a lesson about the power of *hesed* to enrich lives— and transform suffering into productive and meaningful work.

ARTHUR'S MOM

I recently read a true story about two best friends, Joe and Arthur. During their school years, they were inseparable. After graduation, they shook hands and said good-bye. Arthur, coming from a wealthy family, attended the University of California to start his premedical training. Joe, however, was poor. So he had to get a job and forsake his dream of becoming a doctor.

During World War II, the pre-med student joined the Air Force. One day, his mother received a fateful telegram: Arthur's plane had been shot down.

Her son (and only child) was dead.

The mother was inconsolable. She grieved and mourned continually. "Why?" she asked. "Why did this have to happen to my little boy?"

Then, one day, she picked herself up and decided to take action. She wrote a letter to her son's old best friend.

"Dear Joe. By now, you must have heard of Arthur's death. I remember you when you were playing together and I remember how fond you were of each other...

"Like him, you wanted to be a doctor, to ease human pain and suffering. But your family needed your help, so you did the only thing you could do at that time...

"If you are still interested in becoming a physician, I want you to be one. I want you to take Arthur's place at the University. Nothing would make me happier than to pay your way, every bit of it, and thus do for Arthur's best friend, what I had hoped for him... I have thought of it as sort of a living memorial to him, and I know it is what he would want..."

This woman turned her misery and despair into fulfillment and tranquility. She turned her horrible pain and suffering into meaningful joy and compassionate loving-kindness. She turned her darkness of night into a ray of a new dawn. How? She thought about her son Arthur's friend Joe and how she could help him live the life he dreamed of for himself and the life she dreamed of for her son. She took action and used her inner strength to overcome her lonely despair. She reached beyond herself to touch the life of her fellow human being.

Arthur's living memorial became realized through the life of Joe, his best friend. This woman made that happen. Instead of what could have been envy and jealousy, her feelings were kindness and love.

Her response was *hesed*. And this *hesed* can boomerang back to her in the form of warmth, of fulfillment, of love and of meaning.

M.A.D.D.

Candy Lightner lost her daughter to a drunk driver. Her response? She started M.A.D.D. — Mothers Against Drunk Driving. This organization has rapidly become world famous.

Candy proved that one person can make a difference. By responding to her own personal tragedy, her own suffering, with kindness — Candy Lightner showed the world that the healthiest and most productive response to suffering is kindness...and that personal tragedy and misfortune can be used as a springboard to help end the suffering of others.

THE WAXMANS

On Monday, October 10, 1994, Nachshon Waxman, a nineteen year-old Israeli Soldier, was taken hostage by *Hamas* terrorists.

They demanded the release of two hundred fellow terrorists in Israeli jails, as well as a Sheik. They made a video tape. In it, Nachshon was shown captive and bound, as masked terrorists pointed an automatic weapon at his head.

The video was shown in Israel and all over the world. *The world watched* as Nachshon's mother, Esther, an American born woman and the daughter of Holocaust survivors, sat watching the video in horror. Her hand over her mouth, she swayed back and forth in agony. Her husband, Yehuda, also the child of Holocaust survivors, sat by her side, speechless.

On Friday, October 14, 1994, in the last hour before the deadline, Israeli soldiers raided a house in Ramallah, just two miles from Waxman's home in Northern Jerusalem. Their explosives did not work properly. Nachshon, and two other Jewish soldiers, lost their lives.

Just seven weeks later, this was the Waxmans' reaction. Said Esther:

"My husband is interested in opening an educational center now (for Arabs) to get them young, to teach these children, these

Hamas people, about human life and values universal to all religions. He (her husband) feels that by the time they're teenagers – however old these kids were who took Nachshon — it's too late. Even their own parents can't get them anymore".

Mrs. Waxman said: "My son was everybody's son. People in this country tend to be very extreme, and they see the religious community as an extreme, fanatic group. But we're practicing, religious Jews who are also part of modern Western Civilization and maybe that hit a chord. Maybe people are lacking that element of faith, and grabbed onto it when they saw it in so-called normal people".*

How did these two people respond to Hamas killing their nineteen year-old son point blank in cold blood? By putting themselves out and building an educational center for Hamas youth to help them and give them a common set of morals.

SUMMARY

Indeed, hesed is a healthy response to suffering. Paradoxically, one of the healthiest responses to personal sorrow is to practice acts of kindness. By putting oneself out and focusing on others, there is a kind of natural healing that occurs.

Focusing on oneself often creates feelings of bitterness, regret and depression. On the other hand, the hesed that one does while in pain has a way of reversing itself as it provides psychological and emotional fulfillment for the giver. When we are suffering, acts of kindness can enrich our lives and help us deal with our own pain.

— 4 —

The Liberating Effect of Giving

I n Bibical Hebrew, "venatenu" means "and they shall give."
When you take the census of the people Israel, then they shall give (venatenu) each man, ... half a shekel (Exodus 30:12).
The word *venatenu* can be read both backwards and forward. This is called a palindrome — the letters of the word are symmetrical. Whether you read it from left to right or right to left, you have the same word, the same message: giving.

Furthermore, the cantillation note on the word "venatenu" is called a *kadmah ve-azlah,* which literally means "going forward and backward".* Is this a hint to the hidden power, the paradox of giving, the "boomerang" effect of giving, that the recipient of what is being given is a giver as well, and that the giver is receiving back just as much?

"WHY AM I SPEAKING?"

I recently was asked to introduce Rudolph Guiliani, the Mayor of New York, to a group of successful business people. It was a fundraising event for a charitable organization, and it took place in a well-known bank on Fifth Avenue in New York City.

Needless to say, I was very anxious and nervous before the speech. Questions were crossing my mind, a-mile-a-minute:

Who am I, to speak before these successful people?
Why should they listen to me?
What do I know about this organization?
How will I be able to properly honor or introduce the Mayor of New York?
When will I get up to speak?
How much time will they give me before they decide that I'm not a worthy speaker?
What are my qualifications?
What will they think of me?
Am I dressed adequately for this?
Why, in the world, did I agree to this?

Then, I remembered an important public speaking idea from a book I had read about six years earlier. In my own words: "Do not think about yourself. Think about why you are giving this speech. Is it to look good? To impress people? To boost your own self-confidence? If any of these are your motivations, *stop and sit down* because you will most certainly be nervous and overly-anxious."

"However, if your purpose in speaking is to give, you can relax. Are you speaking to inspire others? To present them with new information? To enrich their day? To share a personal event that will make them laugh or cry or give charity or react in a positive, ethical, compassionate, honest or giving way?"

"If this is your purpose, stick to it. Focus on it. Concentrate. Design and write your speech, knowing that it is a means to give, and you will be liberated from fear, liberated from anxiety. Keep in mind that your purpose is to serve others. By focusing on them, on their receiving, you de-focus from yourself, your image, your ego, your adequacy, your competence or your qualifications."

"Catch yourself criticizing and judging yourself and just think: I am here to serve others, to give of myself (my learning, experience, research...) to them. Now, what will it take to give over this information in the most impactful way?"

It is liberating to give. It liberates us from fear and from worry.

YEARNING TO GIVE

I recently read an article about a couple which considered adopting a baby.

They were very anxious to have another child. They were worried about the adopted baby's genes. People are born with "natures" and this, they felt, had a lot to do with what kind of individuals those people become.

They worried about love: Will they truly love this baby as their own? Will this child ever really love *them* and feel that they were his or her parents? Or will there always be an unspoken tension, a kind of eerie silence, a stigma attached to the child?

Then, the couple thought carefully. What was their purpose in wanting a child? It wasn't ego. They were not yearning to boost their image. *They were not looking to gain something.*

They decided that they wanted a child because, in their own words...

"....*We were yearning to give something* (love and a good home). Now that we knew what we wanted most—to give a child a loving and good home — biological origins became completely unimportant. . . given that we wanted to give to a child much more than we wanted to receive from one, that ceased to worry us. It is remarkable how liberating it is to want to give more that to want to receive."

LAST PIECE OF BREAD

A holocaust survivor (Dr. Victor Frankel, in *Man's Search For Meaning*) writes:

> We who lived in the concentration camps can remember the men who walked through the huts comforting others, giving away their last piece of bread.
> They may have been few in number, but they offer sufficient proof that everything can be taken away from a man but one thing: the last of human freedoms to choose one's attitude in any given set of circumstances, to choose one's way. *

Hesed is the only true human freedom. *Hesed* can liberate us and enrich our lives.

— 5 —

Hesed and Longevity

HESED AT ONE HUNDRED

A woman was celebrating her hundreth birthday. When asked "to what do you attribute your longevity and good health?", she replied, "I loved my husband and my children the best I knew how. I love the Lord... and I always try to keep busy and do whatever I could to help out — as I do with Miss Sadie."

"She's the lovely little woman down the street. She'll be eighty-eight next week, but, poor thing, she broke her hip last month. So I go down to her house every day just to check up on her. Yesterday, I brought her some of my nice homemade biscuits. What a dear one she is."

Can you imagine a one hundred year-old woman baking biscuits for her eighty-eight year old neighbor? Can it be that her kindness not only keeps Miss Sadie's hopes and spirits up, but her own as well? Can it be that when a one hundred year-old woman gives of herself, paradoxically, there is more of her to go around? This is the boomerang effect of *hesed. It enriches everyone involved.*

TWO HUNDRED PINTS

In June of 1995, I lay on a table in the blood bank of New York Hospital, donating blood. I noticed a woman in her late sixties also donating blood. She looked so young and vibrant. She was so friendly and cheerful. She asked me about myself, my family. Then I overheard her telling the doctor "I'm already over two hundred pints!"

This lady had donated blood more than two hundred times. She understood well that all human beings are connected, and that when she gives a pint of her healthy blood, she gives the gift of hope and the gift of life to a fellow human being— without regard to race, gender or creed.

I wonder how she stays so healthy. Could it be that by taking care of others she naturally gets "taken care of?" Can it be that her acts of *hesed* have some mysterious way of keeping her healthy and cheerful? Can it be that her *hesed* boomerangs back?

I wonder.

— 6 —

Hesed is Forever

A parable is told about a man who had three friends.*
He loved the first very much and spent the majority of his
time with him.

The second friend he loved less and spent less time with.

The third he spent the least time with and loved him even
less.

Once, the King issued a summons for the man. He was very
afraid. He needed a friend to testify on his behalf.

He called friend #1, the one he loved most. However, this
friend refused to go with him to the palace.

Desperate, he went to friend #2. This friend agreed to accompany him and protect him on his way to the palace, but refused
to testify for him before the king.

Finally, he approached the third friend. This one replied,
"don't be afraid. I'll go with you; I'll come to the king and testify
on your behalf, and you will be saved."

Who are these three friends? What does the parable's metaphor represent? What is its lesson?

Friend #1 is the man's money, his *material possessions* which he loves the most, but which leave him on the day he dies.

Friend #2 represents his family and relatives, who accompany him to the grave, then take their leave and depart.

Friend #3 is his good deeds. In terms of time, he spent the least amount of his time and had the least amount of passion for this part of his life. *Yet only this friend accompanies him to the "king"* and testifies to the Lord on his behalf.

As stated in Isaiah (58:8):

And your righteousness shall go before you.

A GOOD MAN CAN NEVER DIE

Dr. Bernard Siegel, in *Peace Love and Healing,** writes:

> *It lies within you to see to it that those you love keep faith with life. No matter how much they grieve for you, they will know that you live on in them. Love defeats death and makes us immortal. In Saroyan's novel The Human Comedy, the young hero grieves for his brother Marcus, who has died in the war. Homer feels that with Marcus's death the whole world is different, lacking something, altered for the worse, but a friend gives him good counsel:*

> *"I'm not going to try to comfort you," Spangler said. "I know I couldn't. But try to remember that a good man can never die. You will see him many times. You will see him in the streets. You will see him in the houses, in all the places of the town. In the vineyards and orchards, in the rivers and clouds, in all the things here that make this a world for us to live in. You will feel him in all things that are here out of love, and for love — all the things that are abundant, all the things that grow. The person of a man may leave — or be taken away — but the best part of a good man stays. It stays*

forever. Love is immortal and makes all things immortal."
We live on through love. We achieve immortality through
hesed.

IN OUR DAUGHTER'S EYES

Dr. Seigel* tells another wonderful story:
"Bill Bolsta sent me a poem he'd written to his wife after her
death, entitled 'In Our Daughter's Eyes.' Six years had passed and
he'd been waiting to share it with someone. I'll quote from part of
it:

"And you said, "Look for me in our daughter's eyes,
And you will find me there.
I never will leave you, so honey don't grieve,
It's more than I can bear.
And I thank God for our time together,
And the joy you brought to my life.
"And then you closed your eyes, and I whispered,
"Good-bye
My best friend, my woman, my wife."
Well, last night our daughter said her prayers, and climbed
into her bed.
She lay down on her pillow, and then slowly turned her
head.
I gazed into her face as you came climbing through her
eyes,
I felt a warm embrace like a breeze from summer skies.
My disbelief gave way to grief, I brushed away a tear,
And then I heard you softly singing, rich and crisp and
clear.
You poured your music on my soul, it blossomed like a
rose.
Those gaping wounds of empty rooms began to heal and
close.

And when at last your music passed, and your caress was
gone.
I sat quite still, not moving, until I heard our daughter yawn.
I noticed that her blanket had been pulled up to her chin.
She smiled and said, "Goodnight, Daddy. Mommy tucked
me in."

Feelings of love don't always create acts of kindness, but acts of kindness always create feelings of love. When feelings are combined with acts of *hesed*, our lives are enriched and the effect of our actions lives on forever.

— 7 —

Are We Giving – Or Receiving?

As far back as I can remember, every experience I had that was *fulfilling*, enjoyable and memorable was an experience in which I "put myself inside-out". This means that whenever I put aside my own personal, individual subjective needs and desires and focused my energy and my time on others, the experience became one of joy.

It is the mystical, magical paradox of *hesed*. When we focus on giving, who benefits the most? We do.

CAMP SIMCHA

All around me, were the little faces of beautiful children having a great time. But, a careful look revealed more. This was Camp Simcha. There were children in wheelchairs, children without legs, children balding from chemotherapy and radiation treatments. The children have life-threatening diseases including cancer, AIDS, hemophilia and all kinds of lung and liver diseases.

Many of the children here have come straight from the hospital, and after three weeks, they will return to the hospital. Many of the friendships that are built in Camp Simcha last a lifetime, but sadly, some of these "lifetimes" are too tragically short. When people say "good-bye" in Camp Simcha, sometimes it is for good.

The visit to Camp Simcha made me sad. But it also warmed my heart.

It made me sad for all the suffering of the little children, who may or may not make it through the year. But it made my heart warm when I saw the counselors who volunteered their time and who were constantly giving of themselves to these children, whom they know they might never see again.

OUR LIVES / THEIR LIVES

We can leave Camp Simcha and go on to our regular, everyday lives. I can go on to my family, my business, my classes. The children of Camp Simcha, however live very different lives after the camp is over. They return to hospitals. *They* return to I.V.'s, chemotherapy, radiation, surgery, drugs.

Their lives are not normal.

I looked across the room and I saw a little girl in a pink dress, her head shaven, her hair almost all fallen out from chemotherapy, kissing and hugging one of our counselors, and the counselor hugging her back. I saw a tear roll down from the counselor's eyes. As the tear rolled down her cheek, I realized that this little girl was saying good-bye.

I met a fifteen-year-old girl who was wearing a hair-piece and who was frustrated with the camp because she wanted to start socializing. She wanted to meet a boy. My heart was torn apart, imagining that she would have to hide the fact that she had cancer, and that she was bald underneath her hair-piece.

I met the mother of a young girl who passed away very suddenly from stomach cancer. This forty-six-year-old woman told me in detail every stage of what had happened to her daughter. I sat with her for over an hour, listened to her, talked to her about her sorrow, her sadness and her *will to go on*. To this day, she jogs every day, and has competed in many marathons. She is determined to go to medical school and to become a doctor. The woman said to me that she could almost hear her daughter say to her: *"Mom, stop talking about me, go on with your life. Stop talking about me. It's not going to get you anywhere. Use my energy to further your life and enrich your life."*

At Camp Simcha, I was overcome by pain and sorrow, but on the surface, I smiled and clapped, I danced with the children, and ran around with them. I made believe with them that everything felt normal so that they could live a somewhat normal life for the few days and weeks that they have in Camp. I tried to have fun even though I was in pain. The only reason I tried to have fun was so that the kids could have fun. I knew that the stress from isolation and from being alienated from lack of friendships and relationships causes disease and aggravates it, so I did my best to smile and to play. I played basketball with them, ran relay races, and ran around during the singing and dancing.

I know that every child needs the opportunity to find that strength inside; to seek that energy, that life-blood that allows us to heal. I know that the singing and hugging, the fun and joy and connections we build will create a type of energy that is not radiated by the warmth of the sun, but by the love and support of other human beings. I pray that this energy will give these beautiful little kids the strength to reach inwards, the perseverance to deal with the pain and the hope to go on.

LOOK UP AT THE STARS

Rabbi Elimelech Goldberg, the camp's director, constantly speaks to the children about hope. He tells the children to look up at the stars and notice that *the light of every star cuts through a tremendous amount of darkness.* He tells them that the stars are able to do this because they have an energy inside and that they "know this". These stars, he says, send their lights out and they pierce through the darkness.

Rabbi Goldberg tells the kids (we paraphrase): *When you have darkness in your lives, look up at the stars. Remember that they, too, have the energy inside to burst out and cut through the darkness. Remember that no star is alone; that every star has company. Each one of your stars is next to mine,* and together, with the help of God and with the power of love and friendships, the stars will shine brightly.

Rabbi Goldberg told us the story of one little girl who went through a very complicated liver transplant. After five hours of surgery and six times in the hospital, she was too weak to eat. Her mother called Rabbi Goldberg and asked him to speak to the girl. The mother told him that if her little girl refused to eat she would die within a week.

He called the girl and spoke to her about their experience together in Camp Simcha. Then she told him that she remembered to look up at the stars. She told him "I know what you said about the stars and their energy is true. I'm trying to find my own energy. I'm trying so hard Rabbi, but I know that whatever happens we will always be together". He told her that she needs to eat so she can get healthy and come to Camp next Summer. After those few minutes on the telephone, she started eating, determined to go forward again.

THE STRENGTH INSIDE

A tenth degree black belt and grand master of Karate had been in camp the week before. He stood before the children, lifted a big stone and held it in his hands. He meditated for fifteen seconds over it, and, without even looking as if he was applying pressure, *broke it in half.* He then told the kids: "I did this to show you that our true power is the strength that lies inside of us. It isn't the strength in our muscles; it is the strength in our souls, and each one of you has this power."

LESSONS

The entire day at Camp Simcha I was thinking about my own children. I thanked God for blessing me with my healthy children. I started to understand the meaning of gratefulness. I promised myself that I would be a new father and a new husband; more tolerant, more patient, more loving, more forgiving. I promised myself that I would not let this day at Camp Simcha just come and go in my life with no change in me. It had to affect me. I have to be a new person for it. My life would change. *My life would be enriched.* The people around me will feel my love and tolerance and patience. They will feel my connectedness to them, my thankfulness that they exist; that they are in my life. They will sense my prayers for them, my happiness when they are happy, my sadness when they are in pain, my trust and loyalty to them as people, and my respect for them as human beings. After all, we are here for just a short stay and then we leave. We all leave. *We are all terminal.* It is just a question of "when".

THE NEED TO GIVE

There is something very special about the children in Camp Simcha. There's a strength, a light, a beauty to them.

The lesson of Camp Simcha is the lesson of *hesed.* A lesson *that what you give is what you get.* In life, the more we take, it seems, the less happy we become. The more we look to *receive,* the less we actually satisfy our true needs. I realize that every human soul must be nourished spiritually. This creates a desperate need to give, to love, to be compassionate, to be altruistic. And that desperate need, unless satisfied, tears us apart.

The ironic thing is that we think that when we give (when we become compassionate and tolerant and giving and loving) it takes away from us *–that we lose something.* We think that when we give charity we actually lose money; when we extend ourselves to somebody it takes away from what we can give to ourselves. *This is the illusion.* In reality giving is really receiving in disguise. To spend a day with terminally ill children, children with life-threatening diseases, to cheer them up, to make them happy, to love them, to let them be *"kids"* for a day, *enriches our lives,* makes us better people, more loving, more considerate, more grateful. *It gives us perspective.* It sets us up for true happiness, for contentment, for fulfilment.

Hesed not only can boomerang back– it is integrally a "receiving". The act of giving, itself, is an act of receiving, which far outweighs what you could possibly be giving.

Spend the day in Camp Simcha, and you are spending the day enriching and feeding your soul, nourishing your spirit. You are satisfying the part of you that yearns and needs to give love... and to help others.

Have we "given" or have we received?*

— 8 —

Two Visits

This book is dedicated in memory of Joseph D. Beyda, *alav hashalom*. Joseph's work in Sephardic Bikur Holim is legendary.

Joseph's untiring efforts and eloquent words inspired me to do *hesed*. As a result, my visits to the poor, the lonely, the sick and the elderly changed me forever. The people I met touched me.

Let me introduce you to two clients of Sephardic Bikur Holim. I hope, after you meet "Rachel" and "Betty" , you will be touched as well.

"TODAY I HAVE HOPE"

My name is Rachel and I live in Brooklyn, New York. My parents were born in Aleppo and moved to the United States in 1920. I have light brown hair and blue eyes. I'm in my thirties and recently divorced, but I plan on remarrying soon and building a family.

Eight weeks ago I was leaving work and a car came speeding

through a red light and hit me. It was what they call a *hit and run.* I was knocked to the ground. They rushed me to Bellevue only to learn that I was in a *coma.* Medicaid does not provide a hospital attendant to sit by me. My head injuries were *so painful* that in the middle of the night I would thrash around from side to side *unable to control myself.* The nurses decided to tie me up at night with my bedsheets. My arms and legs were tied to the bedposts. With no attendant to help me, I was left alone in the hospital bed lying in my own waste, tied down to the bed, *left to die* in a coma all the doctors thought I would never awake from.

All my hopes, my dreams, *my life, were disappearing.*

I was a *vegetable.*

A family, children of my own, would never be a reality for me. I had no insurance. My mother, who I was taking care of, was now alone. She was without her only child and her only means of support. It seemed, in one short moment, in one fateful accident, life turned into the darkest most horrifying nightmare.

Somehow Sephardic Bikur Holim found out about me.

They called my mother. Within twelve hours there were Sephardic Bikur Holim volunteers at my bedside. They untied the bedsheets so I could sleep like a human being.

They cleaned me so I could live or die with dignity.

They held my hand.

They whispered in my ear.

"We love you."

"We're with you."

"There's so much more to live for."

They prayed for me.

There I was, four weeks in a coma, abandoned by doctors and professionals, but not by Sephardic Bikur Holim.

Within two weeks I snapped out of the coma. Sephardic Bikur

Holim arranged for *government aid* to pay my medical bills. They took me to a *rehab center.* They provided us with *food vouchers* and *paid our rent.* They spent time with my mother and helped her cope with the situation. After another two weeks, when I first was able to *recognize* my mother, I told her:

> "Hi mom.
> I'm back.
> I'm here again and I love you.
> Don't worry, It'll be O.K.".

I *really am* going to be O.K.

I am thankful to God for giving me back my life and to Sephardic Bikur Holim for giving my life *meaning.*

Where would I have been if Sephardic Bikur Holim would not have been there to help me?

Today, I have hope. I want to fall in love again and have children. I want to tell my children about my experience and teach them to be caring, loving, sensitive, giving people. I pray my dreams will come true and I'm thankful I now *have dreams.*

"IN LIFE, MY CHILDREN, IN LIFE"

My name is Betty. My parents were born in Syria and moved to New York in 1930. In 1975, I married my husband. We were very much in love. In 1980, I developed breast cancer. I underwent a masectomy. Needless to say I felt disfigured and unfeminine. I was a little depressed. Before the operation my husband told me, "Don't worry honey, everything will be O.K." After the operation he became resentful. Then, he started to see other women. My daughter, Sarah, and my son, Mikey, didn't understand.

"How come Daddy isn't here?"

I lied to them over and over: "Daddy is working late again."

One Friday night he came into our bedroom and told me,

"get out! You sleep with the kids". He was repulsed by me. I felt worthless. What choice did I have?

The man I loved actually kicked me out of our bedroom.

Well, even if my marriage was in ruins, I was going to try *to think positive.* My cancer was gone and I had two beautiful children. What more could I ask? So I tried to forgive my husband for *their* sake. I tried to make our marriage work.

It got worse.

About one year ago, his girlfriends began calling the house outright. He had a picture of his latest fling on his key ring. One day my eleven year old son Mikey picked it up and asked me "Who is this, Ma?" I didn't know what to say. My husband finally left me to live with his girlfriend.

Not being able to cope with his anger, Mikey started urinating all over the house.

It was then that I developed terminal chest and lung cancer. I asked the doctor how long I would have to live. He wouldn't answer me. Finally the doctor looked into my eyes, shook his head, and said, "not long."

"How long?" I shouted.

"I need to know."

"I have to make plans!"

He whispered, "Six months to a year" and he left the room.

"Six months to a year." It thundered in my mind over and over. "Six months to a year".

While I sat in the hospital bed waiting for chemotherapy, I thought about my kids. Who will take care of them? How would we pay our bills? We were desperately poor, with nothing. I felt bad I couldn't send them to Yeshivah with the rest of the community. How will they ever forgive me? How would they ever forgive their father?

When the hospital told me that I'm not being covered and I had no money to pay the bills, my beautiful thirteen-year-old daughter, Sarah, came to my bedside and held my hand. Her blue eyes were still glassy from crying. She whispered to me, *"Ma, what are we going to do?"*

I called Sephardic Bikur Holim. The next day, Ruthy, a Sephardic Bikur Holim social worker, was by my side. She turned to me in tears and said: "Don't worry, I'm with you. I'm here for you."

Bikur Holim helped me pay my rent and food bills, they helped me get government aid for my medical bills. They put my family in therapy. They had Judy Tawil, a Sephardic Bikur Holim volunteer, come over. She was what they call a "Big Sister" for my Sarah.

They put my kids in the community center camp for the summer so they didn't have to sit home with me all day depressed.

Ruthy taught me that there is hope, that God is really here and is watching over us. I now have the power to keep on going. Six months ago I wanted to disappear. All I knew was pain and suffering. All I knew was poverty and loneliness. Today I know what love is. Ruthy is always here for me, comforting me, taking me to the hospital, consoling and preparing my children for my death. Sephardic Bikur Holim has given me the courage to keep on going.

I know I must die soon, but I'm going to really try to live longer and to thoroughly enjoy my life. I pray to God every day now and I know there is hope."

This is not the end of Betty's story.

I went to visit Betty and her children about three weeks ago with Ruthy. As we walked into the house, her daughter and son ran to greet us yelling, "Ruthy! Ruthy! Hi Ruthy!" and hugged kissed her.

Betty smiled and introduced herself to me. I couldn't believe how beautiful she was. This was the woman who was saying goodbye to her children? This was the woman who had just a few months to live? *I was in shock.*

We sat and talked for while and what did she have to say?

"You have to have faith in God" she said.
"You have to have courage to fight the pain.
"I really never imagined, that there are people in the world like
Ruthy and the people at Sephardic Bikur Holim.
People who are giving and caring.
People who love me unconditionally.
If Sephardic Bikur Holim wouldn't have been there for me, I
would be on the street.
I don't even want to think where my kids would be.
But Sephardic Bikur Holim told me, don't worry, we can help
you and you did.
God bless you."
Her eleven-year-old son Mikey turned to me and said, "My
mom is the greatest".
I said, "Yeah, I see".
Then he said, "No, I mean she's really great!"
I said, "I know, I know".
He said, "No, I mean she's a poet and an artist and a sculptor".
I thought, "This poor kid is making up stories".
"O.K. sure, sure..."
Then Betty turned to me and said: "No, he's right. I am."
"Show him Ma, show him your stuff!"

As we walked around the house Mikey held his mother's hand
and Sarah held Ruthy's.
Betty proudly showed us her artwork and her sculptures.
She was truly gifted.
"My mom's the best", he kept on saying.
On the door to her bedroom there was a birthday card.
He said: "Read them your poetry Ma, read it to them!".
I quickly read the birthday card to myself.
It was from Mikey.
It said,

"Dear Mom, Happy Birthday, I love you
and I want to stay with you always.
Thanks Mom, for everything.
Please stay with me.
And please, *don't die*."

He saw me looking at the card and said,
"No, not *that*, this *poem*, my mom wrote it to us.
Read it to them Ma."
With tears in her eyes, Betty turned to us.
"I wrote this to my children one month after I met Ruthy.
Would you *really* like to hear it?"
I nodded and she shared it with us.
This was her gift to me and I'd like to share this gift with you:

In life my CHILDREN, in life.
If you love me, tell me how much.
In life my CHILDREN (in life!)
Don't wait until I die for you to give me flowers or to tell me
how much I mean to you.
I need to know it now while I'm still alive.
Please hold me in your arms and let me feel your love .
Don't wait for me to die so you can appreciate me or under-
stand me.
In life my CHILDREN (in life!).
Make me part of your life
Let me laugh and cry with you.
Never visit the cemetery and fill my grave with tears and flowers.
Fill my heart with your love.
In life my CHILDREN, in life!

This is Betty and her story.
Her warmth and strength are symbols of the human spirit.
In the short time I spent with her, she truly enriched my life.

Summary of Part One

THE NATURAL PARADOX

R alph Waldo Emerson once said:
> *It is one of the most beautiful compensations of life that no man can sincerely try to help another without helping himself."*

I often feel that the universe is a dynamic, flowing, moving stream of energy. It seems to me that when you give of yourself, you create a temporary imbalance that must be corrected.

Could it be that, like the molecules of air rushing to fill a vacuum, the universe strives to replace the good you have given out? Could it be that the flow will come back to you from a totally unexpected source?

The *Hesed Boomerang* theory means that every time you extend yourself outward, the universe extends itself to you. This Law of Reciprocity is probably as natural as the law of gravity.

Whenever you put another person first, the universe puts you first. The more you give, the more you receive. This seeming paradox is natural.

It is "the ripple effect" of throwing a pebble into a lake.

The *Law of Conservation of Energy* is a rule of physics that states that "matter cannot be destroyed".

Now according to Einstein, energy is matter ($E=MC^2$), thus energy as well cannot be lost. Perhaps a positive act will create positive energy and the repercussions will vibrate back to you. Perhaps the *hesed* boomerangs back to us just like an echo would. Perhaps. We can't prove it.

"Everyone who shows compassion to his fellow creatures is himself granted compassion by Heaven" (Shabbat 151b). This ancient truth that has been taught to us by Jewish tradition is being reaffirmed by current-day psychologists, physicians, psychiatrists, and those who are doing research in glandular and hormonal function. The practice of kindness enriches many lives. *Hesed* seems to boomerang back in a beautiful way.

Modern medical professionals are proving scientifically that the practice of kindness (such as volunteer work) is healthy. It creates happiness. It promotes a strong immune system. It relieves us from stress and anxiety. It can ease our pain.

Giving liberates us. It calms us. It gives our lives meaning. As Robert Byrne once said, "the purpose of life is a life of purpose." Acts of altruism and loving-kindness are part and parcel of our purpose in life for they transform the world and make it a safer place to live.

One of the older definitions of the word "kind" in the Oxford English Dictionary reads: "To act according to one's nature... The manner or way natural or proper to anyone."

Acts of kindness give us hope: Hope that, in the perpetual struggle between good and evil, between decency and cruelty— that good and decency will prevail. When we witness kindness, we are encouraged that the world can become a safe, peaceful, loving place.

Just like throwing a pebble into a pond, practicing *hesed* sends a ripple out into the world that becomes magnified by every life it encounters.

Hesed is our ultimate reminder of what life could and should be all about.

Hesed is the strongest force in the world.

It can dissolve anger and fear and turn enemies into friends.

It breaks down the barriers and creates unity and love.

Hesed is the ultimate answer for society.

It is the ultimate therapy for individuals.

Feelings of love do not always create acts of kindness.

But acts of kindness always create feelings of love.

Thorton Wilder, in The Bridge of San Luis Rey, ends with a very important statement: "There is a land of the living and a land of the dead. The bridge is love, the only truth, the only survival."

Hesed infuses life with meaning.

Hesed creates light where there is darkness.

It brings hope where there is despair.

It warms and comforts where there is grieving.

It nourishes the soul where there is emptiness.

It provides human dignity where there is shame.

It brings joy where there is sadness.

Hesed builds love where there is isolation.

Hesed makes everything it touches sacred and sanctifies life.

Acts of kindness are never wasted.

They always make a difference.

Hesed most often blesses the receiver.

But *hesed* always blesses the giver.

The natural boomerang effect of *hesed* is so powerful it can literally transform our lives.

Part Two

STANDING UP AND SPEAKING OUT

— 9 —

When Will We Wake Up?

*H*esed can naturally boomerang back to us. So can cruelty, selfishness, carelessness and apathy. The world's ecological systems suffer when people abuse the earth. When people waste natural resources and deplete the ozone layer, we all suffer. Our children will suffer. We humans seem to despise nature. We show very little concern for the welfare of our world.

The United Nations estimates that hundreds of thousands of baby girls are disposed of every year in China. From 1990 through 1995, it is estimated that over three million infants were murdered by their own parents.

About twenty five percent of all infants who die are murdered on the day they are born. In Great Britain, Germany, Japan, Scandinavia and France children under the age of one year are murdered at four times the rate of the rest of the population.

When are we going to wake up and speak out?

Today (or on any typical day) in the United States*:

• 1,370 teenagers attempted suicide and 69 people actually committed suicide.

• Every 6 minutes a woman was raped.

• Every 27 minutes someone was murdered.

• Every 76 seconds someone was robbed.

• Every 26 seconds a woman was beaten or abused.

• Every 5 seconds, a child was reported abused or neglected.

• Every 2 seconds somewhere in the world, a child starves to death or dies of malnutrition. Just think about that for a minute. As you read the last sentence a child, somewhere in the world, may have just died of malnutrition!

• In the United States alone, 15 million children are going to bed hungry each night. That is one out of every four children!

Very often I wonder to myself, "when are we going to wake up? Who is going to speak out against the cruelty that is permeating our culture? When will the human being realize that he was empowered with sensitivity, with kindness and a divine soul? When will humanity understand its true purpose in life? When will it see its role in nature as a nurturer, as a lover of the world, as an unselfish, thinking, caring being that is transcendent?"

Instead, we use our minds to create cruelty. We use our divinely- given intelligence to create technology to make others suffer. We design bombs and gas that can slowly kill women and children. We allow our fellow human beings to sleep on the streets and to die hungry. We stand back and watch, as racists and terrorists murder and rape innocent women and children. We say nothing when political maniacs kill and maime innocent, civilized citizens. We stand idly by as our fellow humans are tortured for no reason other than the color of their skin or their religious beliefs.

In its 1996 annual report, Amnesty International provided a detailed account of four hundred forty one new human rights violations—just in the twelve months of 1995. One hundred and forty one of the new cases were torture, sixty were "disappearances", one hundred thirty two of the cases were judicial execution, and one hundred three of the new cases were political killings.

Amnesty International Regional Action Networks deal with human rights abuses in every country of the world. During the year, more than two thousand three hundred eighty local groups participate in the regional networks, and work on the cases of thousands of victims of human rights violations. At the end of 1995 there were four thousand and twelve long-term assignments, concerning over seven thousand individuals, including prisoners of conscience and other victims of human rights violations.

Amnesty International reports on human rights atrocities committed every day somewhere in the world. The most vulnerable victims are the poor and disadvantaged, especially women, children, elderly people and refugees.

Instead of outrage, the world's reaction is apathy. Unless our response is *concerted action*, the abuses, the massacres, the mutilations and rape will continue.

Society must begin to realize that it cannot tolerate cruelty and evil and expect to survive. The apathy must end. There must be more people who are willing to stand up and speak out against injustice. We must create a better world for our children; a world that stands for timeless principles of decency, of love, of peace and of *hesed*.

Otherwise, we are doomed.

—10—

The Power Not To See

The sage Abba Binyamin stated (Berachot 6a): "If the eye had the power to see (all the harmful forces around us) nobody could stand..."

There, he is referring to actual *mazikin*, invisible forces of evil. They are so numerous, that, had they been visible, we could not stand.

By the same token, man does not "see" all the pain and suffering in the world. We each have a psychological defense mechanism. This defense mechanism prevents man from absorbing all the sorrow on this planet. God withheld from man the "power to see all the evil" in order to protect him *psychologically*. Man would not be able to handle it. It might drive him over the edge. Like so many victims or survivors of disaster, he might go mad.

So, we have the innate ability to put other people's pain (as well as our own) far away from our mind and heart. Just by virtue of our humanity, we have this power.

Taken to the extreme, we can rationalize cruelty and torture.

We can "close our eyes" to the suffering of innocent people every day — and we do.

The human being was given the power to rationalize. We can rationalize others' suffering and cruelty with very little difficulty. We close our hearts to the pain of others and our minds take over. If Nazi Germany can teach us one lesson it would be that "normal", intelligent, well-bred, cultured, educated citizens, like you and I, can rationalize suffering. We can cause pain to people and our minds can say "it is O.K.". We've been "educated" in our universities that we don't "think" well when we are "emotional". That is, when we're using our hearts. Perhaps that is true. Perhaps the power of our minds and hearts are mutually exclusive and compete for "energy" or "quality time". If we focus our minds on ourselves long enough, we can actually block out the screams and cries of others.

Nazi officers had homes near concentration camps. They could live completely "normal" lives (school, piano playing, films, shopping...) totally ignoring the screams on the other side of the fence.) They cooked their meat dinners and drank their wine while innocent people starved to death one hundred feet away. They played with their children, while, nearby, Jewish mothers had to decide which of their children would be gassed to death for no reason at all.

In 1982, I visited the Dachau concentration camp, where hundreds of thousands of innocent people were murdered in the Holocaust. The one-hundred-year-old homes which I saw there are not any different from ours. The people who live there are not devils. They are "normal" just like you and me.

Fifty years ago, men went to work and women played cards within sight of the smoke from the camps. People shopped for the latest in fashion clothing, while, in the camp, soap was being made from human flesh.

Dachau is and was a physically beautiful little community with cute little houses, big sweeping porches, lawns, and swings for the kids. It is very tranquil. People just outside the concentration camp lived a very "normal" life. Kids were taught to play the piano, and on most nights, parents would go out to the movies.

We can do this. You and I. Yes — you! After all, we can block out our own pain. We forget our pain quickly— it's a defense mechanism. This defense mechanism of our minds gives us the ability to go on after the loss of a loved one. If, God Forbid, you have ever experienced the death of a loved one (or any tragic saddening event) you know that *time heals all wounds*. Over the course of time, your mind blocks out the pain and sadness. You can still mourn and cry a year later but it's not the same pain. The power of forgetfulness is incredibly strong.

If your mind has the power to block out your own pain, can it not block out the pain of other people? It's a cinch.

What happened the last time you saw someone suffer? Did you ever see a starving child on the news? What was your reaction? If your first reaction was to *change the channel,* you are normal. If someone shows you a photograph of the inside of a concentration camp and you turn away in disgust, you are normal. Our minds don't want us near any picture of pain. Our minds have a clearly defined, focused job description: to redirect our thoughts away from pain, away from negative emotion, away from sadness and away from pity and mercy and compassion.

We can enjoy a Sunday afternoon with our family in the park while women and children are being tortured and starved to death all around the world. It's just a question of distance, of number of miles.

In Dachau, people sat three miles from the gas chambers. In New York, we sit six thousand miles away from other types of concentration camps. How different is it really? How far away do we sit from the homeless? In the last two seconds, somewhere in the world, a child may have starved to death. What did you do about it? Anything? How many more kids will die before you and I decide to do something about it? How many innocent people will have to suffer and die before you and I decide to make a change?

The Nazis (and the three hundred million bystanders who lived in Nazi occupied Europe and watched six million Jews murdered without speaking up) were not abnormal. *They were exactly like me and you.* No different. To refuse to acknowledge this is to miss the lesson of the Holocaust and doom ourselves to repeat it. But what, essentially is the Holocaust? It is the persecution of innocent people. It is a lesson in the human mind's power over the heart. It is the victory of the power to rationalize over the power to feel and to pity.

I often ask myself, "when will our hearts, our compassionate 'human' side win out over our minds and our 'rational' side? When will we decide to *act* to defend the cruel suffering of innocent people and innocent living beings?"

Then I remember that all people are interdependent, that whatever happens to one human being, happens to us all. So we must begin to stand up and speak out.

Shortly after World War II, the German Protestant pastor Martin Niemoller was released from a Nazi concentration camp. He said:

"In Germany:
They first came for the Jews and I didn't speak up because I wasn't a Jew.
Then they came for the Communists and I didn't speak up because I wasn't a Communist.
Then they came for the trade unionists and I didn't speak up because I wasn't a trade unionist.
Then they came for the gypsies and I didn't speak up because I wasn't' a gypsy.
Then they came for the Catholics and I didn't speak up because I wasn't a Catholic.
Then they came for me. And by that time, there was no one left to speak up".

—*11*—

"I Went Back to Bed"

On the night of March 13, 1964, at about three A.M., a twenty-eight-year-old woman named Catherine ("Kitty") Genovese was returning to her home in a quiet middle-class section of Queens known as Kew Gardens. She parked her car in the lot and started to walk the one hundred feet to the entrance of her apartment on Austin Street.

Kitty noticed a man lurking near the parking lot. Nervously, she walked up Austin Street toward a police call box to telephone for help. The man followed her and grabbed her. Kitty screamed. Lights went on in the ten-story apartment house. Windows slid open. Then Kitty Genovese screamed again: "Oh my God, he stabbed me! Please help me! Please help me!"

From one of the upper windows a man called out: "Let that girl alone!" The attacker, Winston Moseley, a twenty-nine year old man, shrugged his shoulders and walked away.

Kitty struggled to her feet and tried to run to her apartment. Moseley returned and stabbed her again. Kitty screamed again and again. "I'm dying!" she shrieked, "I'm dying!"

Windows opened again. Lights went on. Moseley slipped away. A city bus passed. The lights went off. Kitty struggled to her feet again and crawled to the back of the building.

Moseley returned a third time and stabbed her again. Then he drove away.

Thirty-eight people witnessed the entire thirty-five minute episode. Thirty-eight people. *And not one of them even called the police* from the safety of their homes, to save her life. When someone finally did call, the murderer was gone and Kitty Genovese was dead.

What did these thirty-eight eye witnesses have to say when asked why they didn't even call the police? Here were their responses:

"I didn't want to get involved".

"I don't know" (the majority of the answers)

"Frankly, we were afraid".

"I put out the light in our bedroom and we were able to see better".

"I WAS TIRED. I WENT BACK TO BED".

Just one phone call would have saved her life. *Just one person who cared.* One person who would not rationalize apathy. One person out of thirty-eight who would not tolerate cruelty and injustice.

One person who would speak out.

Instead, thirty-eight "normal, decent" people were silent, as a ruthless killer stabbed a sweet, beautiful and innocent twenty-eight year old girl to death, in three separate attacks during a thirty five minute period. *These thirty-eight people knew her.* They were her neighbors, her friends.

One of these neighbors on Austin Street responded with a sigh: "Let's just forget the whole thing."

I can't forget. We cannot forget. This incident should slap

us in the face and wake us up.

Will we allow the mind's *power not to see* to hold sway over us?
Will we *go back to bed?*
Or, will we *WAKE UP?**

— *12* —

The Cursed Earth

The Bible depicts the murder of Abel by his brother Cain. God turns to Cain and says, "what did you do? The voice of the blood of your brother is crying out to me from the earth! Therefore, you are cursed more than the earth, which opened wide its mouth to receive your brother's blood from your hand." (Genesis 4:11).

Rabbi Yehudah the son of Rabbi Hiyah taught (Sanhedrin 37b): From the day the earth opened its mouth and received the blood of Abel, it never again opened its mouth.

Jewish tradition teaches that when human beings observe the wonders of the world, they are often inspired to praise the Creator. People observe a beautiful sunset and are they are inspired with awe and reverence for God. Perhaps this is the meaning of: "The heavens declare the glory of God, and the expanse of the sky tells of His handiwork" (Psalms 19:1). This is how the creations of God can "open their mouths" and praise God.

The earth, however, teaches Rabbi Yehuda, has been cursed

never to "open its mouth" again. In other words, people will not be inspired to praise God by observing the earth. Why? When the blood of the innocent murder victim (Abel) fell to the ground, the earth covered it. The crime was therefore hidden. It was as if the earth was an accomplice.

The Talmud (Gitin 57b) tells of the murder of the prophet Zechariah which took place in the holy Temple. The blood of the murder victim was not swallowed up by the earth. Miraculously, the blood bubbled furiously on the surface of the earth until it was avenged. In the Holy Temple, the earth, so to speak, "acted out" on behalf of the innocent man who was unjustly killed. It "stood up and spoke out" on behalf of the injustice. It did not merely soak up the blood and allow the murderer to walk away unnoticed.

However, in the world's first murder (and, ever since then, except for that one miraculous event in the Temple), because the earth witnessed the murder of an innocent man (Abel) by his own brother, and did nothing, because it just received the blood in a natural way — it was cursed. Rabbi Yehuda teaches us that when people look at the events in the world, the events seem to lack any semblance of moral order. Because the earth allowed evil to exist without any fight, it lost its ability to praise God in a natural way.*

Why was the earth cursed? Because it did not *stand up and speak out.*

—13—

Outrage

There is an odd and perplexing case in the Talmud (Menahot 37a) of a two-headed son. Does he get a double share of familial inheritance or a single share? "Let them pour boiling water on the head of the one and let us see if the other will scream in pain. If the second does not feel the suffering of the first, then they are two separate individuals (and shall receive two shares)."

The Talmud quotes Psalms (91:15): "I am with him in his travail". Perhaps the Talmud is implying that when we feel the pain of the suffering of our neighbor, we are like one person.

In this vein Rabbi Joseph Soloveitchik writes (in *Kol Dodi Dophek*):

If boiling water is poured on the head of a Moroccan Jew, the prim and proper Jew in Paris or London must scream. And, by feeling the pain, he is loyal to the nation.

Elie Wiesel was born on September 30, 1928 in Sighet, Romania. For the first fifteen years of his life, Wiesel lived a "normal" life as a student. In the spring of 1944, his life turned upside down.

The Germans deported all the Jews of Sighet to Auschwitz. In Auschwitz, Elie Wiesel's mother and younger sister Tsipora were separated from him and burned alive in the ovens. Elie marched with his father from Auschwitz to Buna, Birkenah, and Buchenwald— four concentration camps in less than one year. On January 28, 1945, Shlomo Wiesel, Elie's father, was starved and beaten to death in front of sixteen-year-old Elie's eyes.

After the war, Elie lived in an orphanage in Normandy. He then studied in France and became a journalist. In 1956, before writing anything on the Holocaust, or anything else of significance, he was in a terrible car accident (on 46th Street opposite the U.N.) in New York City.

The first hospital the ambulance drove him to refused to admit him for two reasons: first, his physical state was seemingly beyond repair, and second, he had *refugee* papers.

He finally was taken to New York Hospital.

Wiesel was in a coma. Elie Wiesel, survivor of the Nazi final solution, with "A-7713" tattooed on to his left arm, was left to die in New York Hospital. He was an unknown with no family to speak of (besides his two surviving sisters who were in Europe).

Wiesel, the 28 year old "refugee", the failed journalist from France, lay in a coma.

Dr. Paul Braunstein, an orthopedic surgeon at the hospital noticed the tattoo on Elie's arm and decided not to give up on him. He put Wiesel's broken body back together. He whispered in his ear words of hope. Within a few days, Elie awoke from his coma. He then spent a year in a wheelchair.

This was the tumultuous and tormented life of Elie Wiesel until 1956. Then he made a decision. He decided to *stand up and speak out.* He decided to open himself up and start talking .

In the book *"Night",** Wiesel revealed his true feelings:

Never shall I forget that night, the first night in camp, which has turned my life into one long night, seven times cursed, and seven times sealed.

Never shall I forget that smoke.
Never shall I forget the little faces of the children, whose bod-
ies I saw turned into wreaths of smoke beneath a silent blue sky.

Since 1958, Elie Wiesel has written more than 36 other books. In 1969 he married Marion Rose in Jerusalem and in 1972 his son "Shlomo Elisha" was born. "Shlomo" was the name of his father, "Elisha" means "God is salvation" in Hebrew.

Elie Wiesel's personal suffering and pain propelled him and strengthened him to *stand up and speak out* against torture, cruelty and evil. In his words, "being a witness moves me to write, teach and speak... *so I am responsible not only for myself... every moment*, therefore, is *a moment of grace*, and I must justify it... . Once you have that conviction, it's easy... Once you enter the world of Auschwitz, you become obsessed; You are no longer the same person."

On April 19, 1985 president Ronald Reagan presented the *Congressional Gold Medal of Achievement* to Elie Wiesel at a ceremony in the White House. The medal recognized Wiesel's chairmanships of the U.S. Holocaust Memorial Council. It praised him as a world leader, a man who advances the cause of human rights, a literary scholar.

Reagan had planned to visit Bitburg, West Germany, on May 4, 1985, to place a wreath at a cemetery of German soldiers and members of the S.S. He said that he "did not want to visit the (Dachau concentration) camp, in order not to reawaken memories" and "*that most German soldiers in the cemetery were as much victims of the Nazis as were the Jewish inmates of the camps.*"

Reagan presented the medal to Wiesel, who addressed the country and the president with: "That place (Bitburg), Mr. president, is not your place. Your place is with the victims of the S.S. ... for I have seen the S.S. at work, and I have seen their victims. They (the victims) were my friends. They were my parents."

Wiesel said: "*I have learned the danger of indifference, the crime of indifference... .*" He used the opportunity to express his outrage over the president's decision to ignore the plight of human suffering. He criticized the president of the U.S.A. in the White House in front of the entire Western civilization, even as Wiesel was being awarded and recognized for his leadership.

Against the vehement pressure of American Jews, Elie Wiesel decided to "speak truth to power". He didn't listen to his fellow Jews. Instead, he spoke out for the victims of unspeakable cruelty.

On December 10, 1986, Elie Wiesel accepted the *Nobel Peace Prize* for speaking out about various humanitarian causes.

In his acceptance speech in Oslo he said: "...When human lives are endangered, when human dignity is in jeopardy, national borders and sensitivities become irrelevant. Wherever men or women are persecuted because of their race, religion or political view, that place must – at that moment – become the center of the universe".

Elie Wiesel was among the first to speak out for Soviet Jewry. In 1966 he wrote a book called *"The Jews of Silence"*. He has since spoken out about atrocities in South Africa, Argentina, Cambodia, Biafra, Ethiopia, Bosnia and about the maltreatment of the Vietnamese "boat people". He has traveled the world to bear witness to the pain, and has spoken up from their silence.

After the My Lai massacre in Vietnam, Wiesel chartered a plane to get there and help. He recently visited the Miskito Indians of Nicaragua to obtain first hand reports of their suffering under the Sandinista regime.

In Wiesel's own words: "...Whenever I became aware of an injustice, I tried to learn, first of all, as much as I could about it. Speak about it, write about it. Take a position. I was in South Africa; I wrote about the Sowetos. I wrote of my shame as a white person... *the outrage one feels*. Biafra. Miskito Indians. It's the Jew in me that felt the outrage... ."

Elie Wiesel, like others, could have blocked out the pain and suffering of others. He, too, could have let the *power not to see* crush his feelings toward people in pain. But , he didn't. He stood up, and spoke out.*

Elie Wiesel understood, intuitively, that when one human being is suffering, he must *scream*. When boiling water is poured on the head of a human being anywhere in the world, others must scream. They must be in pain.

Our response to cruelty cannot be apathy. It must be *outrage.*

— 14 —

Abraham's Response to the Suffering of Others

The Torah tells about three instances in the life of Abraham, our forefather, that exemplify his attitude toward the suffering of other people.

The first incident took place when he heard that his nephew, Lot, was taken captive. The second was when he heard of Sodom's impending destruction. The third: when he found out that the wives of Abimelech, king of Gerar, were stricken with infertility.

We will discuss each of the three incidents.

HIS "BROTHER"

The Torah describes the rescue mission of Abraham to save his nephew, Lot. Abraham had heard that Lot was held in captivity and needed help. He immediately strove with all his might (and with his three friends) to rescue Lot and his possessions from captivity. He succeeded.

On the surface, it seemed like a basic courtesy that anyone would do for a beloved nephew. But, as usual, the Torah has a deeper meaning when we look further.

Abraham knew that his nephew, Lot, had made a mistake by moving to Sodom. Abraham could easily have rationalized: "You got yourself into this, you get yourself out!" Or better: "It would be better for you to solve your own problems. I can't keep bailing you out! I'm going to abstain — for your own good!"

Further, Abraham could have thought to himself: "The last time I saw Lot, we split up. As the Torah stated: "Lot looked up and saw that the entire Jordan plain all the way to Tsoar, had plenty of water... it was like God's own garden, like the land of Egypt. Lot chose for himself the entire Jordan plain. He headed eastward and the two separated" (Genesis 13:10-11).

Abraham *could* have felt a little bitter at the separation and seeming greediness of Lot.

Now, remember, at this time, Abraham was not a young man. He was about 80 years old. He could have thought, " I'm an old man. Can I really go after these kings and risk my life to save Lot?"

Yet, Abraham understood that the human tendency is to rationalize *hesed* out of our lives. Quickly, he chose not to judge Lot or rationalize apathy. The Torah records Abraham's hearing of Lot's predicament, and Abraham's action in the *same verse*. This is for emphasis.

Did you ever see a homeless man on the street begging for a quarter? Did you ever say to yourself: "If I give him money *what would be the use*? He is just going to buy cigarettes or alcohol with it! Giving him the money is really *not* helpful or healthy for him! I'm not giving him my money — *for his sake!*"

Or perhaps you thought (or rationalized): "This man should take a shower and get a job and support himself. He's not crippled or handicapped. If I give him a quarter, I am, in effect, approving of his lazy, hopeless attitude. In fact, if I give him a quarter, he'll probably keep begging. So, it follows, that if I give him any money, I'm really not helping him — I'm hurting him!" (Just a side note: I just read that thirty percent of New York City's homeless are families, forty two percent are children).

The fact is, when we see a homeless person our human hearts should empathize. As it says in Psalms (34:19): "The Lord is close to those who are broken hearted..." Our *hesed* should overcome our rationalization. Abraham did not just *think* about helping Lot. He didn't weigh the pros and cons. He acted. He took three of his friends and went to rescue Lot.

Furthermore, the verse that describes Abraham's reaction to hearing the news about Lot is very telling. The Torah (Genesis 14:14), understood literally, says: "When Abraham heard that his *brother* was taken captive...". Now, we know that Lot was not Abraham's *brother*. Perhaps this is a lesson to us about the value of human life. The Torah might be hinting to us that when a human being is in danger; when an innocent fellow human being is taken captive — it is not a time to make judgments or rationalize. It is time to consider him your *brother*.

"SHALL THE JUDGE OF THE EARTH NOT ACT JUSTLY?"

Later, God tells Abraham that the city of Sodom will be destroyed.

Abraham knew that Sodom was a cruel place. According to the Midrash, they actually tortured their visitors. They had rules against hospitality! The people exemplified the antithesis of compassion. They banded together in their intolerance and hatred. If somebody was different, or not a native of the city, he would be treated with cruelty.

Abraham was not ignorant of the crimes against humanity that went on in Sodom.

How, then, did Abraham react when he found out that Sodom would be destroyed?

His reaction is legendary. It remains the paradigm of the truly human reaction to evil and suffering:

He approached (God) and said, "Will you actually wipe out

the innocent together with the guilty? Suppose there are fifty innocent people in the city. Would you destroy it, and not spare the
place for the sake of the fifty good people inside it? It would be
sacrilege to ascribe such an act to you — to kill the innocent with
the guilty, letting the righteous and the wicked fare alike. *Halilah
Lechah —It would be sacrilege to ascribe this to you! Shall the Judge
of all the earth not act justly?"* (Genesis 18:23-25).

Abraham then continues to plead with God not to hurt innocent people. "...Let my Lord not become angry, but I will speak just
once more. Suppose ten (innocent people) are found there?"

God agrees with his logic. (Perhaps one can say that God was
"testing" Abraham to see if he would respond as he did.)

Abraham hears about the impending destruction of others and
reacts with compassion and outrage.

When we read about the murder of innocent people all over
the world, how do we react? Is it with apathy or with empathy? Is it
with calm, rational, disconnected understanding — or is it with
outrage, compassion and action? When we hear that every two seconds, somewhere in our world, an innocent child starves to death
(or dies of malnutrition), what goes through our minds? *How did
you react reading that last sentence?* Are you outraged? Are you
prepared to stick your neck out to help save some of these children? This year twenty million people will die of malnutrition. What
are we prepared to do about it? What would Abraham have done?

Perhaps this is why the Torah describes Abraham as having
walked in the ways of God. The way of God is compassion. It is
mercy and kindness. It is to feel outraged at evil and sympathetic to
the suffering of others (no matter who they be).

HOW DO WE RESPOND?

While I was writing this book, a very tragic and horrible incident occurred. On April 19, 1995 a few fanatics blew up a Federal
building in Oklahoma City, killing hundreds of innocent men,
women and children. Young working mothers had just dropped off

their babies and toddlers at a day care center on the second floor just minutes before the blast. They turned around in horror and saw their children blown to bits or crushed.

A few days after this happened, I was asked to speak at a youth seminar on the topic of *hesed*. I asked these sixty high school and college students (and myself) a few disturbing questions:

"How did we react to this news? Was it with more or less emotion than, let's say, hearing that your home team lost the play-offs last year?"

"Was it with less or more outrage and sadness than the day it rained on your vacation? Or how about the outrage you showed on your last drive on the highway when you were cut off or stopped for a ticket that you "really didn't deserve"? ('Everyone else on the road was going 75 miles per hour too! Why did the police officer have to single me out? It's not fair!')."

The students responded honestly. A very memorable lecture turned into a very revealing one. We ended with the conclusion: The difference between a human being and an animal is our power to *choose*. It is our power to *decide our priorities* and to improve our sensitivity to the spiritual and our compassion towards others. It is to feel outraged at evil and sympathetic to the suffering of others.

The Torah tells us of another incident in the life of Abraham: his visit with Avimelech, the King of *Gerar*. At the conclusion, the Torah tells us (Genesis 20:18): "for God had closed up all the wombs of the house of Avimelech because of (the incident concerning) Sarah, Abraham's wife."

God was punishing the families of the king by making all his wives barren. Infertility is a terribly tragic situation. What is very interesting is Abraham's reaction (Genesis 20:17): "and Abraham prayed unto God, and God healed Abimelech and his wife and his maids and they bore children".

Here we have another type of response *to human suffering*. Abraham's reaction to other people's pain is *prayer*. He knows that he can't cure their physiological infertility, so immediately he turns to God and prays for their health.

How many people do you know who, when struck with a disease, *go and pray for other people* to be cured of it? Abraham could have felt "misery loves company"! He *could* have been unsympathetic to Avimelech's problem. Somebody else would have said: "My wife has been barren for our entire marriage. I'm ninety nine years old and I still do not have a child with Sarah. And I was promised to have one years ago! Why should Avimelech complain?"

No. Abraham responds with empathy and turns to God to pray for his friend's recovery. Perhaps we can say that, because Abraham himself was suffering, he better understood Avimelech's predicament. *His personal pain sensitized him to the pain of others.*

The next incident described in the Torah begins (21:1-2): "And God remembered Sarah as He had said and God did unto Sarah as He had spoken. And Sarah conceived, and bore a son to Abraham in his old age at the set time of which God had spoken to him..."

The premise of the Rabbis is that the Torah does not necessarily describe its incidents or "sections" (or "Parashiyot") in chronological order. Thus, the Talmud states (Bava Kama 92a): "This section (about God remembering Sarah) adjoins the preceding one (about Abraham praying for the house of Avimelech to end the infertility). This is to teach you that anyone who seeks mercy (or prays for mercy) for his fellow man (any human being) when he himself is in need of that very thing, he is answered first. As it is stated, 'And he prayed, etc...' which is immediately followed by: 'and God remembered Sarah.' 'For He had already remembered her before He healed Avimelech'". Can this be the "boomerang effect" of a proper response?

THE "CHILDREN OF ABRAHAM"

The Jewish people were charged with a mission. It must become "the light among the nations". As Jews, we must strive to exemplify true *hesed*. As the descendants of Abraham, we must continue his mission of responding to the suffering of others with immediate action. We must stress the virtue of empathy, of tolerance, of kindness, of mercy, of compassion — to our children. We must tell them about Abraham; that he knew when to be sympathetic and understanding, when to be hospitable, when to stand up and speak out against cruelty, suffering of innocents, and injustice of all forms. We must let them know that Abraham knew when to plead with God and when to cry to God on behalf of other human beings. He also knew when to respond with direct action against aggressors.

The sages of the Talmud* went so far as to say that "whoever is merciful to his fellow man is certainly of the children of Abraham". Compassion was indisputably the most indispensable and most distinguishing characteristic of the Jews, who were called *rahamanim benei rahamanim* — "compassionate ones, children of compassionate ones."**

Another word for compassion in Hebrew is *rahamim*. The verb is *raham*. It has the same root as the noun *rehem* (womb). Perhaps its original meaning was "brotherhood" or "brotherly feeling."

The sages wanted the Jewish people to be concerned with compassion and mercy. One of the ways they stressed this was to say that, if you don't act compassionately, you should be suspected of not being a Jew! To the sages, a Jew must be a compassionate human being. The Jewish people have the paradigm of Abraham to emulate, and his legacy to uphold.***

LEARNING FROM HIS OWN PAIN

The world renowned N.Y. Times journalist (and editor) A.M. Rosenthal had a heart operation in the fall of 1994. He wrote in his column**** that he had been given too large a dose of anesthesia. He felt a kind of paranoia. People (doctors and nurses) were sticking him with things and touching him and he felt that they were all out to make him suffer. He said it was a terribly painful experience — more emotionally and psychologically than physically. "I did not understand why all these people were hurting me, why nobody stopped them. I was not just frightened, but in total enveloping terror. I felt it as an overriding bottomless pain. The agony was that since I didn't know why I was being made to suffer so, I could not conceive of the end of the suffering.

"I catch my breath at the memory of those long hours."

He also said that he hopes he will *never forget* that experience. Why? Most people don't want to remember how pain felt! Most people want to forget it as fast as possible and go on. But A.M. Rosenthal felt that he now had first-hand understanding of what a mentally handicapped person feels like. In his words, "I will never forget, I hope, because it gave me a brief taste of the anguish of people who cry in the street because they do not know where their pain is coming from."

He wrote that if you break your leg they call an ambulance, but if you break your mind they leave you on the street to go homeless and die. In his words, "New York State permits severely disturbed people... to remain on the streets weeping, unfed, without medicine."

A.M. Rosenthal, at age 70, felt a certain sense of fulfillment in his own personal suffering. A.M. Rosenthal used his pain as a light to illuminate the pain of others. He now was able to act in an even more sympathetic, sensitive, caring way to the mentally ill and homeless. He makes recommendations to the public and to law makers to help end the suffering all around us. "When it happens," he writes, "we will no longer have to pass the bodies of people with broken minds, or avert our eyes not to see their faces."

A.M. Rosenthal stands up and speaks out about the persecution of *all* people.

"A double crime is being committed," he writes.* "The crime of persecution... and the crime of the accepting witness..."

"As long as passivity lasts, so long will persecution (and injustice and suffering and cruelty) continue. It has always been so."

"WAIT UNTIL I UNLOAD MY MULES"

In the second century, there lived a Tanna, the teacher of Rabbi Akiva, named Nahum Ish Gamzu. He used to respond to every occurrence by saying *"Gam Zu Le-Tovah"* - *"This too is for the best"* (Taanit 21a).

The Talmud (Taanit 21a) relates, that, toward the end of his life, Rabbi Nahum explained to his students why he was made to suffer so much pain.

He was once on the road with three mules laden with food, drink and various delicacies. A poor man approached him and asked for food. Nahum told him, "Sure, but wait until I unload my mules." Before Nahum finished unloading, the man died.

Nahum fell on the man and cried out:
"May my eyes which had no compassion on your eyes, become blind.
"May my hands, which had no compassion on your hands become crippled! "May my feet, which had no compassion on your feet become crushed!
"May my whole body become covered with sores!"

Now what exactly did Nahum do wrong? Did he refuse the poor man food or drink? Was he really responsible for the man's death?

Evidently, Nahum felt that by making the man *wait*, by rationalizing apathy, by not acting swiftly in response to the suffering of another human being — he was guilty of murder. What Nahum exemplified by cursing himself to suffer is that he understood the true message of Abraham our forefather. He understood what Judaism's response is to suffering and he was actually thankful for his eventual pain as recompense for his own apathy.

"WHAT HAS BECOME OF OUR HUMANITY?"

Shervin Pishevar was a six-year-old Iranian boy in 1980 when Iraq began bombing his country. "I'll never forget my fear," he said to New York Times columnist Anthony Lewis on November 22, 1994.

Eventually his family escaped Iran and moved to America. His father went from being an important television executive to driving a taxi, and his mother worked as a maid.

At age twenty, Shervin was a student at the University of California, in Berkeley, majoring in plant genetics. "My brother, who is 26, is a lawyer. My sister, 24, is getting her Ph.D. in clinical psychology. And my father, who's 56, is working on a Ph.D. in mass communications," he said.

Was he bitter about the suffering his family had to go through? Can such a family make a contribution to the world after all the hardships they have gone through? Could they become successful in a foreign country, knowing no one and not speaking the language? Could they turn their sadness and struggle into joy and fulfillment? Could they make any significant contribution to society?

Two days before Thanksgiving 1994, columnist Anthony Lewis received a telephone call. It was Shervin, who asked him how he could reach a Sarajevo children's doctor who had been mentioned in one of Lewis' columns. "I want to help," he said.

"Every Thanksgiving, my whole family sits down, we say our prayers and each of us talks about what we've been through and how important we are to each other. And we always talk about how we have responsibility for other people.

"One of the Persian poets, Sa'di Shirazi, said: 'The sons of Adam are limbs of each other, having been created of one essence. When the calamity of time affects one limb, the other limbs cannot remain at rest. If thou hast no sympathy for the troubles of others, thou art unworthy to be called by the name of man.'

"That's what Sarajevo is about. We all have a responsibility to each other."

Shervin also works as a volunteer in the emergency room of a children's hospital, running for supplies and helping the children to stay calm. "The doctors and nurses have enough stress trying to save the child's life." But now, Bosnia is on his mind. He wants to reach the doctors in Sarajevo and offer to come and help in the children's clinic.

"A couple of days ago, I saw a picture of a seven-year old boy in Sarajevo, who had been shot in the head. I don't know how we can ignore the killing of children.

"What has become of our humanity?

"I'm afraid we have lost the sense of responsibility for people who are being murdered by hate. I don't know what has happened to us. America has a history of helping those who are suffering.

"Just fifty years ago we saw the horror of mass murder that happened because people hated those who were different. I can't understand why we haven't learned".

If this is the sentiment of an Iranian immigrant, what should *our* feelings be? Can we learn something about who we are, and what we are supposed to be thinking about, from this twenty year old boy?

Just as he asked, so should we: *What has become of our humanity?*

—15—

A Seasoned Hesed Professional

E veryone knows the story of Noah, his ark and the flood. God tells Noah that He will be bringing a flood to destroy all the people (and animals) of the earth. Then, He tells Noah to build an ark, so he and his family would be saved.

After the forty days of the flood, the world was still not ready for Noah, his family and the animals on the ark to dock and descend. The flood-waters were still too high. In fact, it took a full year on the ark from the first day of the flood until Noah descended.

What happened during the year Noah and his family spent on the ark? Noah immersed himself in *hesed*, as he cared for the thousands of creatures who needed his help.

In fact, the Torah calls Noah *ish tsadik, tamim*, a *righteous, perfect man*. That is quite a compliment! What was the reason for this fantastic description of Noah? What did Noah do so well or so ethically that he merited such a fine compliment?

The Midrash tells us that it was nothing other than Noah's compassion for other living things. According to the Midrash (Tanhuma, 58) Noah was called a *tsadik*, a righteous man, because of his extraordinary care of the animals on the ark.

Another Midrash (Genesis Rabah, Noah 31:14) tells us that Noah was unable to sleep because he was worried– were all the animals on the ark fed at their proper time?

In effect, God had replaced the old , self- serving, violent world with a new one, led by a seasoned *hesed* professional.

"The world is built on *hesed*" (Psalms 89:13). The world cannot sustain itself without kindness. Noah had the "*hesed*-training" for one year on the ark. Perhaps we all could use a little "*hesed*-training" as well.*

— 16 —

Why Moshe?

M oshe Rabbenu was the greatest leader of the Jewish people. He is described as being able to speak with God "face to face". The Torah tells us that there never was a prophet like Moshe.

What was the most important moral quality that Moshe possessed to give him this ability? Why did God decide to choose him to lead the Jews out of slavery? Why did God give His holy Torah through Moshe? Did Moshe have superior physical skills? Was he a great public speaker? Did he know how to persuade or "win friends and influence people?" What was it that caused God to choose this man?

The Midrash (Shemot Rabah 2:2) tells us through a story:

While our teacher Moshe was tending the sheep of Jethro in the wilderness, a kid, a baby goat, ran away from him. He ran after it until it reached Hasnah. Upon reaching Hasnah it came upon a pool of water (whereupon) the kid stopped to drink. When Moses reached it he said: "I did not know that you were running because (you were) thirsty. You must be tired." He placed it on his shoulder and began to walk. The Holy One, Blessed Be He, said: "You are compassionate in leading flocks belonging to mortals; I swear, you will similarly shepherd My flock, Israel".

The Midrash clearly implies that Moshe was not chosen for his public speaking, political skills, physical skills... but for one reason: *his compassion.*

This compassion had two very different dimensions. One is a gentle sensitivity to others. The other is a sense of outrage, motivating him to take action against evil.

If we look carefully at the events in Moshe's life, both dimensions of *hesed* stand out.

• "... and Moshe grew up and went out to his brothers, and he saw their burdens. And he noticed an Egyptian striking a Hebrew, one of his brothers. So he looked around and saw that there was no one, then he slayed the Egyptian and hid him in the sand" (Exodus 2:11-12).

This is the first incident the Torah relates about Moshe. The most compassionate of men knows when to stand up and use physical force.

• The second incident appears just in the next verse (2:13): "And he went out on the second day, and behold, two Hebrew men were fighting. And he said to the man that was in the wrong, "why do you hit your fellow man?'"

Moshe knew when to stand up and speak out against evil. *Hesed* is not standing by and "tolerating" strife. To practice true *hesed,* one must know when to stand up and speak out.

• When Moshe ran away to Midyan, he witnessed the male shepherds of Midyan driving away the women shepherds from a well.

Moshe's response was clear: "And Moshe *stood up* and saved them, and watered their flock (for them)". He knew when to stand up against cruelty and help those who are in need.

These three incidents introduce us to the personality of Moshe, our leader. He was a man who knew and practiced the true concept of *hesed.* He knew how and when to stand up and speak out against evil and cruelty.

The Midrash stated above asked the question "why Moshe?" "Why did God choose Moshe?" It gave its answer through the anecdote of Moshe saving a helpless, thirsty sheep. The message was clear: because he was a man of compassion. *He was concerned for all living things.*

Yet, one might ask a simple question. It was evident from the three incidents in Moshe's life preceding God's revelation to him why God chose him: He was a leader who knew when and how to speak up against evil, injustice and cruelty.

Why does the Midrash even ask the question?

Perhaps the Midrash understood that one might see those leadership qualities and mistakenly think that Moshe was not a man of sensitivity and compassion. One might think that being compassionate means tolerating evil and complacently standing by, or pitying the evil-doer.

The Midrash wanted us to know that the leader who decided to kill the Egyptian murderer was the same person who took a thirsty sheep on his back to find it water. True compassion understands when to be tolerant and loving yet when to be intolerant to injustice. The sensitivity that brought Moshe to help defenseless women (or a thirsty sheep), was the same sensitivity that brought him to speak out against cruelty and act physically against inhumane treatment of his fellow man.

Rabbi Samson Rafael Hirsch, in *Horeb* (Vol. I, pp 54-55), writes:

> *Do not suppress this compassion, this sympathy, especially with the sufferings of your fellowman. It is the warning voice of duty, which points out to you your brother in every sufferer, and your own sufferings in his, and awakens the love which tells you that you belong to him and his sufferings with all the powers that you have.*
>
> *Do not suppress it! ... See in it the admonition of God that you are to have no joy as long as a brother suffers by your side.*

This attribute of standing up and speaking out, Moshe exemplified again and again. At the time of the sin of the golden calf, God tells Moshe (Exodus 32:9-14): "I have seen this people and they are stiff-necked people. Now, let me do what I want and my anger will destroy them and I will make of you a great nation."

Moshe immediately pleaded with God on behalf of the people (Exodus 32:12), "...Turn from Your anger and turn from the evil against Your people. Remember Abraham, Isaac and Israel, Your servants to whom You swore to multiply their seed as the stars of the heaven". Then, again, Moshe puts his own life at risk and begs God to forgive the Jewish people (for the sin of the Golden Calf) and spare their lives. "And now, if You will forgive their sin. And, if not, please blot me out from Your book which You have written!" (Exodus 32:32)

Moshe, our leader, was unafraid to stand up and speak out on behalf of the people. It was this sense of kindness, of *hesed*, that enabled him to assume the leadership of the Jewish people.*

—17—

The Choice is Ours

One of the greatest, most prolific thinkers in history is Moses Maimonides, the Rambam. He writes:*
"...the purpose of the laws of the Torah is to promote compassion, loving-kindness and peace in the world".

The Hasidic leader Rabbi Moses Leib of Sassov epitomized the concept in his famous statement "to know the needs of men and to bear the burden of their sorrows — *that is the true love of man.*"

We can't stop all the suffering in the world in one fell swoop. The task seems enormous. But can we make a *few small decisions?* What is under our control?
We can choose what we do for a living.
We can choose to volunteer to help others.
We can choose our friends.
We can choose which causes to fight for.
We can choose what to open our minds to.

We can choose which organizations to support and volunteer for.

We can choose which industry to support and who to buy
from.

We can choose which type of cruelty to renounce.

We can choose to be ecologically careful, not to waste.

We can choose to find out about and speak out against
any and every form of cruelty and suffering.

When you were born, *you were crying* and the world rejoiced.
Your goal should be that when you die, the *world will be crying* and
you will rejoice.

If your life is a statement of compassion your death will not
sadden you. It will sadden the world which will miss you. On the
other hand, if your life is merely spent in the pursuit of your own
selfish goals, what did it mean?

I often ask groups of high school students to write their own
epitaphs. "What do you want written on your tombstone?" I ask
them. Their responses tell the story of their real values.

What do *you* want written on your tombstone? Should it say,
"here lies John Doe, he had a big house, a fancy car, and a sizable
bank account?" Should it say "he took a nice vacation every year"?
Should it say "he spent hours each week in the office"?

Imagine if it said: *He sought out the pain and suffering of
others. He fought against cruelty. His life was spent pursuing compassion and freedom. He saw his life as an opportunity to increase
the love in the world and to decrease the callousness and pain.*

When a person with this dream and life purpose dies, how
does the world respond? *It cries, for it has lost a great human being.*

Just ask yourself: *Would the world be a better place with me
in it or with me out of it? Would there be more or less suffering?*

We look back at the past and we are shocked by the lack of
fair play. Women and blacks could not vote. Women were not allowed into college, and blacks were segregated. What will they say

about *us* one hundred years from now? They might look back in disgust at our generation. They might say that we had little or no respect for our fellow human beings, for the environment, the soil, the water, natural energy, or the lives of other living things.

They might say that we continually ignored and tolerated evil in all forms. We stood by and watched as innocent women and children were massacred in Bosnia and in other parts of the world. They might also say that we had the choice to be kind, to live lives of compassion but we chose not to. As per the quote attributed to Edmund Burke:

"All that is necessary for the triumph of evil is for enough good men to do nothing."

Can our lifestyle be as fulfilling without destroying our world? What makes life meaningful? *Perhaps we can measure how meaningful our lives are by evaluating how connected we are to everyone and everything around us.* When we close off our hearts to anyone or anything we pay a price. Our ability to love and to feel gets lost. We lose our connectedness to life and life ultimately alienates us from it, cuts us off and *leaves us with less.*

If there is hope for our world, it is found in our ability to choose the path of *hesed,* the way of God. If we want to create a better, safer place for our children, we must follow the biblical examples of Abraham, or Moshe, and the other great leaders. We can choose to bring more *hesed* into our lives. We can choose to be sympathetic, to be caring and kind. We can also choose to stand up and speak out against the injustice and apathy.

For us, human beings created with free will and the ability to choose, the *choice is ours.*

Summary of Part Two

Today, we are living in a world that is permeated by cruelty, injustice and terrible apathy. This threatens our survival. Tragic and unnecessary suffering and death can be avoided if people decide to stand up and speak out. Let us realize that, as human beings, we were born with the ability to rationalize, to justify, our apathy. Consequently, we must fight back the urge to ignore the pain of others.

Abraham, our forefather, taught us that true *hesed* is kindness, but it is also the ability to stand up and speak out against cruelty and evil. Moshe, our leader, was chosen for his understanding of this balance. Moshe knew when to be sympathetic and kind and when to fight injustice and apathy.

Finally, we must realize that we human beings do have a choice. We can choose to ignore the plight of the poor and the less fortunate, or we can choose to stand up and speak out. When we choose the latter, we create a better, more loving world for our children.
The choice is ours.

Part Three

Everyday Kindness

— *18* —

Everyday Kindness

In Judaism, there is a legal principle called *tadeer veshe-eno tadir, tadir kodem.* This means: if we are faced with two alternative actions, one that occurs often and another that occurs only seldomly, we act first on the one that is more frequent — and then act on the one that occurs less often.

Perhaps this principle can be applied to *hesed* as well. We should be careful not to underestimate the opportunities to do *hesed* that present themselves most often.

Hesed should start in the home. Start with your immediate family. Your business associates. Your closest friends. *Then* go out and "save the world."

48 HOURS

How many opportunities do you have to practice random acts of kindness? Each and every day we are faced with literally thousands of situations that can call for *hesed.*

Here was the last 48 hours for me:

• A car waited and hoped to get into my lane on the highway.
• A person ran, hoping to catch the elevator that I was standing in.
• A woman dropped her change on the subway and hoped I would help pick it up for her.
• My children wanted ice-cream cones.
• My wife needed to know if I still thought she was pretty.
• My sister needed to know that I trust her decision making ability.
• My mother needed to know that I don't blame her for how nutty I turned out.
• My employee needed to know if I still value her opinion.
• My brother was hoping to spend some quality time with me.
• My wife's close friend was hoping I would write a speech for her non-profit organization and deliver it (to help raise funds for children with Attention Deficit Disorder).
• My business associate was hoping I would call "just to say hello and see how things are."
• Two of my nieces were hoping to stay with us in our summer home for the weekend.
• One of my vendors needed to sell me his product and make a small profit.
• I interviewed a fine young woman for a marketing position. She needed to know that I appreciated her experience and her skills.
• A close friend needed to hear me say that he wasn't crazy, and that I had feelings similar to his.
• There were ten of my employees who needed to know that I valued their work, their extra effort.
• There were two homeless people on the street near my office who were hungry.
• My close friend's two year old daughter was diagnosed

with leukemia. I needed to visit, to talk to my friend, to encourage him, and to *be there for him.*

• A business associate needed to "vent." She needed me to listen to her and to empathize.

• Thousands of strangers (other human beings) needed me to *smile.* This would mean that they're not *invisible.* They matter.

• My brother-in-law was hoping to talk to me about his business career.

• One of my students called, hoping that I could give a special class in her home for her friends.

• The cashier at a store was hoping for some acknowledgment.

• My friend needed a loan.

• My close friend's wife had just given birth to twin girls and it was time to share in his joy, visit, bring gifts and congratulate him.

• My wife is sleeping as I write this. I have to be careful not to disturb her sleep or awaken her.

• An elderly man needed a lift home from synagogue. Did I happen to have room in my car for him?

• A young couple came to me to ask my advice about the purchase of their first home.

• Every person that I came into contact with needed me to either pay *attention,* show *affection* or express *appreciation.*

"I'M JUST A REGULAR GUY"

Very often, people think that they must do something *spectacular* in order to feel accomplished. Most people associate *hesed* with major campaigns such as *Feed the Children,* giant projects like the fight against homelessness, or heroic altruism like risking your life to save Jews from the Holocaust.

It is actually very dangerous to think this way. The *more* that people believe that *hesed* is beyond them, or that *hesed* is only for the heroes, the *less* they will feel that they can practice *hesed* themselves.

I can't tell you how often someone responds to one of my speeches or lectures with, "that was a beautiful speech, Jack. I was moved. But, you see, *hesed* is for people like Jerry Lewis. Real *hesed* is done by my Rabbi or my doctor. *I'm just a regular guy.*"

How many of us *regular guys* feel that our lives are too busy, too normal, too restless to think about random acts of kindness and compassion? Our view of ourselves usually determines how we act. If we believe *hesed* is only for "other" people, we then disassociate from it. We label ourselves as "regular" or "normal" or just "busy". Then we dismiss *hesed* from our lives.

I am fortunate to have many good friends. Every year, on my birthday, an "anonymous" friend plays *Happy Birthday* music on the voice-mail in my office. This thoughtful person makes sure that the first message I hear on March 7th is not another obligation I might have to undertake. Instead, it is a delightful and humorous *Happy Birthday* tune that cheers me up and makes my day a little more special.

So, my anonymous friend, Steven Giller, wherever you are, thank you for being so considerate. Thank you, Steve, for brightening up my day and for teaching me that *a simple act of kindness can go a long way in someone's heart.*

Steven Giller and I hardly spend time together. We are friends from high school. Yet, I know that Steve's life is a statement of compassion. I know that we are connected in a spiritual way. How? By magical, mystical, yet simple acts of courtesy and kindness. Altruism builds and maintains normal acts of *hesed* that make the world a nicer, more enjoyable place to live in.

Thanks again, Steve.

My cousin and friend, Sara Sultan, who personifies the meaning of kindness, has typed (and retyped and retyped...) the vast majority of this book. When you call Sara and she is not available, her answering machine plays a song:

> You've got to get up every morning with a smile on your face and show the world all the love in your heart.

Her message cheers you up and really puts a smile on your face! Sara teaches me how important small acts of kindness are. They always make a difference. Thanks, Sara.

HESED IN THE LITTLE THINGS

We can find opportunities to do *hesed* in the little things. *Hesed*, loving-kindness — is found in a real handshake. It is found in a sincere "thank you." *Hesed* is found when you open the door for someone, or you let your neighbor park his car in your driveway. *Hesed* is withstanding the temptation to honk your horn when the "idiot" in front of you goes too slow; withstanding the temptation to curse when the "moron" going faster than you passes you by. (And *hesed* is *not* referring to your fellow human beings by those names, or others, just because they are not moving at your exact pace in life).

FIVE KIND WORDS

Our lives are nourished by kind words and gracious behavior. A simple *excuse me* can calm down a tense friend. A simple, sincere, *thank you* can make someone's day.

My wife taught my six-year-old daughter Annette, to look at the five fingers of her hand and to count her "five nice words". My daughter counts her fingers and names them "please, thank you, excuse me, hello and good-bye". She smiles with pride as she "shows off" how well she remembers her five precious friends, her "five nice words" of courtesy that will bring *hesed*, love and kindness into the world.

THREE-STEP HESED TECHNIQUE

I recently read an interesting book on love and relationships. The author discusses a simple, proven, *three-step* way to build or rebuild the love in a relationship. Her formula is to take just three minutes, three times a day, and do three things: (1) Pay *attention* to your spouse. (2) Show *affection*. (3) Express *appreciation* (say "I love you" or "I love the way you..." or "I'm sorry for..." "Thanks for being so forgiving, so kind, so patient with me...").

Do you think this three-step technique can improve the quality of your relationships? Of course it can. These three steps are three acts of everyday (*every minute*) *hesed*. They are three simple acts of loving kindness that, if done often, can transform a bad marriage and end the *hostility*. Everyday, "normal", simple, random *hesed* habits will enrich lives.

42 IDEAS FOR EVERYDAY KINDNESS

1. Get up and give your seat to the woman or elderly person on the train.
2. Spend fifteen minutes in a hospital emergency room and help someone.
3. Help someone walk across the street (the blind, seniors, kids).
4. Listen to people with eye contact, truly attempting to understand.
5. Put your shopping cart back, at the supermarket, when you're finished with it.
6. Write a "thank you card" to someone unexpectedly.
7. Send a greeting card to someone unexpectedly.
8. Take someone's picture with a Polaroid camera and give it to him/her as a gift.
9. Drop off a plant at your local police station.
10. Call someone just to say "I miss you".
11. Pick up trash from the sidewalk and put it where it belongs.
12. Give your waiter an extra-generous tip.

13. Give someone your parking spot (not because you're pulling out, but even when you need one, too).
14. Allow another driver to merge into your lane on the highway.
15. Send a bouquet of flowers to someone unexpectedly.
16. Buy someone an ice-cream cone on a hot day.
17. Allow the person behind you in line at the store to go ahead of you.
18. Pay the toll for the car behind you at the bridge.
19. Order a gift and send it to someone unexpectedly.
20. Make an anonymous donation to a local charity.
21. Slip $20 into the pocketbook or pocket of a needy friend.
22. Sit with a homeless person on the street and listen to him or her.
23. Gather all of your old clothes and give them directly to homeless people.
24. Spend an hour in a hospice or hospital visiting the sick.
25. Bring your secretary a cup of coffee.
26. Find someone doing something right and praise him or her.
27. Smile.
28. Pay for someone's lunch.
29. Pay for the next person in line at a store or museum.
30. Get your kids to donate their old toys to kids who might need and appreciate them more.
31. Pick up the mail or a newspaper for your next door neighbor so he or she doesn't have to bother.
32. Be first to greet everyone today.
33. Do talk to strangers.
34. Say "thank you".
35. Hold the door open for someone.
36. Give someone a hug.
37. Lend someone money.
38. Call your mayor's action volunteer line and find out places to volunteer your services.
39. Hold back the criticism and tolerate other people's weaknesses.

40. Help your spouse with the kids.
41. Teach a kid to ride a bike or catch a ball.
42. Baby-sit for someone.

William James wrote, *"I am done with great things and big plans, great institutions and big success. I am for those tiny, invisible loving human forces that work from individual to individual, creeping through the crannies of the world... Which, if given time, will rend the hardest monuments of pride."*

Everyday *hesed* is found in what is most regular. Everyday kindness is found in the most *normal,* everyday events.

NEW YORK CARES

In 1986, in a living room on the Upper West Side of Manhattan, six friends gathered and discussed their frustration with established volunteer agencies in New York City.

Their meeting led to the formation of *New York Cares,* which connects willing volunteers with dozens of projects in and around the city.

Nine years later, New York Cares had enrolled 13,000 volunteers, and its model had been replicated in twenty six cities, with a total membership of seventy five thousand people. They since have created a national umbrella organization known as City Cares Of America to help form new groups and spread successful ideas.

New York Cares' purpose and mission are to make charity work attractive by simplifying the process of volunteering and removing the coercion and guilt. They make volunteering easy, meaningful and fun. They insist on direct involvement in the community and they provide instant gratification for the volunteers. Many of the projects double as singles clubs for the socially conscious and have led to a number of marriages.

Every December, New York Cares collects winter coats for the poor. In 1994, they collected *seventy-one thousand coats.*

At Hands On Atlanta (an offshoot of NewYork Cares), each month there are about two hundred projects, including park clean-ups, tutoring programs and soup kitchens. Hands -On Atlanta was started in 1989 by a group of twelve friends, and in 1995 has a volunteer membership of eleven thousand people, and a one million dollar budget.

The key to their success is simplicity. "Keep it simple," is their motto and their mission.

Simple, pure *hesed.* That is what enriching lives is all about.

THE HESED BOOMERANG PRINCIPLE

The *hesed boomerang* theory is rooted in Jewish tradition. We are promised that acts of altruism will not go unrewarded. Both the written Torah and the oral tradition are replete with assurances and anecdotes to this effect. The concept of *what goes around comes around* is a universal message, but its roots lie deeply within Judaism.

The Torah and the Prophets promise us that kindness is high on God's list of priorities, and that God will repay the giver. The Sages promise us again and again that the rewards of *hesed* in this lifetime and in the world to come are innumerable.

God has promised that our *hesed* will protect us; that its rewards include health, wealth, long life, family, love, a fine reputation, and the promise of our prayers being answered.

The Sages tell us (Shabbat 151b): "Everyone who shows compassion to his fellow creatures is himself granted compassion by heaven." *(Kol hamerahem al haberiyot, merahamim alav min hashamayim).*

The Zohar *(Perashat Emor)* expresses this in an interesting way: "The act below stimulates a corresponding activity above... thus, if a man does kindness on earth, he awakens *hesed* above... similarly, if he performs a deed of mercy, he crowns that day with mercy, and it becomes his protector in the hour of need... happy is the man who exhibits the proper conduct below, since all depends on his act to awaken the corresponding activity above."*

We see a similiar idea in the prophets.

Say of the righteous that it will be well with him; for he shall eat the fruit of his doings. Woe to the wicked. It shall be ill with him, for the work of his hands shall be done to him (Isaiah, 3:10).

The Sages understood Isaiah to mean: if a person, during his lifetime, is in the habit of not having pity on others, he reinforces the attribute of strict heavenly justice. Then, when he is in need of benefits or pity, *he is paid back* "measure for measure" with his own attitude.

The Midrash (Ruth Rabbah 2:14) declares: "Rabbi Ze-era said. The scroll (of Ruth) tells us nothing of ritual purity or impurity, or prohibition or permission. For what purpose was it written? To teach how great is the *reward* to those who perform deeds of kindness."

In commenting on the verse in Kohelet, 7:2, it states:

And the living should put it to his heart. This is referring to God, who lives forever, and who rewards man for every single step that he takes in doing hesed.

The Midrash rewards acts of *hesed* with all the *blessings promised in the Torah.* When the Torah (Deut. 28:22) says, "and all these blessings shall come upon you and overtake you if you will listen to the voice of God," The Midrash (Tanna Deve Eliyahu chapter 26) comments: "When will all these blessings come upon you? If you will obey God and walk in His ways, the ways of heaven."

The following three true stories are good examples of how acts of kindness can "boomerang back". These three examples are not intended to be a comprehensive, nor a statistically significant study of the boomerang effect of *hesed.* Nor do I intend to "prove" or to state unequivocally that acts of *hesed* always return.

I would hope that most people do not need to read stories

about *hesed's* rewards, and would practice *hesed* without a thought about recompense. Yet time and again I hear similarly true and beautiful stories about people who credit their good fortune to a good deed they had done. I would like to think that these are not isolated incidents, that *hesed* does have an almost mystical way of returning to us. I would like to think that everyday kindness can protect us, fulfill us and sustain us. This is God's promise, and it is being kept.

DOLLAR FOR DOLLAR

In 1976, Morris C. Benun was returning home from a business trip. As he approached the toll booth at the Verrazano bridge (on his way from New York to New Jersey) he suddenly realized that he had misplaced his wallet and had no money at all. The toll at the time was a dollar, and Morris was very embarrassed. The cars behind him started honking.

At that moment, he noticed that there was a friend, David Mamiye, several lanes over, in his car, waiting to pass through the toll. Morris hoped that David would help him. He got out of his car, ran over to David's car, explained his embarrassing predicament, and asked him for a dollar. David smiled and immediately gave Morris a dollar bill for the toll.

In 1988, Morris' wife had just given birth to a baby girl in Mount Sinai Hospital in New York City. As Morris walked out of the hospital and over to his car, he noticed a meter maid ticketing cars whose meters had expired. He noticed that the car behind his was about to be ticketed. "I wanted to do something nice for someone, so I placed four quarters into the meter to save the owner from getting a ticket.

"As I was doing this, the owner, David Mamiye, was exiting the hospital and arrived at the scene. It so happened that David's wife had *also* just given birth in Mt. Sinai Hospital and he was just returning from a visit with her. David looked at me and smiled... as we both remembered how he had given me that important dollar bill twelve years earlier."

FLAT TIRE

In May of 1996, *WINS News* reported an amazing event. Multimillionaire tycoon Donald Trump was driving (without his chauffeur) on the New Jersey Turnpike when he got a flat tire. He pulled over to the side of the road and tried to wave down speeding passersby for help.

Finally, a middle-age man stopped and quickly changed Mr. Trump's flat tire. Then he smiled and got back into his car to leave. Donald thanked the unassuming man and asked him if he would accept payment. The man refused. Mr. Trump begged him to take *something*, anything. The man finally told him: "If you really want to thank me, you can do something. Send my wife some flowers!" Donald took down the man's address and he left.

About a week went by, and the man forgot about the incident. He had no idea that the man he helped was Donald Trump, one of the wealthiest men in America.

Two weeks went by and no flowers.

About three and a half weeks after the flat tire incident, a messenger appeared at the door of the man. The messenger had a bouquet of flowers from Donald Trump. There was a note attached to the flowers. It read:

"Thanks for your help.
Sorry for the delay with the flowers.
You see, there were a few complications.
But now, I have settled everything.
I think you will be happy to know that the mortgage on your home is paid in full."
Enclosed is a copy of a confirmation from your bank.
Your house is now 100% yours.
Congratulations, and thanks again."

I have paraphrased the news report. But the message is clear: Mr. Trump decided to show his gratitude with an incredible display of generosity. The unassuming man who did a simple act of kindness was paid back a thousand (or a hundred thousand) times!

"WE'LL TAKE TURNS"

On May 4, 1994, a twelve year old Hasidic girl from Brooklyn named Suri Feldman, was with her school on a hike in the woods in Massachusetts. The girl got lost. It was a Wednesday. Buses came from Jewish communities all over the East Coast to help search for her. About two weeks earlier, a thirteen-year-old-girl got lost in the woods and they recovered her body parts in three different places. The police said she was raped and her body was cut into parts. Can you imagine the anxiety and suffering that Suri's parents must have been feeling?

Wednesday night they searched for Suri all night long. No sign of Suri. Hundreds of thousands of Jews helped, by either searching or by reciting the Book of Psalms with all their hearts. They prayed in the synagogues that they would find Suri alive.

Thursday came and went and still no sign of the young girl. When the Friday morning sun rose, most people (i.e. reporters, police) had serious fears for Suri's safety. Could a twelve year-old Brooklyn Hasidic girl have managed to stay alive without food, all alone for three days in the forest?

On Friday afternoon Suri was found. She was rushed to the hospital and released. She arrived at her home in Boro Park, as hundreds of people waited to celebrate her safe return. Her family, friends and neighbors were singing and dancing in the street. As she approached them they greeted her with hugs and kisses. Some were crying. On her apartment building, there was a giant banner, about three stories high. It contained one simple sentence, one verse, that expressed how everyone felt:

Hodu Lahashem Ki Tov, Ki Le'olam Hasdo.
Thank God for He is Good. His hesed is eternal.

One newspaper reporter attempted to turn the Suri Feldman

story into a scandal. He found out that she is one of thirteen children, and that her family is strictly Orthodox. "Perhaps", he wrote, "she was really running away from home! Perhaps this twelve-year-old had a plan that might explain how she stayed alive for three days. Perhaps she prepared enough 'running away food' in advance."

He did a little more research and found out how she managed to stay alive. At the beginning of the trip, she had told her six friends that she would not mind holding all their lunches. "We will take turns", she said. She volunteered to hold them first as they hiked over hills and in the forest.

After she was lost, she rationed the sandwiches and ate them sparingly until she was finally found on Friday afternoon.

Her act of simple "everyday" *hesed* (carrying their sandwiches) actually kept her alive.

HESED GOAL-SETTING

Of all the things in the world King Solomon could have asked for, he asked God for "an understanding heart". Perhaps he understood that practicing true *hesed* takes training and skill and patience. And when one practices *hesed*, he or she has the whole world (and the next world) in the palm of the hand.

To be good at anything, we have to practice it. We need a game plan, a strategy. To increase the *hesed* in our lives, we need an organized way of building it up. We must monitor how well we are doing with *hesed*, just as we would monitor how well we are doing with our investments.

Any good business person would want to set business goals and monitor them on a daily or weekly basis. When it comes to spiritual goals, seeming "intangible success", most people do not set goals, nor do people check to see how they are progressing.

It is time to decide to increase the *hesed* in our lives. It is time to make a game plan. Our individual game plans are subjective and should be personal. Keep track of your successes and failures. Build small wins and don't be discouraged if you slip.

The verse in Psalms (23:6) comes to mind: *"May only good and hesed pursue me all the days of my life..."* Perhaps, after a person accustoms himself to doing *hesed*, it becomes second nature to him. So, even when the person is not thinking about doing *hesed*, it is as if *hesed* "pursues" him. When people start to increase the *hesed* in their lives and train themselves to do *it*, opportunities for doing *good* and for doing *hesed* seem to appear more often.

It is as if *hesed pursues them.*

THE DAILY HESED PRACTICE CHART

The following is my personal *hesed* practice chart. I have used it to keep myself on track. Feel free to photocopy and adapt the chart to your specific needs. Let the chart guide your daily activities and focus you on *hesed*. See if you can build more 'everyday' *hesed* into your life, and watch the wonderful results.

DAILY HESED PRACTICE CHART

ACTS OF HESED - GENERAL	SUN	MON	TUES	WED	THUR	FRI	SAT
Listen with empathy							
Do a favor for someone							
Drop expectations							
Drop judgments							
Drop criticism							
Forgive mistakes							
Show patience			.				
Tolerate what usually annoys							
Help another - standing side by side							
Sympathize with problems and pain							
Compliment (Praise every small sign of growth)							
Show appreciation and thanks							
Build self-esteem							
Share joy							
Give honest advice							
Give a gift							
Give a card							
Teach and enrich							
Lend money							
Give charity							
Raise charity							
Do not gossip							
No anger, don't lose temper							
Exhibit fair play							
Visit the sick, elderly, lonely, grieving							
Hospitality							
Volunteer							
Help out in school							
Pray for someone							
Hug someone							

DAILY HESED PRACTICE CHART

HESED TOWARDS KIDS	SUN	MON	TUES	WED	THUR	FRI	SAT
"I Love You"							
Give a bath							
Tickle them							
Change diapers							
Get kids dressed							
Get kids undressed							
Read kids a book							
Tell kids a story							
Help kids with homework							
Praise kids for their efforts							
Help kids with they play or their sports							
Take kids to recreation							
Sing with kids							
Teach kids							
Play with kids							
Give your kids a hug							

HESED TOWARDS SPOUSE	SUN	MON	TUES	WED	THUR	FRI	SAT
"I love you"							
"I just called to say I miss you"							
Baby-sit so spouse can go out							
Go to dinner together							
Do household repairs							
Help with shopping							
Help with car (gas, tokens..)							
Take out trash							
Help clean up house and keep it neat							
Make quality time							
Wake up with the baby in the middle of the night							

— *19* —

Taking Notice of Others

WHEN DOES THE DAY BEGIN?

There is a legal debate in the Talmud (Berachot 9b) as to when the day officially begins. The first opinion is: "When you can tell the difference between blue wool and white wool". The second opinion is a variation: "When you can tell the difference between blue wool and wool dyed the color of leek." (Leek is greenish blue. You would need more light to distinguish between these two colors, hence the morning would legally begin later).

Other opinions are brought, as well.

The third Sage said: "A new day begins when you can distinguish between a wolf and a dog".

The fourth opinion is a variation: "When you can distinguish between a donkey and a wild donkey".

The final opinion is "when you can see and recognize the face of your friend from a distance of four *amot*" (approximately six feet).

The Talmud declares: Rabbi Huna said, "the law follows the last opinion."*

This debate was a legal one. The Sages needed to define their terms objectively so that Jewish law could determine when night has ended and the day has begun; and when we can recite the morning prayers (such as *shema*), wear *tefillin* (phylacteries), etc. This debate is the basis of the *halachah* (Jewish Law).

However, we can also apply this discussion symbolically. When will the night of suffering end? When will there be a dawn of a new day?

When we can recognize the face of a friend from a distance. When we can see another human being and *recognize* him as our *friend* — *then* a new day has come.

As the generation after the Holocaust, we realize that the Nazis were celebrated musicians, poets and artists. They were also very scientific. Among the Nazis were some of the greatest, most brilliant doctors and scientists in the world.

Art and science did not prevent cruelty and suffering. The Nazis had a very sophisticated culture. The lives they lived were full of torturing and obscene, barbaric cruelty.

There is an ancient Greek (Stoic) dilemma. Our answer to it exemplifies the unique perspective of Judaism relative to other cultures. The dilemma goes as follows: *You come across two starving men in the desert, both dying of thirst. You only have enough water in your jug to save one of the men. One man is a philosopher, and the other is your father. Now, should you save your father or the philosopher?*

The Greeks, of course, reasoned that you must save the philosopher. This is because they believed that the wisdom of the philosopher alone will build a better world.

We as Jews, understand, that reason alone does not bring man to morality. The ancient Greeks, with all their reason and wisdom, used to leave deformed and ugly children on mountaintops to die. Greek writers said that the Jews were barbarians for keeping their children alive. The Greeks only kept aesthetically pleasing ones alive. Judaism, however, taught, that all human beings were created in God's image. The Jew knows that he must save his father. Building a better world starts with compassion and gratitude, not philosophy and culture.

When will the night of sorrow, of pain, of suffering, end? When will there be a dawn of a new day? When we are able to go beyond ourselves, *see and recognize the face of our friend*, the face of our fellow human being who needs *our* compassion, our concern.

When we make a covenant of compassion and concern with life, we find it gives us just more inner strength and power. When we are able to see our own face in the face of our fellow human being, to see *our own* needs in his, to feel for others as we would feel for ourselves, *then* the morning has arrived for us. The new rays of light have then cut away the darkness (the selfishness, the self-pity, the sadness and restlessness) and a new day has begun.

What could have created light in the holocaust was one person who could see another human being and recognize him as his "friend", as his "brother".

When one person decides that compassion and tolerance will lead the way, it is a sign of a new dawn.

No, it is not art or science. It is brotherhood and compassion that enlightens and brings man out of the lonely darkness and cold into the warmth and the rays of the sun.

THE CHAFETZ CHAYIM AND A COLD CHILD

I recently heard a true story about a well known Rabbi who had gone to visit a wealthy philanthropist for a donation. He asked the man: How did he come to support so many institutions of Torah learning? The answer....

"I was a wild teenager. My parents sent me to apply at the Yeshivah of the Chafetz Chayim zs"l. I wasn't accepted. Since I could not stay in the Yeshiva, I needed a place to sleep for the night. The Chafetz Chayim said: 'You can stay at my place'. So, I went home with him.

"The place was a two room shack. The Chafetz Chayim *gave*

me his own bed. It was cold and dark. He was obviously very poor. His apartment had no heating system, no electricity.

"I was just a young boy. I was cold and trying to sleep. Then the Chafetz Chayim walked into the room (as I pretended to be asleep). He must have thought, "oh, it's a little cool in here for him". He then took off his long jacket (that he was going to sleep in) and put it on me, over the covers.

"Years later, I became a very wealthy man. Even though I never became an observant Jew, I never forgot the feeling of that jacket of the Chafetz Chayim on me that night. The feeling of being cared for and loved by a total stranger never left me. I was so touched by that one act that whenever an institution of Torah learning approaches me for charity, I remember that night at the little house of the Chafetz Chayim, and give from my heart."

The message: You just never know how taking notice of people can change them. It can touch the lives of everyone around us (especially our children). *It can inspire us with a feeling we might never forget.*

The Chafetz Chayim thought this boy was asleep, but *noticed* that he was cold, so he responded with *hesed.* Now, hundreds of thousands of students of Torah have the opportunity to study, as a result of that kind deed.

Acts of *hesed* never die. They can live on and on and snowball *and boomerang.*

SUGAR FROSTED FLAKES

For *hesed* to boomerang back to us, it must start with *taking notice.* Let's take a good look at the face of our friend. Is he in pain? Does he need help?

The Talmudic sage, Rabbi Tanhuma, used to buy two portions of food and vegetables: one for himself and one for the poor.*

Learning from this, a father taught his family to do something similar. Each time they would go shopping at the supermarket, they would buy one extra item— a can of tuna, a container of milk, etc. They then kept these extra items and delivered them to one of the local pantries which distributes food to the hungry in their city.

One day, in the supermarket, the father took a box of Cheerios from the shelf and said: "This will be our food gift for today."

His son, who was about six-years-old, picked up the box from the shopping cart, put it back on the shelf and said, "no it won't."

The father was amazed. "Why not?" he asked. "What's wrong with a box of cereal?"

"Today we are getting *Sugar Frosted Flakes*," he said as he reached for that cereal. "Because there are hungry *kids* out there, too. And kids like Sugar Frosted Flakes better than Cheerios."

The six-year-old son had truly seen the faces of the people he was helping to feed.

The darkness of night ends and the morning begins—*when we begin to see the faces of our brothers and sisters.*

BIRTHDAY GIRL

To put *hesed* into action is to take the time to notice people; to appreciate their unique beauty, their growth, their warmth. Dr. Leo Buscaglia, in his *"Living, Loving and Learning"* (page 33) cites Thorton Wilder's *Our Town...**

Our Town

In this play, there is a scene where little Emily dies. She goes to the graveyard and is told "Emily, you can return for one day in life. Which day would you like?" She said: "Oh, I remember how happy I was on my twelfth birthday. I'd like to come back on my twelfth birthday."

All the people in the graveyard said, "Emily, don't do it. Don't do it Emily".

But she wanted to. She wanted to see her mother and father

again. So the scene switched, and there she is, twelve years old, gone back in time to that wonderful day she remembered.

She came down the stairs in a pretty dress with her curls bouncing. But her mother was so busy making the cake for Emily's birthday that she *could not stop long enough to look at her.* Emily said, "Mom, look at me. I'm the birthday girl." And her mother said: "Fine, birthday girl. Now sit down and have your breakfast." And Emily stood there and said, "mom, look at me." But her mother did not.

Her Dad came in and he was so busy making money for her that he did not look at her either, and neither did her brother, because he was so involved in his own things.

The scene ends with Emily standing in the middle of the stage saying, "please somebody, just look at me. I don't need the cake or the money. Please look at me." And nobody did. Nobody stopped to notice her. She turned to her mother once more and said, "Please Mom?" Then she turned and said, "take me away. I've forgotten what it was like to be human. Nobody looks at anybody. Nobody cares anymore, do they?"

Hesed starts by taking notice of others! Let's take a good look at the face of our friend. Is he in pain? Does he need help?

JOEL'S DAY

Dr. Buscaglia goes on (page 215-216) to tell the story of one of his students named Joel. Joel asked Dr. Buscaglia: "*What's there to do?*"

He brought Joel to a convalescent home "to do something for somebody else". Here's his story:

".... I brought him inside and there were a lot of aged people lying around in beds in old cotton gowns staring at the ceiling. Senility doesn't come from old age. It comes from not being loved and not feeling useful.

"...Anyway, we walked in, and he looked around, and he said,

"What'll I do here? I don't know anything about gerontology." I said, "Good! You see that lady over there? You go over and say hello."

"That's all?" "That's all."...

"And he sat down and they started to talk. Oh, my goodness, the things she told him! This woman had known so many wondrous things about life, about love, about pain, about suffering. Even about approaching death, with which she had to make some kind of peace. *But no one cared about listening!*

"He started going once a week and pretty soon that day began to be known as "Joel's Day." He would come and all the old people would gather.

"You know what that wonderful woman did? She asked her daughter to bring her a lovely dressing gown. And there she was propped up in her bed one day for Joel in a beautiful satin dressing gown. She'd had her hair done again, which she hadn't done in ages. *Why have your hair done if nobody sees you?* The people in that home don't look at you. They "do" to you. I don't want to be done to. Don't do me any favors. Better you should look at me and say, "how are you, Buscaglia?" and mean it, than do for me.

"Wonderful things began to happen on Joel's day. And probably the greatest triumphant moment in my educational career came one day when, without knowing it, I walked out on campus and there was Joel, like the Pied Piper, with about thirty little old people following him, hobbling to a football game!

"What's there to do?" *Look around you.* What's there to do? There's a lonely person next to you to touch. There's a hassled saleslady that needs you to tell her that she's great. What's there to do? It isn't monumental. It's teeny little things that make the difference. Small things, side, by side, by side."

TAKING NOTICE AND TAKING ACTION

One cold February night in 1995, the Sephardic Bikur Holim chinese auction committee was in the office making calls to solicit raffles and coupon packages for the auction.

If you have ever tried to call someone at 9 PM, after a full day of work, and persuade them to donate $500 or $1000 to charity, you know how difficult this is. Worse, when you get rejected, you begin to lose your drive. After three or four calls without raising money, your morale starts to fade.

I was in the office that night making calls. The volunteers around me were losing their enthusiasm. This was the tenth night in the last eleven upon which we left our families and worked in the Bikur Holim office, attempting to raise money. I was desperately trying to "psyche people up". After someone would succeed at a call, we would cheer and pat him on the back — encouraging him to make another call.

I remember what motivated me: I just pictured in my mind the tiny apartment of a Bikur Holim client whom I had recently visited. I pictured the time the client opened an empty refrigerator and was too ashamed to admit that he had nothing to offer me except a warm can of Coke. This is what kept me going. I would picture the horrendous circumstances our poor lived under and I would push myself to ask for financial support. After all, it's relatively easier to sell a product that you really believe in and understand.

Not everyone had that kind of motivation.

I'll never forget what happened next. Joseph Beyda, the man to whom I dedicated this book, walks in and greets everyone with a warm smile and words of encouragement. He talks with us and makes us feel proud to be on his team.

And then he asks for a list, sits at a table and proceeds to make calls. "Joe," I told him, "It's 10:15 PM, it is kind of late to call people. We are really just wrapping up and calling it 'quits' for tonight. We'll be here again tomorrow night and every night until the auction."

Joe just smiled and said, "Jackie, watch this!"

He then proceeded to call one prominent community leader after another. He asked us for the most challenging calls to make. "Who refused you guys tonight?" He asked. "I'll call him. Who didn't give you what you got last year? Who put you off and told you to call back next week?" Then he would call and wake them up. "Don't make believe you're sleeping. Wake up. I need $5,000. We are selling these raffles... It is Bikur Holim; do I have to say anything more? These kids are in the office working for the community, and you're in your cozy bed. Listen! I'm not hanging up until you give me $1000 more than you did last year...." Joe went on and on until after 11 PM.

Most of us just watched in awe. Some of us cheered after each call. Joe seemed to just "conquer" each call, in away we all dreamed we would be able to do.

When he was through (not because he was tired, but because he thought it really wasn't nice to call people too late), we added up what he had just accomplished: $60,000. He had just raised $60,000 for Sephardic Bikur Holim in that one hour.

As I look back on that night I have many thoughts. Perhaps most of all I realize that he wasn't there that night just to raise money for Bikur Holim. He was there primarily for us, the volunteers. He knew we were having a very difficult time raising money. He knew that we were almost burnt out.

He took notice and took decisive action.

He wanted to inspire us. But how? Was it with a depressing story about a sick or poor client? No. Not this time. He knew that the best way to encourage us was with action. So he rolled up his sleeves, sat at the phone and asked for names to call– not just any names, but the most intimidating, the most difficult. As a true leader, he exemplified what we had to do. Fearlessly, he conquered each potential donor with enthusiasm, humor, passion and love. It seemed as if he was in love with us, with SBH, with the people he called, and with the entire community.

When he finally finished his magnificent work that night I remember that I just came over to him and gave him a big hug. I was overjoyed, inspired, encouraged. He not only helped the poor, he not only gave people the merit and opportunity to give, he helped each one of us in the room that night.

As I make cold calls for many charities, to this day I think back on that cold night in February, and how Joseph fearlessly and passionately raised $60,000 in about an hour. Joseph Beyda passed away on April 19, 1997, at the young age of 54. I know that if he were here with me right now, there would be tears in his eyes and he would admit that he did it for us. He would admit that he knew we needed him to show us "how it's done". He would tell me how important it is to notice people and to take action to help people when you notice that they are in trouble. He would encourage me to follow in his footsteps and do the same.

Thanks Joe. Our community thanks you. The poor and sick thank you and we, the volunteers, thank you forever.

"IF THIS WERE MY MOTHER"

Ronnie Tawil is a successful international businessman as well as a learned Torah observant Jew. He is also one of my closest friends. He recently told me about the time he had to go out with his son to the pharmacy to get a prescription for his wife. As he left, he noticed an elderly woman sitting on his neighbor's porch. He asked her if she needed anything. She was lost and wanted to get home. He took her in his car and she gave him an address that didn't exist. He took her around and asked her if anything seemed familiar. She said she lived near a big synagogue. He drove her to the closest synagogue, to no avail...

Finally, Ronnie took her to the police station. The sergeant said: "You can go now Mr. Tawil, we'll take over from here. Someone will call for her no doubt soon." Ronnie said: "No. My mother is about her age. If she were lost or in trouble I know I'd like someone to be with her". So he stayed with her. "Are you hungry?" he asked her, and then proceeded to buy her a yogurt and a soda. About one hour later, someone called the station and said he was looking for his lost mom.

Two days later, Ronnie got a call from his mother. "You're never going to believe what happened to me…" She had locked her keys in her car. It was dark outside and she was in a bad neighborhood. Just then, two Hispanic youths in tank tops approached. Mrs. Tawil imagined the worst. She was almost ready to hand them her purse. But instead of harassing her, they went to the gas station for her; then they tried another and convinced the gas station attendant to come to the car and help open the door for her. She was very appreciative. She tried to pay them. One of the young men replied: *"We won't accept money lady - you just stay safe. If this happened to my mother I'd want someone to help her out"*.

Is there a connection between Ronnie's act of *hesed* and the *hesed* done for his mother? Could it be that when we help others some type of help really boomerangs back to us? We can't know for sure. What we do know is that Ronnie Tawil took the time to notice a simple old lady who needed help. He would not leave her alone. He cared. We also know that those two Hispanic boys, *at the same time, on the same night,* had also taken notice of an elderly woman who just happened to be Ronnie's mom.

The darkness of night ends and morning begins when we start to *notice* and help other people.

— 20 —

Smile and Watch the World Smile Back

"*Good Morning!*"
The Talmud (Sotah 8b) asserts: God deals with man measure for measure. The priest's blessing in Numbers (6:25) "The Lord shall make His face shine upon you" is granted to those who "shine their faces" upon their fellow men.

Greeting people properly is another act of *hesed* that is guaranteed to boomerang back to us.

The Mishnah (Avot 1:5) advises us to "greet every man with a pleasant expression of countenance," to (Avot 3:16) "receive everyone cheerfully," and (Avot 4:20) to "take the initiative in greeting any person you meet." The Talmud (Berachot 17a) relates that no one ever greeted Rabbi Yohanan ben Zakai before he greeted them, not even a stranger in the marketplace.

Rabbi Yohanan was attributed (Ketuvot 111b) with the saying: "It is better to whiten one's teeth for his friend (i.e. to greet him with a friendly countenance, with a smile that reveals the teeth), than to serve him milk."

Very often, just a cheery, sincere "good morning" can brighten up the day of a person who feels dejected. When we greet people with a friendly smile, we show that we care about them and that we're happy to see them.

The Talmud (Berachot 6b) goes so far as to say that if someone greets you and you fail to return the greeting it is considered sinful.

Avot DeRabi Natan (13:4) states that if you give a person charity with a sad or sour expression on your face, it is as if you gave him nothing. Conversely, if you just greet your friend with a smile, *even if you physically gave him nothing*, it is as if you gave him all the beautiful presents, physical blessings and assistance in the world.

FROM THE OUTSIDE IN

Jewish Tradition (for example, Mesillat Yesharim, by Rabbi Moshe Haim Luzzatto) teaches us that outer feelings bring on inner ones.

This means that by changing our actions, we can change our feelings. By "acting happy" - our minds get convinced that we are so. Our feelings then begin to change, and we become happier.

Psychologist William James stated that "action and feeling go together; and, by regulating our action, which is under the more direct control of the will, we can indirectly regulate the feeling."

Dr. Robert Zajonc, a psychologist at the University of Michigan, has scientifically proven that putting a smile on your face produces the feelings of joy. He also has shown that putting on a sad face creates sad feelings. This means that facial expressions are not merely signs of our emotions, they actually *contribute* to the feelings themselves.

Dr. Paul Ekman, a psychologist at the University of California Medical School at San Francisco, found similar results. He has shown that, when people mimic different emotional expressions, their bodies produce distinct physiological patterns, such as changes in heart rate and breathing rate.*

SMILE WHEN YOU AWAKE

When you awake in the morning, try, just once, to force yourself to smile.

Look in the mirror and smile. Trust me on this. When the first thing you do in the morning is smile, your day will be a whole lot happier.

Your brain will no doubt tell you: "Why should I smile? What is there to smile about? I don't even want to get up, let alone smile. This guy is nuts."

Don't listen to it. Just try to stretch your lips apart and smile. Why smile? What is there to smile about? Well, look at yourself. Can you see? Can you hear? Can you smell? Can you walk? Talk? Eat? How is your breathing? Can you use your hands? Your fingers? Your arms and legs? Can you get up and walk? Can you go to the bathroom? Are you free?

What is there to smile about? *ARE YOU ALIVE?*

How many people wake up each day but are not able to see? Can everyone speak and hear and walk? Are there people you know who can't properly breathe without aids? Do you know anyone with colitis or Chrone's disease who has difficulty going to the bathroom? How many people wake up each day in a prison cell or in a country that will not grant them basic human rights?

When you awake tomorrow, and your brain tries to convince you not to smile, just ask yourself:

"Am I free?"

"Can I move my body?"

"Is my blood flowing properly today?"

"Can I breathe?"

What is there to smile about? No matter how painful you feel your life is, no matter how bitter you are, just ask yourself one question: *Could it be worse?* Is there anyone out there who woke up this morning in a more painful, more bitter predicament? Could your life be worse? Is there anyone out there who could not (or did not) wake up this morning?

Can you smile because you're alive? Can you wake up and smile to show how thankful you are for your life and your breath? Smiling magically transforms your spirits.

Consider These Nine Facts About the Human Body — and smile!*

1. The average heart beats one hundred thousand times a day, pumps six quarts of blood through over ninety-six-thousand miles of blood vessels.

2. The six quarts of blood are actually twenty four trillion cells and make about four thousand trips throughout the body every day.

3. Seven million new blood cells are produced every second.

4. With all the heat, it maintains constant temperature of 98.6 degrees!

5. The skin has four million pores cooling the body.

6. The brain is comprised of more than twenty-five billion cells

7. The wisdom of a single cell is said to exceed all the accumulated knowledge of the human race to date. Yet, it can not be seen without a microscope. The smallest cell is one billion times the size of its smallest component! The cell is the site of more chemical reactions than all the chemical factories in the world combined.

8. Inside a cell is a nucleus, that has chromosomes, that contain genes that are made up of DNA. All the DNA in your body would be the size of an ice cube, yet if it were unwound and joined together it would stretch 80 billion miles long (800 times the distance between earth and sun).

9. Approximately three-hundred billion old cells each day are replaced with new ones (the "old" toxic cells are removed through bowels, bladder, lungs and skin).

Every time I read these facts about my body, an overwhelming sense of gratitude and happiness sweeps through my mind. I can't help but smile. When we realize how blessed we are, we can sit back and smile with satisfaction and appreciation. *Try it. Do it now. Go on. Sit back and smile! How does it feel?*

Smiling and laughing give your brain an "oxygen shower". When you smile, your facial muscles contract and you increase the blood flow to the brain. Your tears of laughter at the end of a laughing spell actually relieve the build-up of blood supply to the brain.

SMILE WHEN YOU GREET SOMEONE

The second most important time to smile is upon greeting someone. Try to smile sincerely when you say "hello" to someone.

To smile is to say "I'm glad. I'm glad to be alive. I'm glad to see you. I'm glad to say 'hello' to you. *I'm happy you are alive too with me today".*

How would you feel if someone you work with one morning came over to you and said: *"Hi, good morning. I just wanted to let you know that I'm happy you are alive. I'm happy to see you. I'm happy to have you in my life."*

How would that feel? Of course, it would feel wonderful. Yet, how difficult is this to actually say to someone? It is really hard to speak as beautifully as that. Yet a simple smile does it! That's the power of a smile. A smile brightens up their day and yours. *Smile and watch the world smile back!*

Try this simple test: Walk over to someone today — maybe it can be a close friend or acquaintance or business associate or even a cashier at your local store — and *smile* at them. Smile sincerely and mean it.

Now, watch the face of the cashier or your friend. Watch them smile back! Try it. It's like magic! Just smile and watch the world smile back.

THE VALUE OF A SMILE
(Author Unknown)

It costs nothing, but creates much.

It enriches those who receive, without impoverishing those who give.

It happens in a flash and the memory of it sometimes lasts forever.

None are so rich they can get along without it, and none so poor but are richer for its benefits.

It creates happiness in the home, fosters good will in a business, and is the countersign of friends.

It is rest to the weary, daylight to the discouraged, sunshine to the sad, and Nature's best antidote for trouble.

Yet it cannot be bought, begged, borrowed, or stolen, for it is something that is no earthly good to anybody till it is away.

And if in the exciting rush of our busy store, some of our associates should be too tired to give you a smile, may we ask you to leave one of yours?

For nobody needs a smile so much as those who have none left to give!

GOOD MORNING, HERR MUELLER

Near the city of Danzig lived a well-to-do Hasidic Rabbi, (Rabbi Samuel Shapira, Chief Rabbi of the Polish village of Prochnik), scion of prominent Hasidic dynasties. Dressed in a tailored back suit, wearing a top hat, and carrying a walking cane, the Rabbi would take his daily morning stroll, accompanied by his tall, handsome son-in-law. During the Rabbi's morning walk, it was his custom to greet every man, woman and child whom he met on the way with a warm smile and a cordial "Good morning." Over the years the Rabbi became acquainted with many of his fellow townspeople this way and would always greet them by their proper title and name.

Near the outskirts of town, in the fields, he would exchange greetings with Herr Mueller, a polish *Volksdeutsche* (ethnic German). "Good morning, Herr Mueller!" the Rabbi would hasten to greet the man who worked in the fields. "Good morning, Herr Rabbiner!" would come the response with a good-natured smile.

Then the war began. The Rabbi's strolls stopped abruptly. Herr Mueller donned an S.S. uniform and disappeared from the fields. The fate of the Rabbi was like that of the rest of Polish Jewry. He lost his family in the death camp of Treblinka and, after great suffering, was deported to Auschwitz.

One day, during a selection at Auschwitz, the Rabbi stood on line with hundreds of other Jews awaiting the moment when their fates would be decided, for life or death. Dressed in a striped camp uniform, head and beard shaven and eyes feverish from starvation and disease, the Rabbi looked like a walking skeleton. "Right. Left, left, left!" The voice in the distance drew nearer. Suddenly the Rabbi had a great urge to see the face of the man with the snow-white gloves, small baton and steely voice who played God and decided who should live and who should die. He lifted his eyes and heard his own voice speaking:

"Good morning, Herr Mueller!"

"Good morning, Herr Rabbiner!" responded a human voice beneath the S.S. cap adorned with a skull and bones. "What are you doing here?" A faint smile appeared on the Rabbi's lips. The baton moved to the right — to life! The following day, the Rabbi was transferred to a safer camp.

Years later, the Rabbi remarked about this incident: "This is the power of a good-morning greeting."

SMILING FOR LIFE

Paul Pearsall, in his *Super Joy*, tells of a Holocaust survivor who used to take a "smile walk" every evening in the concentration camp. She would walk near the barbed wire, smile, and feed one of the guard's dogs with some of her sparse food. She told fellow prisoners why: "I smile for life, for hope, for staying alive."

The New York Times, on August 22, 1997, reported the passing of a 122 year old lady in France. She had been interviewed and asked what she thought kept her alive so long. Her answer? "SMILING. I love to smile. I smile everyday. That is what has kept me alive and feeling so young!"

"I AM SURE HE IS STILL IN THERE"

There is a story told about a slaughterhouse in South America that is run by a certain Mr. Samo.

Every night, before closing up for the day, he checks the building to make sure everything is in order. One evening, he was about to close up the building when the night watchman, Alex, approached him and told him not to leave. "Mr. Samo, with all due respect, you can't close up yet. You see, there is still one slaughterer in the building!" Mr. Samo told him, "I have checked this building every night for many years. I checked it tonight and there is no one here."

"I'm sure he is stilll in there," Alex said. "O.K. Alex, if you insist, I'll check again." Mr. Samo re-entered the slaughterhouse and checked the entire building. There was no sign of any human being. "I checked again. There is no one in there. Trust me. Maybe he left when you weren't looking."

"Please, Mr. Samo," Alex pleaded. "I am positive that the man is still in there. Maybe he's in some kind of trouble. Can you please go back and check again a little more thoroughly?"

"O.K. Alex. I'll go back in and check again. But this is the last time." Mr. Samo was touched by the genuine concern of the simple night watchman.

Mr. Samo went back through the building, searching every inch. There was nobody in sight, no trace of anyone. Just as he turned to leave, he passed by the freezer. He thought to himself. "This freezer certainly is huge. It is definitely big enough for a person to walk inside. What if there is someone locked inside? Let me go in and take a look."

Mr. Samo opened the freezer door and discovered not one, but three slaughterers inside, nearly frozen to death. He quickly called for an ambulance which rushed them to the hospital.

Earlier that day, the slaughterers had entered the freezer to check the meat. When they were ready to leave, they found that the door would not open. They banged and yelled for hours, to no avail. No one heard a sound. Finally, they gave up and resigned themselves to a cold death. Just then Mr. Samo found them, and their lives were saved.

A few days later, Mr. Samo approached Alex the night watchman. "How could you possibly have known that there was someone in there? Also, why didn't you tell me that there were *three* people in there. If you knew about one, surely you knew about three."

Alex responded proudly. "Ever since those men came from Israel a few months ago, one of them always greeted me with a kind 'Good Morning' when he came in everyday, and a sincere 'Good Evening' when he went home for the day. He has done this every single day without fail. That day, I remembered that he had greeted me in the morning, but he hadn't wished me a good night. That is how I knew he was definitely still in there. I really didn't know if anyone else was inside."

A simple greeting not only saved this slaughterer's own life, but the lives of two of his colleagues.

— *21* —

Hesed With Our Speech

There is so much *hesed* that can be done with our speech. The Mishnah (Avot 4:3) advises: "Do not separate yourself from, or treat disparagingly, any word (of your own)." In other words, do not speak in haste, without thinking, for you might say something you will later regret. Your words are never unimportant or inconsequential. Spoken words have a way of coming home to roost.

Henry Wadsworth Longfellow (in *The Arrow and the Song*), expresses this concept as follows:

I shot an arrow into the air,
It fell to earth, I knew not where;
For, so swiftly it flew, the sight
Could not follow it in its flight.
I breathed a song into the air,
It fell to earth, I knew not where;
For who has sight so keen and strong
That it can follow the flight of song?

Long afterwards, in an oak
I found my arrow still unbroke;
And the song from beginning to end.
I found again in the heart of a friend.

When we speak, our words can be as harmonious and as pleasant as a song. When we sing the song of *hesed*, when we speak with compassion and understanding, our words are sure to enter into the hearts of other people and create happiness.

HELPING THE "POOR"

Hesed is helping the poor. Yet the word "poor" (*dal*) has been interpreted by the Sages to mean many things. We can help the *materially* poor, the *physically* poor (the sick), the *spiritually* poor (the irreligious), or the *intellectually* poor (the uneducated).

Helping any of these "poor" people, by providing them with what they lack, is considered *hesed*. Much of this *hesed* is done with our speech.

TEACHING PEOPLE

Abraham is described as having "walked in God's ways". One reason: He converted people and educated people to the wisdom of monotheism. Teaching is one example of *hesed* that can be done with our speech.

The Talmud (Sukkah 49b) uses the verse in Proverbs (31:26): "She opens her mouth with wisdom and the Torah of *Hesed* is on her tongue", to say that studying Torah in order to teach others is considered a "Torah of *Hesed*". So, teaching others Torah is an act of *hesed*.

The Talmud (Ta-anit 24a) tells us that God accepted the prayers of an unknown *hazan*, before accepting the prayers of the great Sage, Rav. Why? Because *he taught children without asking to be paid*. If they could not afford it — he did not demand payment. Also, he bought gifts with his own money to reward the children and encourage them to learn more.

CALMING PEOPLE, CREATING PEACE AND LOVE

Interceding on behalf of a friend, and stilling somebody's anger is an act of obvious *hesed* that can be done with words.*

If you speak sympathetically to someone and allay his or her anxieties, you have performed *hesed*. You can use your words to soothe and to comfort — to show good will with sincerity and respect.

Creating peace between feuding friends or brothers or husband and wife (as God did with Abraham and Sarah) is another way to use speech to create *hesed*.

PREVENTING HARM

Anything one can say or do to prevent harm from befalling another person is an act of *hesed*. The Torah tells us that (Genesis 20:13) Abraham asked Sarah to do *hesed* for him by telling people that he and she were brother and sister, not man and wife, in order · to protect him.

The Zohar (Leviticus 46b) declares: "Just as a person is punished for speaking evil (gossip, slander), so too a person is punished if he has the opportunity to speak up, if he can talk, but chooses not to."

MOTIVATING TO DO HESED IS HESED TOO

If you convince or motivate someone to do a favor for another person (or if you do one yourself) you have done *hesed*.

GOOD ADVICE

You can help someone by giving them good advice This, too, is considered *hesed.*

FUNDRAISING

You can use your words to persuade people to give charity or help in community volunteer projects. The Talmud (Bava Batra 10a) asserts: "Greater is he who causes others to act, than he who acts alone".

PRAYING FOR OTHERS

When you pray to God for another person —you are doing a great act of true *hesed.* The Midrash (on Deut. 33:1) says that Moshe was not called "Man of God" until he spoke out in defense of (and prayed for) the Jewish people.

The Talmud (Bava Kama 92a) declares: "Anyone who requests mercy for his friend, and he himself is in need of that mercy, *he is answered first.* . . as is written in the book of Job (42:10), 'and God returned to Job as he (Job) prayed for his friends.'"

Abraham knew how to respond when he heard that Avimelech's wives were stricken with infertility: *prayer.* He prayed to God to end their infertility. And, He did. The Midrash* depicts the angels crying out to God: "Master of the Universe! Sarah (Abraham's wife) is barren for all these years. Avimelech's wife is barren. Abraham now prays for her (Avimlelech's wife) and she becomes fertile along with his other midwives. *These* women you remember and you hear, but Sarah still remains barren? Is it justice?" Immediately, "and God remembered Sarah." (Genesis 20:17-18)

• The sage Abba Hilkiyah and his wife, both prayed for rain. Soon, the rains came. But the other Sages noticed that the clouds which brought the rain were above the wife. In other words, her prayers were stronger. They asked Abba Hilkiyah for the reason.

He answered: she is always home. She gives bread to the poor. I only give money. Also, I prayed that the evil people should die. She prayed that they repent (which they did).*

•As we have mentioned above, Jewish tradition considers the act of praying for the sick *part and parcel of the mitzvah of "Bikur Holim"*. If one spends time visiting the sick, but does not spend time praying for divine mercy, he has not fulfilled the mitzvah completely.

•The prophet Isaiah (54:9) says, "because these are like the *waters of Noah* to me." The Zohar (Noah 67:2) writes: "When God told Noah that He would save him and his family from the flood if he would build an ark, Noah did not pray for the world. Because of this, the flood was called by his name 'the waters of Noah. Noah would go down in history as the man who did not pray for others. Even if there were no righteous people left in the world, he still could have felt some pain, some sympathy. He could have cried out to God for help.

•The Talmud (Berachot 12b) credits Rabah Bar Haninah Saba as saying in the name of Rav: "Anyone for whom it is possible to request mercy for his friend, but does not, is called a *sinner*".

•Referring to the book of Ruth, the Talmud (Bava Batra 91a) blames Elimelech and his two sons, Mahlon and Kilyon, for their own premature deaths. Rabbi Shimon Bar Yohai says, "Why were they punished? Because they *could have prayed* for (the people of) their generation (who were suffering a severe famine in the land of Israel). They could have requested mercy, but they did not.**

REASSURE THE POOR WITH WORDS

The Talmud*** promises: "Whoever gives a coin to the poor earns six blessings, while one who *reassures the poor with speech* earns eleven blessings." *Poor*, again, can be interpreted to mean any one of the four interpretations we mentioned above (impoverished, sick, agnostic or uneducated).

Similarly, the Midrash (Leviticus Rabah 34:15) quotes Isaiah (58:10): "If you draw out your soul to the hungry..." Notice that the prophet does not say, "If you draw out your *bread* to the hungry!" This teaches us that if you can't do *hesed* with your money (or your material possessions) *then at least you can do hesed with your words.* You can console the poor with kind words, sympathetic words, words that show you have "drawn out your soul" to him in a sincere and caring way.

HESED AND PERSISTENCE IN KEEPING YOUR PROMISES

In 1989, an 8.2 earthquake almost flattened Armenia, killing over 30,000 people in less than four minutes.

In the middle of utter devastation and chaos, a father rushed to the school where he brought his son that morning, only to discover that the building was as flat as a pancake.

He was in shock. All his mind could think of was the promise he made to his son each night as he tucked him in bed "no matter what, I'll always be there for you!". He looked at the pile of debris that was once a school and tears welled up in his eyes. He felt paralyzed, unable to move. All around him parents were screaming and crying, clutching their hearts: "My son!", "My baby!", "My daughter!". He looked around him and all he could see was despair.

Then he decided to act. Quickly, he remembered that his son's classroom was in the back right corner of the building. He rushed there and started digging.

Other parents tried to pull him away. "It's too late." "They're all dead." "Go home." "Come on, face reality, there's nothing you can do!"

To each parent he responded, *"I made a promise and I will keep it.* Will you help me?" Then he proceeded to dig for his son, stone by stone.

The fire chief arrived and tried to pull him off the debris saying, "you're in danger. We'll take care of it. Go home!". The man ignored him and kept digging.

The police came and said, "you're outraged and distraught. It's over. Go home. You're in danger. We'll handle it." The man asked them: "Does anyone want to help me?" No one helped.

He kept digging alone, through the night, through the rain, for 8 hours, ... 12 hours... 24 hours... 36 hours... then, in the 38th hour he pulled back a boulder and heard his son's voice. He screamed his son's name "ARMAND!" He heard back *"Dad? it's me dad. I told the other kids not to worry. I told them that if you were alive, you'd save me and when you saved me they'd be saved. You promised 'no matter what I'll always be there for you'. You did it dad!"*

"What's going on in there?" He asked.

"There are only 14 of us left out of 33, dad. We're scared, hungry, thirsty and thankful you're here. When the building collapsed, it made a wedge, like a triangle and it saved us."

"Come on out, boy!"

"No, dad! Let the other kids out first, because I know you'll get me! No matter what, I know you'll be there for me!"

The determination and persistence of this father in the face of crisis, suffering, chaos, and seeming tragedy is a paradigm of *hesed*. A major component of *hesed* is keeping a promise — and "being there" for those who need us.*

THE HESED BOOMERANG PRINCIPLE

The Book of Proverbs (3:3-4) states: Kindness and truthfulness (with other people) will lead to "finding favor" in the eyes of God and man.

The Mishnah (Avot 3:13) teaches: "If the spirit of other people is pleased with you (i.e. because you act in a courteous, ethical, trustworthy manner), then the spirit of God will be pleased with you. If the spirit of people is not pleased with you, then God won't be either." Acts and words of kindness and love which build and strengthen relationships between people, create a spirit of harmony. This spirit of harmony seems to have a positive effect on how people are treated by God.

The Talmud states (Yerushalmi, Sanhedrin 10:1): "Rabbi Yehudah ben Hanan said in the name of Rabbi Berechya. God said to Israel: "My children, if you see the merit of the patriarchs and matriarchs faltering, go and engage in acts of kindness."

The legend has a sublime message. How would we know when the merit of our forefathers is faltering? Perhaps we can assume it is faltering when we are suffering. Or perhaps when we find ourselves in a melancholic, sad or lonely mood. The Midrash then gives us advice: "Go and engage in acts of *hesed*." Perhaps by doing acts of compassion and loving-kindness, our suffering will be erased, our melancholy will be lessened. Our feeling of sadness might be turned into a feeling of fulfillment by doing acts of love.

Yet perhaps the Midrash means to imply that we can "call on" the merit of our forefathers to help us. But when that doesn't seem to "work" — we must build *our* own merits. We must use *our* own bargaining power. An easy way to do this is to do *hesed* with our speech.

The prophet *Hosea* (10:12) declares : "Sow to yourselves according to your righteousness, reap according to (your) loving kindness. It is time to seek God".

The Midrash (Shoher Tov, chapter 65) comments: "Whoever bestows loving kindness will receive the good tidings that his prayers have been accepted".

They further substantiate this with two verses in Psalms:

"As for me, in the abundance of your loving-kindness will I come into your house" (5:8).

"You answer me with your salvation" (69:14).

The Talmud (Ta-anit 25b) further states that God accepted Rabbi Akiva's prayers before Rabbi Eliezer's, because Rabbi Akiva was described as *ma-avir al midotav* (forgiving of others). Since he was a *forgiving* person, so thus, God acted toward him.

A KIND WORD CAN SAVE A LIFE

A story is told about a famous author who walked along the East River promenade in New York City, very depressed. He felt his life was empty, meaningless. He felt that his life's work, his writing, which he devoted his entire life to, had no value. After all, he thought, what had he accomplished in life? Suicidal, he contemplated climbing over the railing that separated the promenade from the river and throwing himself in.

He stood in the dark, staring at the water, just about to climb the railing and end his own life. Just then he heard an excited voice. "Excuse me, I'm sorry to impose on your privacy, but aren't you Christopher D'Antonio, the writer?" He nodded. "I hope you don't mind my approaching you, but I just had to tell you what a difference your books have made in my life! They have helped me to an incredible degree, and I just wanted to thank you!"

"No, my dear, it is I who have to thank you," he said, as he turned around, walked away from the East River and headed back home.

Part Four

DIMENSIONS OF HESED

Introduction to Part Four

THE WORLD IS BUILT ON HESED

"Rabbi Yohanan said :
'Jerusalem was destroyed only because (its inhabitants) decided cases according to Torah law.' Should they have
instead decided cases according to the law of tyranny?
Rather, say the following: Jerusalem was destroyed because
they limited their decisions to the letter of the law of the
Torah, and did not perform actions that would have gone
beyond the letter of the law (Lifnim mishurat hadin)."
-Bava Metsia 30b

Hesed makes the world go 'round. It is the cement of human
society. Without hesed, society disintegrates. Standing upon the
letter of the law alone leads to ruin. Jerusalem's destruction wasn't
retributive punishment. It was a natural consequence. A wholly
legalistic society, which does not practice acts of altruism, simply
cannot exist.

The *rejection* of altruism, of *hesed*, of "going beyond the letter of the law for others" (*lifnim mishurat hadin*) is characterized
by some as the trait of the evil city of Sodom.* Those who say,
"what's mine is mine and what's yours is yours" in many cases would
be excellent judges. Yet, in situations where there is a need for
their help, these people would refuse. They are thus associated
with Sodom.

Legalistic, uncharitable people who are obsessed with their
private concerns and property create barriers between fellow human beings. *These barriers make society crumble.*

Perhaps this attitude spawned the "baseless and unwarranted
hatred toward others" which ultimately led to the destruction of
Jerusalem.

The Sages (Avot 1:2) tell us that compassion is one of the
three pillars upon which the world stands. In other words, the world
would not be able to continue to exist without people having the
virtue of *hesed*.

For a good part of a person's life, he or she depends on others
for his own well-being. From the time he is a baby and his mother
kindly rocks him to sleep, till the time he is an old man and he
needs help crossing the street – help from others plays a role in his
or her life.

> When someone is sad, he or she is in need of comfort (in
> Judaism there is a specific *mitzvah* of comforting the
> mourner).
>
> When someone is in need of a loan or a job, the Torah tells us
> *you shall uphold him.*
>
> When people travel and need a place to stay, the Torah tells
> us to be hospitable.
>
> When someone is sick, the Torah tells us to visit him.
>
> When someone is hungry, we must feed him.
>
> When someone gets married, Judaism obligates us to bring
> joy to the bride and groom.
>
> Indeed, *hesed* is a cornerstone of our lives — and the world

could not exist without it.

Jewish thought is replete with statements which imply this concept. Here are just a few:
• The Talmud (Eruvin 86a) expounds upon a verse from Psalms (61:8). The verse: "May the world exist in the presence of God. Kindness *(hesed)* and truth *(emet)* shall sustain it." The explanation of the Talmud: When shall the world endure in the presence of God? When *hesed* and *emet* (kindness and truth) sustain it.

• A verse in Psalms (89:3) says, "because I said, the world will be built on *hesed.*" The Midrash (Tehillim 89) compares the world to a three-legged chair that is about to fall. It is as if the *hesed* in the world is the fourth leg that keeps the chair from falling over. It is the view of Jewish tradition that *hesed holds up the world.* It keeps us from falling.

• The verse in Isaiah (51:16) states: "and I have covered you with the shadow of my palm." The sages (Yerushalmi Ta-anit 4:2) explain this to mean that the kindness which a person dispenses with his hand *make him worthy to be covered by the shadow (protection) of* (so to speak) God's *palm*" .

• According to the Talmud (Yerushalmi, Ta-anit), acts of *hesed* bring rain to the world. Without rain, of course, the world would cease to exist.

• *Great is the power of charity since, from the day of creation until now, the world has been held up by charity.*

Indeed, the world is built on *hesed.*

— *22* —

Charity

CHARITY AND THE
HESED BOOMERANG PRINCIPLE

The most obvious and most common form of *hesed* is *tsedaka* (charity). Let us begin this chapter with the promise of Jewish tradition.

"TEST ME!"

Regarding charity, scripture promises (Malachi 3:10): "Bring the whole tithe into the store-house that there may be food in my house, and test me *(ubehanuni na bezot)* now with this, says the God of Hosts, if I do not open for you the gates of heaven and pour you out a blessing immeasurable".

The original Hebrew of "immeasurable" is "ad beli dai." This literally means "until there is not enough." The verse would thus read "... and test me now with this, says the God of Hosts, if I do not open for you the gates of Heaven and pour you out a blessing *until there is not enough."* This would obviously not make sense in context. Rather, the Talmud (Ta-anit 9a) interprets it as a kind of pun in Hebrew: *ad sheyiblu siftotechem melomar dai* ("Until your lips become worn out from saying 'enough'!")

Now, how many people do you know that, when given the opportunity to have more money, say "no, that's enough. I have *enough money*. I don't need any more. Enough!"? The Rabbis of the Talmud understood how seldom anyone would say "enough" to having *more*.

Consequently, the promise of Malachi is: *By giving tsedaka, one will be blessed beyond all rational thinking*, beyond his wildest imagination.

The Torah (Deut. 14:22) demands of us to tithe our crops. The Talmud (Ta-anit 9b) and Midrash (Sifri) find a hint in the double language: *aser te-aser* — you shall *surely* tithe. In the words of the Sages: "give a tithe *(aser)*, so that you will become wealthy *(titasher)*." Jewish tradition promises to fulfill *The Hesed Paradox*: "The more you give – the more you get".

• The Jewish legal code backs this up by stating unequivocally that in giving tithes it is permissible to test God.

THE PRAYERS OF THE CHARITABLE

Rabbi Tanhuma (bar Abba), who lived in Israel in the fifth century, used to declare public fasts when there was a drought.

Once, after many fasts, the rains still did not fall. Rabbi Tanhuma then addressed the public: "My sons, fill yourselves with compassion for each other and the Holy One will fill Himself with compassion for you."

People began giving charity to the poor. They witnessed a man giving money to his ex-wife. The man told Rabbi Tanhuma: (Even though it was a difficult divorce and I have many hard feelings), "I saw that she was suffering, and I was filled with compassion for her."

Rabbi Tanhuma raised his face toward Heaven and declared: "Master of the Universe, this man has no obligation toward the woman, yet he saw her suffering and was filled with compassion for her. You, about Whom it is written, 'merciful and gracious', and we Are Your children, the sons of Your beloved ones, Abraham, Isaac, and Jacob, how much more so should You be filled with mercy for us?"

Immediately thereafter, the Midrash (Genesis Rabah 33:3) relates, the rains began to fall in the land of Israel.

• The Talmud (Yevamot 63a) promises: "Anyone who lends to the poor in his time of need will be blessed with the verse in Isaiah (58:9): "Then you will call and God will answer."

WHOSE MONEY IS IT?

The Mishnah (Avot 3:8) advises: "Rabbi Elazar of Bertota said: Give Him of His own, for both you and whatever is yours are (entirely) His. And so also (in his prayers) did David say (I Chronicles 29:14): "For all things are from You, and from (the bounty of) Your hand we have given You."

Imagine if a friend of yours left one hundred thousand dollars with you to take care of. Later, he asks you to give ten thousand to a poor man. Do you deserve gratitude? Of course not. After all, the money belongs entirely to your friend! In a similar way, God has blessed us with all our material wealth. Should we be thanked or rewarded when we give part of His blessing for tsedaka in accordance with His will?

The Talmud (Ta-anit 24a) records that Rabbi Elazar of Bertota really practiced what he preached. Whenever "charity officials", who were in charge of collecting and distributing funds for the poor, saw Rabbi Elazar of Bertota, they used to hide from him, because he would insist on giving them every bit of money he had with him.

The Talmud (ibid) tells an incredible story. Rabbi Elazar of Bertota spotted the charity officials and took out all the money he was carrying and gave it to them – except one zuz (a small coin), which he used to buy wheat. The wheat which he then put in his store-room miraculously grew and filled the entire store-room, so much so, that it was bursting. After discovering this phenomenon, Rabbi Elazar of Bertota's daughter excitedly ran to her father and told him: "Come and see what your good Friend (God) has done for you!"

THE POWER OF CHARITY

Rabbi Yehudah Bar Ilai, a Tanna of the fourth generation, the student of Rabbi Tarphon, underlined (Bava Batra 10a) the power and importance of charity with a parable.

"Ten strong things have been created in the world," he taught. "The rock is hard, but the iron cleaves it. Iron is hard, but the fire softens it. Fire is strong, but the water quenches it. Water is strong, but the clouds bear it. Clouds are strong, but the wind disperses them. Wind is strong, but the body bears it. The body is strong, but fear crushes it. Fear is strong, but wine banishes it. Wine is strong, but sleep makes one sober. And death is stronger than all of these. Charity, however, saves one from death, as it is written (Proverbs 10:2): 'Charity delivers from death.'"

THE CHARITY OF DOCTORS

The Talmud (Ta-anit 21b) explains why Abba the surgeon's prayers were accepted immediately. He had a private room with a coinbox. After he treated his patients, they could go in and pay whatever they could afford without being embarrassed. Essentially, Abba treated people for free and didn't let them feel any shame. This was his charity. The Talmud saw his *hesed*, his charity, as the reason for his prayers being answered.

There is a story told about a doctor who had devoted his life to helping the under-privileged. He lived over a liquor store in the poor section of a large city. In front of the liquor store was a sign reading:

Dr. Williams is upstairs.

When he died, he had no relatives and he left no money for his burial. He had never asked for payment from anyone he had ever treated.

Friends and patients scraped enough money together to bury

the good doctor, but they had no money for a tombstone. It appeared that his grave was going to be unmarked until someone came up with a wonderful suggestion.

They took the sign from in front of the liquor store and nailed it to a post over his grave. It made a lovely epitaph:

Dr. Williams is upstairs.

THE MONEY WE TAKE WITH US

Indeed, all that we truly keep after we die, are our good deeds. Our acts of *hesed* stay with us forever. The only money we can "keep" after we die is the money we gave to charity. As it says (Numbers 5:10), "...whatever a man gives to the *kohen*, shall be his".

The verse implies that the only money that will remain with man forever will be the charity he gave to the *kohen* (priest). *The donation really belongs to the donor.* When giving to others we enrich ourselves.

The Talmud says (Mishnah, Peah 1:1) that *hesed* stands by man until the end of all generations (Psalms 103:17): "and the *hesed* of God endures forever and ever for those that fear Him").

THE PROMISES OF JEWISH TRADITION

The Rabbis go as far as to say (Tanna Deve Eliyahu Zuta, Chapter 4): If you have given charity, you will acquire possessions. If you have acquired possessions, give them as charity while they are still in your hands... If you do not use them for charity they will soon depart, as it is said (Prov. 23:5): "Shall your eye make it fly away and be gone?"

•The book of Proverbs (21:21) promises: "Whoever pursues tsedaka and *hesed* shall find life, prosperity and honor."

•The Torah further states (Deut. 15:10): "You shall surely give him and your heart shall not be grieved when you give him, for because of this, the Lord, your God will bless you in all your work..."

•A Talmudic saying rewards acts of tsedaka with wise and wealthy children: (Bava Batra 9b): "Rabbi Yehoshua ben Levi said:

He who does charity habitually shall have sons, wise, wealthy and versed in the Aggadah. 'Wise'–as it is written (Prov. 21:21) 'Whoever pursues tsedaka and kindness shall find life'... 'Wealthy' — as it is written (Ibid) 'He shall find prosperity'..."

• The book of Psalms promises rewards to those who give tsedaka. A verse in Psalms (37:26)* states clearly: "Since, all his days, he was gracious, lending to others, thus his children will be blessed".

INDIRECT HESED

Jewish tradition promises us that all resultant, future benefits of our charity will be credited to us (and we will be rewarded for it all).

The Talmud (Bava Kama 9a) tells us that if one act of charity results in multiple benefits— the original act of *hesed* is never forgotten. If, for example, you loaned someone money to start a business ten years ago, and today the business is successful and supports ten families — it is as if you are currently supporting those ten families.

The reverse is also true. Rabbi Yohanan says: To rob a fellow man even of the value of a *perutah* (the lowest monetary currency) is like taking his life away.

The verse in Samuel (I;21:1) says: "It is for Saul and his bloody house, because he put the Gibeonites to death". Saul actually did *not* kill any Gibeonites. He did, though, kill the entire city of Priests in Nov — which used to supply the Gibeonites with food and drink (in payment for the wood and water which the Gibeonites hewed and drew for the altar). So, we see that indirect *hesed* is considered rewarded as direct, and *indirect harm* is considered punished as direct harm.

CHARITY WITH AN ULTERIOR MOTIVE

According to the Talmud**: "If someone says: 'I give this money to charity that my son may live or that I merit the world to come' — he is completely righteous in this act". The same applies whenever one expects, also, to derive some benefit from an act of *hesed*. His mitzvah is not nullified. It is a praiseworthy act to do *hesed,* and there is nothing wrong to wish that God grant you a favor or bless you in return.*

Of course it would be better to perform the mitzvah of *hesed* expecting nothing in return. "Then, the holy power of the mitzvah which has been performed in the most perfect manner possible will so strongly draw forth the heavenly attribute of *hesed* that will extend over all created existence" (ibid).

Psalms (57:11) reads: "For your *hesed* is great unto the heavens," and Psalms (108:5) reads: "For your *hesed* is great above the heavens". The Talmud (Pesahim 50b) understands the first verse to apply to people who do mitzvot for some benefit or ulterior motive. The second is for those who do mitzvot, expecting nothing in return.

THE EFFORT OF CHARITY

The Talmud (Sukkah 49b) teaches that the reward of charity is commensurate with the *hesed* in it, as the prophet Hosea (9:12) says: "Sow for yourselves according to *charity* but reap according to *hesed*". Rashi elucidates this for us: "The gift is the charity. The *effort* in making the gift is the *hesed* (Sukkah 49b).

In Judaism, there are very specific laws of charity. Charity is never accomplished without effort. The Shulhan Aruch (Yoreh Deah 249:3) states: "You must give the charity with a smile, with happiness and with a good heart. And you must feel the pain of the poor man, suffer with him and speak to him words of comfort and consolation. If, on the other hand, you give the charity with a sour or unhappy (or regretful) facial expression, you lose your merit.

EVEN THE POOR MUST GIVE

The Jewish tradition** demands that each and every person must contribute to charity. Everyone should give according to his means. The poor must do *hesed* as well. No human being should feel exempt from the practice of *hesed*. Nobody should live without its blessings and life-enriching effects.

THE EIGHT LEVELS OF CHARITY

The Torah (Leviticus 25:35) states: "And if your brother becomes poor, and his means fail him with you, then *you shall uphold him.*" This verse (among others) provides us with the framework for the mitzvah of charity. According to Jewish tradition* there are eight levels of charity.

The lowest level, or level eight, is when you give a poor person charity and you show that you are sad about it.

The seventh level is when you give less than you should, less than what is expected of you (or less than what the poor man requires), but you at least give it with a smile.

The sixth level is when you give the appropriate amount of charity with a smile, but you do it only *after* the poor man asks you for it.

The fifth level is when you give the charity *before* the poor man asks for it.

The fourth level is when you give charity without knowing who, specifically, will benefit from the charity. The poor people know who give the funds (or the food, etc.) but you, the giver, do not know to whom it goes. (This, of course, saves the poor from embarrassment).

The third highest level of charity is to give the charity anonymously. In this case, you *do* know who will receive the money, but the recipient does not know who the kind donor was. (This is actually better because it does not allow him to feel as ashamed).

The second highest level of charity is when neither the giver nor the receiver know who is who. The donor does not know to whom the money goes and the recipient does not know where the money came from. This is considered a very high form of charity because it preserves the poor man's dignity.

In fact the Talmud** tells of the customs of the first Rabbi Abba. Rabbi Abba used to put money in a scarf and hang the scarf behind him so that the poor could take money freely without him seeing them. He went to great lengths to give charity, and do it without shaming the poor.

Rabbi Yona, another great sage, also found a way to maintain the dignity of the receiver. It was told about him that when a person of a wealthy family became impoverished, he would say to him: "My son, I hear that you have been left an inheritance. Take this money as a loan until you can repay it when you receive the inheritance." However, when the man had taken the money and left, Rabbi Yona would say, "Let it be a gift. He owes me nothing..."

The highest level of charity is *to uphold him*. This occurs when you help find a poor man a job, or when you give him a job, or when you make a partnership with him, or give him a loan. These methods preserve the person's dignity. The goal is to get the man to "stand on his own two feet" and eventually be able to support himself– to strengthen him, so he will never have to ask for charity again. This is truly *to uphold him*. Even if you "uphold" a poor man, by purchasing something from him, you have done a great *Hesed.*

THE ETERNAL INVESTMENT

The Torah (Levit. 25:35) commands us: If your brother becomes poor and his means fail with you then *you shall uphold him."* The mitzvah of "upholding" is incumbent upon us all.*

About ten years ago, a friend approached me for a loan. *He still did not repay the last loan I gave him.* I wondered to myself if I would ever see the money again. My mind was focused on my material possessions (i.e. my money) not on him and his plight. Nor was my mind focused on what might be my future if I did grant him the loan.

The next week, my stock broker called me and told me that he recommend I buy a certain stock that was about to do an IPO (initial public offering). He said it would be a good investment for me. Immediately, I told him to buy the stock for me.

"How much can I buy?" I asked.

For a *stock*, which can be a *good* investment for the future, I did not hesitate to put up the money. For a loan, which will be an *eternal* investment, my mind held me back.

When my friend approached me for the loan, he had little to gain — just money to help him get by. I, on the other hand, as the bestower of kindness, had the opportunity to fulfill a command- ment of the Torah. The "return on investment" is eternal. I should have *rejoiced.*

I should have responded to my friend as enthusiastically as I responded to my broker. I should have asked: *"How much can I lend you?"*

THE HESED TRUST FUND

The Torah states (Exodus 22:24): "When you lend money to My people, the poor man that is with you...". Rabbi Mosheh Alshech has made an interesting analogy: Imagine a man with a big family, who, in his will, left all of his money and possessions to one of his sons. Actually, the man had really intended to appoint this son a *trustee,* since it is reasonable to assume that he would not cut off the rest of his children without anything. The one son, in effect, is holding a trust fund for each of the other children.

When God gives one person wealth, the amount of money in excess of his needs is a trust fund, deposited by God. God has, in effect, appointed him to administer it, take pity on the poor and unfortunate. After all, is it reasonable to assume that God would make one of His children rich and cut off the rest of His children? Aren't we all the children of God?

The rich are thus the trustees to support the poor. The verse above (Exod. 22:24) implies this by saying that the poor is "with you". As if to say, whatever the poor man really needs belongs to him. It is deposited *with you* on his behalf. Therefore, you must not withhold it from him.

"REAL ESTATE"

There is a story in the Talmud (Kallah, chapter 9) about the wealthy Rabbi Tarfon. One day, his friend Rabbi Akiva approached him and asked him, "would you like me to purchase some real estate for you?" Rabbi Tarfon said "yes" and immediately handed him 4,000 golden dinars to secure the investment. Rabbi Akiva took the money and distributed it among the poor.

Some time later, Rabbi Tarfon met him and asked him, "where is the real estate you purchased on my behalf?"

Rabbi Akiva brought out the book of Psalms and opened it before them. They read until they reached the verse (Psalms 112:9): "He scattered abroad, he gave to the poor; his "Tsedakah" (charity) will endure forever."

Then Rabbi Akiva stood up, pointed to the verse and said "this is the real estate I bought for you". Rabbi Tarfon stood up, kissed him and said: "You are my master, my guide; my master in wisdom and my guide in good conduct". Rabbi Tarfon then provided him with additional money to distribute among the poor.

Why did Rabbi Tarfon kiss and praise Rabbi Akiva after the latter had obviously deceived him? Perhaps because he understood that, given the choice of acquiring an *ephemeral* place, or an *eternal* one, he would ultimately be happier with an eternal one. One can acquire a *physical* piece of 'real' estate – or, with the same funds, he can purchase a spiritual, everlasting piece, a *true* estate. *Hesed* lives on forever. Charity is indeed an investment.

THE CURSES OF APATHY

The Talmud (Ketuvot 67b) curses people who close their hearts and refuse to give charity. "He who shuts his eye against charity is like one who worships idols."

The Talmud declares (Betsah 32b): "Rav said: 'The rich of Babylon will go down to Gehinom'. Their sin: they refused to perform acts of charity and kindness."

The Midrash tells us (Leviticus Rabbah 34:12): "Let the mitzvah of helping the poor never appear trivial in your eyes — for its nonperformance evokes twenty four curses, while its performance earns twenty four blessings".

The Talmud (Bava Batra 10a, quoting Jeremiah 16:5) tells us that by refraining from giving charity and acting benevolently, we cause God to withdraw His peace from the Jewish people.

A Good Name

Rabbi Shimon declared (Pirkei Avot 4:13): "There are three crowns. The crown of learning, the crown of priesthood, and the crown of royalty; *but the crown of a good name exceeds them all.*"

No doubt, by perpetuating acts of *hesed*, such as charity, you make your imprint on the world. If you never let a day go by without performing *hesed*, then day after day you are building a "good name", a fine reputation for yourself.

Proverbs (22:1) declares: It is better to choose a good name than riches." The Mishnah (Avot 2:8) agrees. "If one has acquired a good name, he has acquired it for himself".

Shakespeare (Othello, III, 3) wrote: "Good name in man and woman, dear my lord, is the immediate jewel of their souls. Who steals my purse steals trash; ...but he that filches from me my good name robs me ... and makes me poor indeed."

Obtaining a "good name" through charity is a wonderful way to live. When people speak about you in your absence it will be with love, respect and with praise. If you have a *need*, your fine reputation will always precede you and help protect you.

The Nobel Prize

Alfred Bernhard Nobel was a 19th century Swedish chemist and engineer, who developed and exploited the use of nitroglycerin. A relative with a similar name had died and a careless journalist wrote an obituary for Alfred Nobel. It read "He was a merchant of death and a master of destruction. He had amassed a fortune as he armed the nations of the world for war. He was a cold-blooded and ruthless warmonger."

Alfred Nobel read his own "obituary" in the Swedish newspaper. He was so disturbed by it that he decided to make a change. He decided that a good name is more important than riches. He could easily have denied any wrong-doing, rationalized his career and sued the newspaper for libel. Instead, he faced his life and decided to devote the rest of his life to the enrichment and betterment of humanity. With his wealth, he established the international Nobel Peace Prize, and other Nobel Prizes for contributions to literature, art, science and medicine. Nobel was determined to reverse his "obituary" before he left the land of the living. He set out to make the world a better, more peaceful, more loving place because he had lived.

A HIGHER STANDARD FOR OURSELVES

The Talmud (Ketuvot 17a) teaches that a person must do his best to understand the needs of others. Yet, for himself, a person should have as few needs as possible. He should shy away from honor, but bestow honor upon others. One should forego personal pleasure, trust that "God will provide" for financial needs and not worry. One should go out of his way to prevent other people from loss. One should try never to borrow, but should lend money freely. One should try never to accept charity, but should generously give as much charity as possible.*

SHE OPENED THE WORLD FOR OTHERS, AND NOW THE WORLD HAS OPENED FOR HER

A good example of a person with a higher standard for herself would be eighty-eight-year-old Oseola McCarty.** Miss McCarty lived in a tiny house on Miller Street, in Hattiesburg, Mississippi, all her life. She was brought up by her grandmother, mother and aunt. As they fell sick over the years, she cared for them. Oseola had to drop out of school at age eight, and began to work as a laundress to support the family. Her grandmother died in 1944, her mother died in 1964, and her aunt in 1967, leaving her completely alone and poverty-stricken. She continued her meager existence as people brought their clothes to her to clean, but would seldom talk to her.

She lived by herself since 1967, between rows of hanging clothes. She saved as many one-dollar bills as she could, spending very little on herself. She had only left Mississippi once in her life. She had never been on an airplane. In 1995, her arthritis worsened, making it hard for her to work or sometimes even stand. She felt her life was creeping to a sad and lonely ending.

Then, on July 26, 1995, Miss McCarty did something that would change her life forever. She walked into the local bank and told the teller to *give her life savings away.* She instructed the bank to send the balance of her account, all one hundred fifty thousand dollars of it, to the University of Southern Mississippi, to be used for scholarships. She did not ask for anything in return. It was just a very simple, unselfish act of kindness.

Within weeks, every major news organization in the nation had interviewed her. She was on the front cover of *The New York Times.* She was on *Good Morning America,* and was named one of Barbara Walters' *Ten Most Interesting People of 1995.* She was featured in periodicals and on television.

People have been lining up to honor her. Harvard made her an *Honorary Doctor of Humane Letters.* (She says that she is not absolutely sure what that award means, but she is proud to have it). The National Urban League made her a *Community Hero.* The National Institute of Social Sciences gave her a gold medal. She actually carried the Olympic Torch (not far, but she did carry it) and won the *Wallenberg Humanitarian Award.*

Oseola was recently interviewed for a new television show (even though, she says, she never watches T.V.). People, famous and ordinary, sought her out and called her "holy". President Bill Clinton made a point to meet with her, show her his respect and have his picture taken with her.

Longstreet Press of Atlanta compiled a collection of her sayings in a book entitled, Simple *Wisdom For Rich Living.* It is a book of Miss McCarty's opinions on faith, work, clean living, saving money and finding peace of mind.

Here is what the book says on the subject of self-esteem: *"It seems pretty basic to me. If you want to feel proud of yourself, you've got to do things you can be proud of."**

Here is another McCarty quote: *"Building community is not that hard. It just takes ordinary friendliness. The woman who took me to the doctor when my arthritis got bad is a checkout person at my grocery store. When she helped me with my groceries all those years, we spoke. I didn't stand there looking at the floor or the ceiling."* (In other words, she subscribes to our *"hesed* boomerang" theory).

Oseola McCarty's kindness has had a ripple effect on other people. Recently, an elderly woman sent in a ten dollar check, saying that she wanted to be a part of what Miss McCarty had started. Others write to her or come to see her because they want to be close to someone good. Artists and poets have visited her as have preachers and teachers, to draw on her strength and what they see as basic goodness.

At the University, other philanthropists have added more than two hundred thousand dollars to her original endowment of one hundred fifty thousand dollars, and it continues to grow. Her *act of kindness* has inspired literally thousands of people to reconsider giving charity. Because of her gift, her kindness, as many as six students will be going to college next year who otherwise would not be able to afford the tuition.

On Thursday evening, September 18, 1997, at a U.N. dinner, Ted Turner pledged to donate one billion dollars over ten years to benefit United Nations programs. This was one of the largest gifts in philanthropic history.

The money will go to benefit Unicef (which provides water, nutrition, health and education projects for children), the U.N. Development Program (which seeks to eradicate poverty, protect the environment and create jobs), and to other U.N. programs that help the poor, the sick and the suffering of innocent people.

Ted Turner acknowledged that "people love their money, like their houses or dogs." He told reporters that "with practice, it gets easier. I'm trying to set the standard for gallantry... I've never been happier than I am today."

Ted Turner described his decision to donate the money to Cable News Network as a "spur of the moment" decision. When asked who inspired him to this enormous generosity, he responded, "Mother Teresa, Jacques Cousteau, Princess Diana, financier philanthropist George Soros and 'the little colored lady-washer who gave away everything', referring to Oseola McCarty. (The Wall Street Journal, September 22, 1997).

Through all the fanfare, Miss McCarty is still as modest and unassuming as she always was. She still gets down every night on her knees to pray. She still lives a simple life. Yet, her lone simple act of altruism has enriched her life beyond her wildest dreams. *The New York Times* (Nov. 12, 1996) sums it up nicely:

"But an odd thing happened, an unexpected thing. That unselfish gift — she did not even ask for so much as a brick to be dedicated in her name — has infused her life with color and experiences and delivered her from the isolation of her past. Her generosity touched so many people, created such a fuss, that she soon found herself flying all over the country, accepting humanitarian awards, and meeting famous people."

The title of The New York Times article on her is very appropriate: *She Opened the World for Others, and Now the World Has Opened For Her.* * **

—23—

Hospitality

"AND ABRAHAM RAN..."

In Jewish tradition, Abraham is known as *the man of hesed*. When three visitors came to his tent, he convinced them to stay. At first, he offered them merely bread, water and a little rest. Then, he ran to his cattle and prepared for them a huge meal.

On the surface, Abraham seems to be merely a decent, normal person. After all, who would not take in three weary travelers? But we must look further to find a deeper understanding.

How would you feel *two days* after being circumcised? What would *you* do? How would you feel on the third day of your *hernia* operation? Would you sit at the front of your home, and, upon seeing travelers, "run towards them" as Abraham did? .

The Torah, in describing this incident, uses the verbs *ratz*, meaning *ran*, *vaymaher* (hurried) and *Mahari*, (hurry!), a total of four times. The emphasis is on *how* Abraham responded to weary travelers — even while he himself was suffering great physical pain. His response was *hesed*.

Imagine being able to communicate with God, and, in a mystical, prophetic way, being able to hear "a still, small voice". Now imagine that if you hear this voice, if you are approached by God and by guests simultaneously that you have to say (Genesis 18:3)"O my Lord, if I have found favor in your eyes, do not go away from your servant". Imagine telling God: "Please wait just a few minutes. I have to go serve my guests. When I return from helping other human beings, I'll return and talk with You."

This is what the Bible tells us that Abraham did. He was actually conversing with God and saw potential guests. He asked God to excuse him, and went to greet and invite the guests into his home.

Abraham's hospitality was legendary. The Sages say (Bava Metsia 30b, Shabbat 127b) that he built his home with entrances on all four sides, so that passersby on their way would tend to approach it. Abraham would then run to serve them and let them rest in his home.

Jewish tradition holds the virtue of hospitality in the highest regard. The Talmud asserts that hospitality to guests is more important and should take priority even over "welcoming the Divine presence".

There is an interesting Midrash (Exodus Rabah 28:1) that describes what happened when Moshe was about to receive the Torah. The angels wanted to strike him down (and not let him receive it). God then created an image of Abraham and asked the angels, "are you not now ashamed? Wasn't this the man who was so hospitable as to invite you in to eat in his home?" Then God turned to Moshe and said, "the Torah is given over to you only because of the merit of Abraham (and his hospitality)".

Perhaps this is what the Mishnah (Avot 3:21) meant when it declared: "If there is no flour (food), there will not be Torah." If not for the "flour" (the food) that Abraham hurried to prepare for his guests, there might not have been a Torah (or for that matter a Jewish people...).*

AMON AND MOAV

The Jewish people were prohibited from marrying people from the nations of Amon or Moav, even if they converted. The reason? They refused to meet the Jewish people with bread and water as they left Egypt. Their *lack of hospitality* (and compassion) was the reason for their rejection. Perhaps the Torah is trying to teach us a lesson: Individuals without hospitality have no place among the Jewish People.

HOSPITALITY?

The Torah (Deut. 23), when it outlaws the nations of Amon and Moav, simultaneously declares that third generation Egyptian converts *would* be allowed to enter the assembly of Israel. The Torah further commands us to be extra sensitive not to oppress or insult the Egyptians.

An obvious question arises: The nations of Amon and Moav were ostracized for life because they had not provided the Jews with bread and water as they left Egypt. The Egyptians, who enslaved our people for two hundred ten years, killed our children and threw our babies into the Nile — *may* be allowed to join the Jewish people?

Why?

The answer: The Egyptians had provided a refuge for the Jews during the famine. Pharaoh gave Jacob and his family a city (Goshen) to live in, and made sure that they had enough food.

This one act of *kindness*, of *true hospitality*, can never be forgotten. No matter what happened in Egypt later, the fact that the Egyptians had helped the Jewish people will forever allow them a potential place in the assembly of Israel. The Torah seems to be constantly reminding the Jewish people to be appreciative and grateful of all the *hesed* done for us. We are commanded to allow the Egyptians to join us. Their actions "boomerang" back to them.

THE ANTITHESIS

Sodom and Gemorrah were cities that did not know how to treat guests. It was known that these cities actually had laws prohibiting hospitality. The antithesis of hospitality is cruelty and evil. These cities were ultimately destroyed and never rebuilt.

If *hesed* can boomerang back to us, perhaps cruelty, its antithesis, will boomerang back as well.

A HOSPITALITY 'HOW–TO'

Jewish tradition spells out how to perform the mitzvah of hospitality: Many of these procedures are derived from the Torah's story of Abraham's three guests (Genesis, Chapter 18).

• Seek opportunities to be hospitable. Abraham, in physical pain following his Berit Milah at an advanced age, sat at the entrance of his tent, looking for guests.

• Say a little, and do much (Avot, 1:15). Abraham offered the guests very little, ("and I will fetch a morsel of bread"). Yet, after he convinced them to stay, he prepared a full meal for them.

• Hospitality is performed with washing facilities in addition to food and drink. Abraham ordered that water be brought for the travelers to wash their feet.

• It is part of the mitzvah of hospitality to give guests a place to relax and refresh themselves from the fatigue of their travels. Abraham invited his guests to rest from their journey under the refreshing shade of a tree.

• Jewish tradition requires that we receive guests cordially. It instructs the host to immediately place food before the visitors (in case they are too ashamed to ask).

• When serving them, the host should be gracious and not irritable. His conversation should be comforting to them, helpful and encouraging. He should not disclose his own troubles or worries to them, and he should appear to regret that he can't provide them with more.

• The host should slice bread for his guests to prevent them from becoming ashamed or embarrassed.

• The host should not look at his guests while they are eating.

• If the guest sleeps over, the host should give him the best bed available.

• The host must escort his guest out.

The Rambam (Hilchot Avel 14:2-3) writes that it is actually more important to escort the guests out than it is to invite the guests in. The Talmud (Sotah 46b) declares that, if one does not escort the guest, it is as if he spilled blood! Furthermore, the Zohar (Vayera 104:1) writes: "A man should escort his guests out because the entire mitzvah of hospitality (*hachnasat orhim*) is dependent upon it."*

BLOODSHED

The Torah (Deut. 21:6) discusses the following scenario:

A dead body is found between two cities and the elders of each say: "Our hands have not shed this blood, neither have our eyes seen it".

The Rabbis of the Talmud (Sotah 46b) say: "Can it even enter our minds that the elders of the 'Bet Din' (Jewish court) shed blood? Actually, they (the elders) mean to say: 'we did not see him and dismiss him without food, and we did not leave him without an escort'."

Thus, the Rabbis imply that *not performing the mitzvah of hospitality is like shedding blood.***

THE HESED BOOMERANG PRINCIPLE

The Rabbis tells us that the mitzvah of hospitality is one whose "interest" (or "fruit") is enjoyed (or "eaten") in this world, while the "principal" remains intact for the world to come. In other words, the benefits of hospitality abound in this lifetime. After all, hospitality is a beautiful kind of *hesed*, and it can "boomerang" back to us.

For example: when the guests leave Abraham's home, one of them tells him, "your wife Sarah will have a son". The Midrash (Tanhuma, Ki Tetse) tells us that one of the rewards of showing hospitality to guests in this world is having sons.

Another example: When Rebecca saw Abraham's servant approaching in the desert, she offered to give him water to drink and to feed his camels as well (see Genesis 24:14). This was the sign he was looking for. Rebecca was the most worthy to be the wife of Isaac, the daughter-in-law of Abraham. Her simple, honest hospitality and *hesed* changed her life forever. *Hesed* seems to have a way of coming around, going around, and returning to us.

Even hospitality that is done for an ulterior motive (such as to convince someone of something, or to get the person to "owe you a favor") is a blessing. Additionally, even hospitality that is done on a "quid pro quo" basis (in other words, you owe someone a favor so you invite him in to eat a meal with you) is still considered an act of *hesed* that will not go unrewarded.

The Talmud (Sanhedrin 103b) relates: Rabbi Yohanan declared in the name of Rabbi Yosi the son of Kisma: "So great is the food fed to guests, that it pushed away two families (Amon and Moav) from Israel".

Rabbi Yohanan himself declared: "It has the power to push away the close (Amon and Moav, who were the descendants of Lot, the nephew of Abraham our forefather), and bring near to us those who are far away" (the descendants of Yitro, the Kohen of Midyan. They served in the Temple.)

When did Yitro feed guests? When he fed Moshe, who saved Yitro's daughters from the shepherds.

After that incident, Yitro had two good reasons to invite Moshe in for a meal. Firstly, he owed him a favor. Moshe had just helped his family. The *least* Yitro could do was to invite him in. Secondly, the Midrash (Tanhuma on Exodus 11) reminds us that Yitro might have had an ulterior motive: his seven unmarried daughters. So

Yitro says (Exodus 2:20): "Call him and let him eat bread."

The Mishnah (Avot, 4), gives us some insight: "Be as careful to fulfill an easy mitzvah as you are to fulfill a difficult one, for you will never know the rewards of the mitzvot." In other words, even a simple act of *hesed*, even hospitality that is as easy and natural as returning of a favor, can have many beautiful rewards and blessings. Not only, our sages tell us, did Yitro's act of hospitality earn him an entire portion of the Torah named after him (parashat Yitro). In addition, his descendants merited to be included in the nation of Israel and serve in the Holy Temple.

The verse in Ecclesiastes (11:1), "cast your bread upon the waters for you shall find it after many days," has been interpreted (Shemot Rabah 27:6) to refer to the actions of Yitro.

Additionally, after the Exodus, the Torah states: "And Aaron and all the elders came to eat bread with the father-in-law of Moshe before God." Yitro "cast his bread" to Moshe, only to "find it after many days" with Aaron and the elders of Israel.

As noted earlier, escorting a friend is a component of hospitality. The Talmud (Sotah 46b, Shabbat 118a) relates an incident that exemplifies how great is the merit of one who fulfills this mitzvah.

In Judges (1:24), a man points out the entrance to a city, helping the Jews militarily. And, "they went in and smote the city by the edge of the sword, but they let the man go free with all his family". The man then left and built a city called Luz.

The city of Luz is famous, according to Jewish tradition, for being indestructible. A Talmudic passage describes it as "the city against which Sanherib marched without uprooting it, Nebuchadnezar marched without destroying it and through which the angel of death has no permission to pass."

The Sages reason as follows: "Now this Canaanite did not utter a word or walk a step (he merely pointed his finger). Yet, he gained deliverance for himself and his descendants, to the end of all generations. Whoever, then, actually *does walk* with someone to escort him, will all the more so be rewarded.

ABRAHAM'S HOSPITALITY BOOMERANGS BACK TO HIS DESCENDANTS

"Cast your bread upon the waters for you shall find it after many days." (Kohelet 11:1)

Abraham to his Three Guests:	God's Payback in the Wilderness:	God's Payback in the Land of Israel:	God's Payback in the World to Come:
Gen. 18:5 "I will fetch you a morsel of bread."	Ex. 16:4 "Behold I will cause bread to rain from heaven for you."	Deut. 8:8 "It will be a land of wheat and barley; You shall not lack anything in it..."	Psalms 72:16 "There will be a rich field of grain in the land upon the top of the mountains."
Gen. 18:4 "Let now a little water be fetched."	Num. 21:17 "Spring up O' well, sing unto it."	Deut. 8:7 "For the Lord, your God brings you into a good land, a land of brooks of water."	Joel 4:18 "And it shall come to pass...all the brooks of Judah shall flow with water..."
Gen. 18:4 "and wash your feet."	Ezekiel 16:9 "Then I washed you with water" (Before they received the Torah)	Isaiah 1:16 "Wash yourselves, make yourselves clean, put away the evil of your doings..."	Isaiah 4:4 "When the Lord shall have washed away the faith of the daughters of Zion."
Gen. 18:4 "and recline yourself under the tree."	Psalm 105:39 "He spread a cloud for a screen."	Levit. 23:42 "You shall dwell in booths seven days."	Isaiah 4:6 "And there shall be a pavilion for a shadow in the daytime from the heart."

As you can see from the chart, the Sages of the Midrash go to great lengths to impress upon the people that acts of *hesed do not go unrewarded.*

Abraham's acts of kindness and hospitality "boomeranged back" to his descendants hundreds of years later and they will continue to pay dividends in the world to come. Just as the Torah (Exodus 34:6) promises that God "extends acts of kindness for thousands of generations."

The verse in Ecclesiastes (11:1) reads, "Cast your bread upon the waters for you shall find it after many days."

On the surface this makes no sense at all. Would anyone throw bread into the water and expect it to stay edible or retrievable?

The Midrash (Kohelet Rabbah) teaches us an important lesson: This verse is not to be understood literally! Kohelet is reminding the reader to cast his *compassion* into the *world!* Cast not your "bread" but your love, your kindness. Why? Because what *goes* around eventually *comes* around: *"For you shall find it after many days."*

—24—

Visiting the Sick

A VISIT

Let me take you with me on a visit. It's July 24, 1990. I look around the room . Old, used furniture. A small, dark, and dingy one-bedroom apartment. Jack lays in bed. His arms and legs look more like thin bones than body parts. His right arm is completely paralyzed. He's talking to me. What is he trying to say? "M. S." Jack wants to tell me he has multiple sclerosis, a disease that takes away from him the power to move his muscles.

Kathleen, his caretaker, turns to me. "You know, Jack has a great memory and a great mind. Ask him some questions!".

"Are you in pain, Jack?" He shakes his head.

"Do they take good care of you?" He nods.

"Where were you born? Syria or the U.S.?' He musters all his strength to get a word out. I can't understand him. I'm trying to read his lips. I'm straining to see what he's trying to say. I can't. He is not giving up. He is determined to tell me something. He won't give up. (Idiot! Why did you make him strain himself and why are you making him suffer? Can't you see he can't speak?)

Kathleen, the caretaker, tries to understand. "Let me go through the alphabet with you, Jack. Okay? A, B, C, D, E - E?" He nods frantically.

"E - Egypt?" He nods again and smiles — a smile of triumph. Ah. He felt good.

"He loves when people come to visit him from Bikur Holim! He loves it when you guys come and talk to him and he loves to talk. Do you know Jack knows Arabic and Hebrew? Wait! Jack is trying to say something again."

He's moving his lips and he's moaning — it sounds like an "I". His eyes are pleading to be understood, pleading with me to make him whole by making him feel understood.

"I?", I hear myself saying. He then swirled his tongue.

Kathleen says "S? I.S.? Israel?" he nods.

"For how long?"

"TEH" "Ten? Ten years?"

Yes, he's happy. He rests.

"What age did you go to Israel?'

"EF" - 5 years old? He nods again.

So you moved to the States when you were 15? He smiles.

"M.S." He manages to say, "Oh, that's when you began to get M.S.?" He nods again.

We are talking. I'm telling him I care.

"He's trying to tell you he has M.S. for 22 years, from the age of 15. You see, Jack is only 37."

"They told me at Bikur Holim you wanted me to help you put on Tefillin. Should I get my Tefillin?"

He nods. He's dangling his left arm in the air. I wrap the Tefillin on his left arm and he smiles.

"He's so happy when you come to visit. He loves the company. He wasn't always in bed like this. First, he had trouble walking. Then, he had a cane. Then a wheelchair. He hates being cooped up in this little apartment. Do you know Jack has a degree? An A.A. in accounting."

"What college is your degree from, Jack?"

"Queeh"

"Queensboro?"

He smiles and nods. He's so proud. He's proud to be alive.

We're sitting and he's holding my hand. His big blue eyes are looking in mine. He's searching me. I feel like he's trying to say something. I look back forcing a smile.

"I think he's trying to tell you something. Do you understand him?" Embarrassed, I shake my head.

With tears in my eyes I say, "what do you need? Are you in pain, Jack? How can I help you? What can I do? Do the Tefilin hurt?"

"Thank", I heard him say. But I think I'm dreaming.

Kathleen says, "He really wants to say 'thank you'. Is that what you're saying, Jack?"

He smiles and squeezes my hand. The tears are rolling down my cheeks and he smiles and looks into my eyes in a sad way, as if to say, "don't cry, I'll be fine. I'll be okay. Thanks for coming."

I took off the Tefillin from his left arm and he helped me unwrap it.

"He's saying 'come again'. Thank God for you people at Bikur Holim. When he found out you would be visiting yesterday he was saying your name all day just waiting for you to come. Now that you're leaving, he's sad."

"I'll be back, Jack. God bless you. Refuah Shelemah" I tell him.

He squeezes my hand again. "Thank", he managed to moan out. He looks at me with his big blue eyes. He smiles and lets my hand go. And I leave.

Visiting the sick is just one way of making our lives into statements of compassion, of incorporating *hesed* into our lives.

As I continued to visit the sick and the elderly, I realized more and more the positive effect my visits were having on my life.

I stopped caring so much about my personal or financial worries. I started to focus on other people, *and I was never the same person again*.

I have to say, there are no more surefire ways of reducing your stress, personal anxiety and sadness than to visit sick people, comfort the bereaved and befriend the lonely.

THE HESED BOOMERANG PRINCIPLE

The Mishnah (Shabbat 127a) relates. "Visiting the sick is a mitzva from which man enjoys the fruits in this world, while the stock remains for him in the world to come".

The Talmud (Nedarim 40a) assures that: "He who visits the sick will be delivered from the punishment of Gehinam." This is derived from the verse in Psalms (41:2): "Happy is he that considers the poor, God will deliver him in the day of evil." They interpret "poor" ('dal') as "sick" (or physically poor) and "evil" as "Gehinam".

The Talmud (Nedarim 40a) relates: After Rabbi Akiva visited and revived a sick student, he declared, "he who does not visit the sick is like a shedder of blood!"

A BIKUR HOLIM PRIMER

Visiting the sick, in Hebrew, is referred to as *Bikur Holim*. Very often I encounter people who want to visit ill people in a hospital or old age home. But, *they just do not know how.* Many people feel uncomfortable visiting a sick person. People ask, "what do I say?" "What should I not say?" "How should I act?" "How do I make it enjoyable?"

Rabbi Eliezer ben Isaac (11th century Germany) wrote in his *Orot Hayim (Paths of Life):* "Visit the sick and lighten their suffering. Pray for them and leave. Do not stay too long for you may inflict upon them additional discomfort. When you visit the sick enter the room cheerfully."

The purpose of this book is to motivate you to do volunteer work, or to dramatically increase the *hesed* in your life. The promise is that it will enrich your life and the lives of others. Visiting the sick is a vital part of *hesed*. It is a skill that needs to be practiced.

I have compiled a list of guidelines for people who would like to visit the sick. These "forty two rules of Bikur Holim" are intended to be used as a primer on the mitzvah of visiting the sick, the lonely, the elderly or anyone else who needs a friendly visit. Please feel free to use these "rules" liberally, and to spread the word and encourage others to visit the sick and enjoy it as well.

They are divided into four parts.

A) How to show respect

B) What to talk about and how to talk about it.

C) Things to do on the visit.

D) What to remember before you leave.

Enjoy!

A. How to Show Respect

1. Respect the elderly, or the sick, or lonely, as people. Respect their points of view.

2. Respect their privacy.

3. Let them feel important, special and loved.

4. *Find something to love* about the person you are visiting. Everyone has some lovable qualities. Make a sincere connection. You won't regret it.

5. *Be Yourself* . You have your own style of speaking to others. *Use it and be natural.* The patient will appreciate your sincerity. Try to speak on the same level and don't forget to SMILE.

6. Give the elderly opportunities to share their talents, their experiences, their potential, their past. *Utilize the interests of the elderly;* help them to develop some new interests or to revive old ones.

7. Do not break an appointment without letting the person know. Do be faithful in your visits. *They mean a lot.*
8. Do not make it a "them" and "us" situation; make it a *sharing* one.
9. Avoid making the relationship one in which material giving takes precedence. Remember that the important thing to them is that you are there.
10. Let them do as much for themselves as possible. They have pride and human dignity. *Don't take that away from them.*
11. Be patient, calm and gentle.
12. Don't be effusive or overly anxious to please. That may seem insincere.
13. Be sincere, be yourself. *Don't use flattery.*

B. What to Talk About and How To Talk About It

14. *Identify Yourself.* Upon entering the room as a stranger, put the person at ease by identifying yourself. Be sure to greet other patients in the room as well. Ask the patient if this is a convenient time to visit. Be prepared to leave if the patient is sleeping, tired, preoccupied, or has other visitors. Do not stay too long. It is the quality of your visit that counts.
15. *Be a good listener.* Establish and maintain eye contact. Position yourself on the same physical level if possible. Focus all your energy exclusively on the other person.
16. *Patient Confidentiality.* Do not discuss the patient's condition unless he or she offers the information first. If the patient does bring up the subject, then encourage the discussion, as this can be very therapeutic.
17. *Be Observant.* Look around the room for flowers, cards, photos and books that you can discuss. Take an interest in the patient and ask him or her about where he or she lives, what he or she does, any hobbies, children and

grandchildren, etc. Encourage the patient to do some or all of the talking.

18. Ask the person: "How are you doing?" and *carefully listen to his or her answer.*
19. *Restate* what you hear the person saying to you.
20. *Ask questions* that will help you get acquainted and will show that you are trying to understand.
21. Ask about family members. Are they visited? Are they lonely?
22. *Do not talk about your problems.* If they ask about your family, talk about it but try to keep the conversation directed toward them.
23. Make light conversation; say positive things; avoid controversial and depressing subjects.
24. Do not speak about death or dying unless an elderly person himself introduces the subject— because of fear, anxiety, or need of clarification on the subject, or because he or she knows that death is imminent. You should be aware of the various possible reactions, such as denial, anger, bargaining, depression and acceptance.
25. *In any situation, you should listen and maintain a stance reflecting hope and positive approach.* You should be careful not to interfere with the religious views of the elderly person and should not impose your own ideas on the subject.
    Remember that the elderly are very realistic.
26. *Do not* give medical advice.
27. Remember that everyone who has lived 65 years or more has had many interesting experiences. Ask about them.
28. Look for similarities, not differences.
29. Give feedback to the person:
    State what you've noticed or learned about the person or his or her situation.
    State what you are going to do about it (if you can do something).

Tell how you feel. For example, "I'm glad I came to see you today" (But only if you are *sincerely* glad!)

C. Things to Do on The Visit

30. *Smile* and enjoy yourself.
31. If appropriate, shake hands to greet the person.
32. *Create an atmosphere of caring, love, acceptance and trust.* Don't judge, criticize, complain or offer advice. Just try to listen, to understand and keep the patient company. Your unconditional presence is all that counts.
33. *Be Prepared for Surprises.* Keep in mind, if you are in a hospital, that you may see unpleasant sights. Prepare yourself mentally to accept them.
34. *Doctor's Orders.* Before responding to a patient's request for water, food or to be moved, check with a nurse or doctor. The patient may be under medication or scheduled for an operation. Also, please do not offer medical advice, just listen.
35. *Proper Hygiene.* Always wash your hands before and after a visit so as not to transmit any bacteria to yourself or to the patient. Never visit if you are sick. Even a cold can be harmful to the patient.
36. Play cards, read out loud, play a musical instrument or bring along some yarn for the client to begin knitting a baby sweater, scarf, etc...
37. Encourage interest in appearance. Maybe she will let you give her a manicure or fix her hair.
38. If it is appropriate, you can ask if they would like to go outside and take a walk.

D. Before You Leave, Remember:

39. Check to see that their needs are being met (and take notes).

Is there enough food?
Do they need clothing?
Do they need weekly visits?

40. *Follow Up.* Ask the patient if he or she (or the family) needs anything, and find out if you can fulfill the request. Upon leaving, wish the patient a speedy recovery.

41. *Prayer.* It is customary to recite *tehillim* or a personal prayer in the name of the patient later that evening. Ask the patient, "would you mind if I prayed for you?" Praying for the health of the sick is actually considered part of the mitzvah. "The visitor perceives their suffering and prays for God's mercy... If one spent time with the sick but forgot to pray for Divine compassion, he has not fulfilled the mitzvah completely."*

42. *Be Proud of Yourself.* You have just taken away 1/60th of the patient's illness. Congratulate yourself on doing a good deed. You have just improved someone's health by showing him that someone cares.

"I AM NOT WHAT YOU SEE"

There is a beautiful poem which is attributed to Laurie Pope Pauly. It is entitled, "I Am Not What You See". It should be considered *required reading* for anyone sincerely interested in visiting the elderly (or even dealing with the elderly):

I AM NOT WHAT YOU SEE!

I didn't always look this way;
all wrinkled and sagging
Hair wispy and gray.

My teeth in a glass,
My muscles grown frail,

My vision fast failing,
Skin sallow and pale.

You might be surprised,
Had you seen me at eight,
With eyes bright and eager,
Awaiting life's fate.

I ran with swift feet,
And sureness of gait,
Each day was so sweet,
Adventures so great!

At twenty, the world,
Was at my command.
My future was rosy
My time in demand.

At thirty, I'd conquered
Many a foe,
Well loved and respected,
By those in the know.

At forty, established,
With wealth and some fame,
My goals half accomplished,
My deeds won acclaim.

At fifty, successful
With future assured,
All systems were, "Go",
All holds were secured.

How could this happen?

How could this be?
How could somebody,
Play this trick on me?

While I wasn't looking,
While I didn't see,
Somehow an old body,
Was traded for me.

I stagger, I tremble,
I drool, I complain,
My limbs won't sustain me,
My body knows pain.

Now dawdling, now dreaming,
What happened to me?
Where is that person,
That I used to be?

You see me defeated,
Exhausted and slow,
My life almost ended,
My time running low.

Be gentle and kind,
As you tend to my needs.
In caring for me
Your are planting your seed.

For someday, it may
Be you in this place,
Submissive and broken.
In need of God's grace.

CONTRACT ON HIS LIFE

Les Brown tells the story of the time he worked as a morning disc jockey at a local radio station. On his way home from work, he would visit sick people in the hospital, and read to them.

One day, he offended someone on the radio (by exposing the truth about a fraudulent activity). They *put a contract out on his life*.

One day the following week, he arrived home at 2AM. A big, tall man suddenly appeared from the side of the house and asked, "are you Les Brown?"

The man told him about the contract, and that he had taken it and *convinced the mob not to kill him.*

Why?

"While I was in jail (Ohio State Penitentiary), my mother wrote to me about a man, a disc jockey, that would visit her and read to her once a week. I found out that it was you who made my mother feel less lonely. I wanted to meet you. When I found out that those people wanted to knock you off, I took the contract and made sure nothing bad would happen to you".

Les Brown's life was saved because of his daily visits to sick people in the hospital. It is just another example of how *hesed* can often boomerang back in a strange, magical and wonderful way.

Sometimes it can even save our lives.*

—25—

Feeding the Hungry

We live in a world that is full of natural resources. There is plenty of food to feed everyone. Yet our world is devastated by hunger.

Based upon the annual reports of Earthsave, Amnesty International, and Feed the Children: Every two seconds, somewhere in the world, a child dies of malnutrition. This means that each and every day, more than forty three thousand children die of not having enough food to eat! Every 53 minutes a child dies from poverty. In the United States alone, fifteen million children (or one in five) are so poor that they are at risk of going to bed hungry each night. Every 32 seconds, in the United States, a child is born into poverty. In New York alone there are more than one hundred thousand homeless people. Forty percent of them are children.

If we want to change these tragic "statistics", we must work together. We must make real changes.

TWO DREAMS

A woman had two very different dreams.

In the first dream, she saw hundreds of sad, expressionless people sitting at a gigantic banquet table. On the table was a vast array of the most delicious foods. *But not a morsel of food had been touched.*

She wondered, "why aren't these people eating? They look so tired and hungry, and the food looks delicious. I don't understand."

Her guide said, "they can't feed themselves. If you will notice, you will see that the people have no joints in their arms. They can hold their arms straight out, but they cannot bend them. No matter how hard they try, they cannot bend their arms to bring their hands to their mouths to feed themselves."

In her second dream, the woman saw another large room. Here, too, was a large banquet table laden with food, with hundreds of people sitting around it. And, here too, each person's arms had no joints — exactly like at the other banquet table.

Yet in this room, the people looked well-fed, happy and content!

The woman asked her guide: "How can these people look so well fed and satisfied when their arms are held straight out, unable to bend to bring food to their mouths?"

The guide said, "look carefully."

The woman looked and saw, that, although each person could not bend his or her own arms, each could grasp food in his or her outstretched hand, and could hold the food and lift it up to a neighbor's mouth.

The people could not feed themselves. But they could feed their neighbors.

Either of the two "dreams" could be our world.

To the extent that we "feed" only ourselves, we all "starve". When, however, we think of others — when we serve our fellow human being, the world can flourish.

The difference between darkness and light, night and day, loneliness and friendship, sadness and joy, restlessness and tranquil satisfaction, hell and heaven, is acts of *hesed*, of love, of kindness. *These acts can boomerang right back to us until we can't keep the love and warmth out of our lives no matter how hard we try!*

A wise man once said "There are two kinds of people in the world: The givers and the takers. The takers eat well — but the givers *sleep* well".

WHY REBECCA?

The Torah tells how Abraham sent his servant to choose a wife for his son Isaac. The servant prayed to God for a sign (Genesis 24:12-14). "He prayed: O God, Lord of my master Abraham... If I say to a girl, 'tip over your jug and let me have a drink', and she replies, 'drink, and I will also water your camels', she will be the one whom You have designated for Your servant Isaac".

Why do you suppose Abraham's servant chose *this particular sign?*

Perhaps, after spending time in the home of Abraham, he understood what character traits were important in a person. Perhaps he realized that the best daughter-in-law for Abraham would be someone who would not only give him a drink, but would continue and say, "let me draw water for your camels". He sought a woman who would believe that feeding the hungry is so important that it applies to all creatures of God. The *hesed* of Rebecca convinced the servant of Abraham that she would make a good wife for Isaac (and a good daughter-in-law for Abraham!).

There was one differentiating characteristic, one fine moral quality that would decide the destiny of Isaac and the future of the Jewish people: *hesed*

The Midrash* explains why Abraham's' servant *ran* to her after watching her fill her pitcher with well water. It says that he saw the water from the well miraculously rise to meet Rebecca.

Now, the question is: Wasn't a woman who was worthy enough to have miracles performed on her behalf, enough for Abraham's son Isaac? Did this servant really need another *sign*, more evidence of her worthiness?

The answer is clear. Only after she performed her acts of *hesed* for the men and the camels was she chosen. It must have been impressive for him to see water miraculously rising to meet her, *so he ran to her.* Yet only after she gave his camels water was he convinced of her worthiness.

MAZON

Mazon is a group of Jewish people dedicated to responding to hunger. They ask people to contribute three percent of the cost of their catered event. The three percent goes toward feeding the hungry. In its fourth year of existence, Mazon (literally meaning food, nourishment) raises one million dollars annually.

FEED THE CHILDREN

In 1996, Feed the Children, led by Larry Jones, delivered more than sixty million pounds of food and other essential supplies to hungry children in the United States alone. This incredible organization touches millions, the world over. Larry Jones makes it so simple to donate to his charity. He describes real cases of hungry children and shows how Feed the Children comes to the rescue. For just thirty five dollars, you can authorize Feed The Children to deliver ten twenty-five pound boxes of food to hungry children in the United States. Feed the Children has a network of more than 6,300 separate organizations. Volunteers from these organizations and an additional 47,000 food pantries and churches then distribute the food directly to the hungry boys and girls and families who need it the most.

TREVOR'S GANG

On December 8, 1983 an eleven-year-old boy named Trevor Ferrell was watching the local TV news, which had a story about the city's homeless people. Trevor was curious. He lived in a town called Gladwyne, in the suburbs of Philadelphia. He asked his dad if they could go out and "see the homeless people who live on the street". His father refused. Trevor insisted, and his father, Frank, finally agreed. They got into the car with the mother, Janet, and two other Ferrell children. They drove to the city to see the homeless people. When they reached the center of the city, Frank locked the car doors.

Then, it happened.

They stopped at a light and Trevor looked out the window and saw a homeless person. Before anyone knew what was happening, Trevor unlocked and opened his door, and, carrying his blanket from home, walked straight up to the homeless man. He rested the blanket on the man gently and said "God bless you". The man responded very gratefully and Trevor got back into the car.

On the way back to Gladwyne, the Ferrells told each other how good it felt to help others.

The next night, they went back to the streets again. This time Trevor brought some food to give to the homeless. The next night they went again, and the night after that, and the night after that, and the night after that. Through rain, sleet, snow and hail, Trevor and his "gang" continued to go out to the streets to do something for the homeless. This has been going on since December 8, 1983. And "Trevor's Gang" has not missed a night since. *Not one single night.*

One cold winter night Trevor convinced his dad to come with him to try to sleep on the street. Trevor wanted to know what it really felt like to sleep on the street as the tens of thousands of homeless people do each and every night. They actually only lasted three hours. It was too cold for them.

People found out about Trevor and his nightly visits. In February, 1984, just two short months after the visits began, a widow donated an old, run-down building to Trevor that he could use for a shelter. On March 18, 1984, on the one hundredth day of Trevor's campaign, "Trevor's Place", a homeless shelter in downtown Philadelphia was opened. As of May of 1988, Trevor's Place, with a capacity for fifty people, has managed to find permanent housing for 84% of the people who come into the shelter and has found jobs for 80%.

The Ferrells work with many different types of homeless people. They worked with one young person who spent every night riding public transportation. Trevor took her in and supported her for two years. She then went to school and graduated pre-med from the University of Pennsylvania.

A local car dealer found out about Trevor. He "leased" him a van for one dollar a year and put the words "Trevor's Gang" on the sides. Now, when Trevor and his gang go out to the city on their campaign to seek out and help the homeless, people in other cars recognize the van and honk their horns in approval.

Once, a policeman pulled over the van and, instead of issuing a summons, he handed Trevor a contribution.

Many times, the Ferrells visit nearby fast-food restaurants to buy food to fill the van. The owners of these restaurants fill jugs with lemonade for free, and give Trevor big supplies of food and utensils to help him on his mission. People have responded to Trevor and his gang with compassion and empathy.

As of this writing, Trevor's gang has fed over three hundred thousand meals to the homeless, and helped countless others all over the streets of Philadelphia. Trevor has virtually made visiting and helping the homeless of that city a *safe* and enjoyable experience. Trevor and his family are not wealthy people. They are not exceptional public speakers. They have no political friends. They are just like me and you.

Trevor Ferrell is learning-disabled, dyslexic. So is his brother, Allen, and his father, Frank. Trevor Ferrell was an eleven-year-old boy who thought he could make a difference. He thought it was cruel to have people "live on the streets" with nobody to help them. So he fed them. And he clothed them. And he covered them with blankets. And he housed them in Trevor's Place. And he put his loving arm around them and told them he will not leave them alone. By the age of thirteen he was running his own homeless shelter.

Trevor describes his mission very simply:

"I am only one, but still I am one.
I cannot do everything, but still I can do something.
And just because I can't do everything, I will not refuse to do something I can do."

What is the lesson of the Trevor Ferrell story? It is a lesson about feeding the hungry; a lesson of *hesed.* Trevor teaches us that acts of altruism and compassion can be very simple. All that's needed is focus and repetition.

LEFTOVERS

Alice Mosiniak is a sixty-five-year-old woman living in Toledo, Ohio. Alice heard that this country discards more than thirty billion dollars worth of food each year. We waste about sixty million tons of grain, fruits and vegetables each year. She read that there is enough good food thrown out to feed more than fifty million hungry people. She knew that there were more than two hundred million hungry people in the world.

So she made a decision. She started an organization called *Toledo Seagate Food Bank.* People can donate extra and leftover food that is still edible. She put together a group of volunteers to help pick up, sort out and drop off the food.

Within a few years, Alice Mosiniak's group was handling *one million pounds of food each month* and feeding *tens of thousands* of hungry people throughout twenty counties in Ohio.

This woman and her volunteers have saved thousands of lives and she has done it very simply.

"Let me have your leftovers and I'll sort them out and feed the poor, the orphaned, the homeless and the hungry."

And that is exactly what she does.

Alice Mosiniak teaches us about transforming waste into value, transforming apathy into care. And she has transformed many hungry people into satisfied, happy and grateful volunteers.

"GLEANERS"

On November 1, 1981, Celeste McKinley walked into a small grocery store near her home in Las Vegas and asked if she could have some leftover produce for her pet cockatoo. The manager gave her some leftovers and invited her back the next day for more.

So Celeste went back the next day for some more leftovers... and the next day and the next. She began to realize that this grocery store, as well as many others like it, were discarding enormous amounts of food, perfectly fit for people to eat.

So Celeste made a decision. She made arrangements to pick up this leftover food and she started feeding people.

Celeste's organization is called "Gleaners". Gleaners *now handles more than 400,000 pounds of food a month* feeding more than *20,000 people a month* absolutely free.

Celeste does not accept any government money. Her basic rule for her work is the *preservation of human dignity.* So she "sells" the food to poor families — she charges 25 cents per family member.

People pay what they can. Some people give her food stamps, which she gladly accepts (and later discards, since the government refuses to cash them for her). Some people volunteer to work certain hours at the food bank instead of paying.

Tens of thousands of hungry and poor people come to Celeste for help. They leave satisfied, content. Food that would have been thrown into dumpsters (slightly dented cans, close or just-expired or dated food that is still legal, slightly damaged produce that can be sorted out, day old bread) helps feed the men, women and children who otherwise would go hungry.

Celeste McKinley was an entertainer, a singer and comedian who "played the clubs" in Las Vegas. She was a successful business-woman who at one time owned two companies.

She gave up her entertainment career. She sold her businesses. She and her husband David live on about six thousand dollars per year. Celeste and her husband made many personal sacrifices for *hesed*. Yet they are living happy, meaningful and fulfilling lives. She probably feels that her *hesed* boomerangs back to her every single day.

DONATE, DON'T DUMP
Kroger Supermarkets ran a print advertising campaign that read:

> *We at Kroger are concerned about hunger in America and we have committed to do our part in solving this national problem. At Kroger, edible food will not be thrown away. Agencies who feed the needy... will be picking up merchandise from our stores. We urge all retailers of the food industry to share our concern and join in the effort to DONATE - DON'T DUMP!*

THE TEN DOLLAR FINE
One cold day, in 1933, Fiorello LaGuardia was presiding as judge at police court. They brought a trembling old man before him, charged with stealing a loaf of bread. The man admitted his guilt and said, "what can I do, my family is starving."

La Guardia turned to the man and said, "I have no choice. I must punish you for your crime. I sentence you to a fine of ten dollars." Then he reached into his pocket, and said, "Well, here's the ten dollars to pay your fine. And now I remit the fine". He tossed the ten dollar bill into his hat. "Furthermore", he declared, "I'm going to fine everybody in this courtroom fifty cents for living in a town where a man has to steal bread in order to eat. Mr. Bailiff, collect the fines and give them to the defendant!".

The hat was passed around the courtroom and the incredulous old man, with a light of heaven in his eyes, left with forty-seven dollars and fifty cents to help feed his family.

Fiorello LaGuardia taught everyone a lesson that day about the value of human compassion, about *hesed* and feeding the hungry. Sometimes we must put the law on hold and take care of the people around us.

"HOW CAN I NOT SIGH?"

The Talmud (Ber. 58b) tells about an incident that occurred after the death of Rabbi Hana Bar Hanilai who lived in Babylonia in the fourth century and was known for his wealth and charity.

After Rabbi Hana's death, Rabbi Hisda and Rabbi Ula passed the site of his house. Rabbi Hisda sighed. Ula asked him why he sighed so sadly. He replied, "how can I not sigh over a house that contained sixty bakers that worked day and night to provide bread for the poor? Hana's hand was always in his pocket, ready to extend help to any deserving poor, so that the poor would not have to wait. This house had four entrances — one on each side. Any person who entered, left completely satisfied. I remember when there was a drought in the land. Rabbi Hana left wheat and barley around the house, in order that whoever was embarrassed to take it during the day, could come at night and help themselves then, without any shame. Now that this house is in ruins, how can I not sigh?"

THE HESED BOOMERANG PRINCIPLE

Jewish tradition promises that *hesed*, such as feeding the hungry, will not go unrewarded. Proverbs 19:17: "*He that is gracious to the poor lends to God and his good deeds He (God) will repay him"*

The Rabbis of the Talmud and Midrash often stress this verse in Proverbs to encourage the people to be kind and bestow mercy.

• The Midrash (Tanhuma Mishpatim 15) tells us: God Himself says... "If the poor man was hungry and was in the throes of death and you helped nourish and revive him, I swear I shall restore a life to you in return. ... I shall remember what you did for the poor man, and I shall save (your children) from death for your sake." God will repay a life for a life.

• The Talmud (Shabbat 156b) tells an incredible story of the power of feeding the hungry. Rabbi Akiva was told by astrologers that, on her wedding day, his daughter would be bitten by a snake and die. On her wedding day, she stuck a large pin into the wall and it entered the eye of a snake that was about to jump out at her, and inadvertently killed it.

The next day, she told her father what happened, and he asked: "You must have done something to be saved from that snake. What did you do?" She replied, "at the wedding, people were busy feasting and celebrating. A poor man came to our door, and I could see he was hungry and nobody was helping him. So, I ran over to him and gave him my portion of food so that he would not be hungry."

Rabbi Akiva then declared to his students that when the verse (Proverbs 10:2) says, "charity saves from death", it refers to natural as well as unnatural death.

• The Talmud tells us (Mishnah, Peah 1:1) that *hesed* stands by man until the end of all generations. As it was written in Psalms (103:17), *and the hesed of God endures forever and ever for those who fear him.*

• The Talmud further states (Avodah Zarah 17b): Rav Huna said: "He who occupies himself with Torah study (alone, without doing acts of *hesed)* is as if he had no God, for it is said (Chronicles II, 15:3): 'Now for long seasons Israel was without the true God'. What is meant by 'without the true God?' It means that he who only occupies himself with the study of Torah is as if he had no God to protect him".

Perhaps the statement of Rabbi Huna can be understood as follows: If one occupies himself with Torah study *without* doing acts of *hesed* it is as if he has no God to protect him and shield him with divine mercy. He has "no God" to show him *hesed* in return and help him in his time of distress and need.

• The Talmud (ibid) says that Rabbi Hananyah ben Teradyon was arrested. He knew that he did not do enough *hesed,* so he was not going to be freed. Rabbi El'azar ben Perata was arrested on five charges, but since he studied Torah and practiced acts of *hesed* he would be freed.

• The Midrash (Tehillim 118) expounds on the verse in Psalms (118:19), "open for me the gates of righteousness" as refering to the world-to-come. They will ask man: "What work did you do" (to deserve to enter this world?) A man answers, "I fed the hungry." They respond: "This is the gate of those that feed the hungry. Enter!" Another replies: "I gave drink to the thirsty." They respond: "This is the gate of those who gave drink to the thirsty. Enter!". . .

• The Midrash (Ruth Rabba, chapter 5) states: "Come and consider how great is the power of those who perform acts of charity. How great is the power of those who do kindly deeds *(hesed),* for they shall shelter neither in the shadow of the morning, nor in the shadow of the wings of the earth, nor in the shadow of the sun, nor in the shadow of the wings of the *Hayot* or *Cherubim* or *Seraphim* (heavenly bodies), but under whose wings do they shelter? Under the shadow of Him at Whose Word the world was created, as it said (Psalms 36:8) 'How precious your loving kindness, O, God! And the children of man take refuge under the shadow of your wings'."

• Another Talmudic saying (Bava Kamma 17a): "Whoever occupies himself with Torah as well as acts of *hesed* will see his enemies fall before him... and he will acquire intuitive understanding like the children of Yisachar (see Chronicles I, 12:32). Joseph is used as the example because he had supplied food to many people during the famine in Egypt. He also took care of his father's funeral. Jacob tells Joseph (Genesis, 47:29): "Do unto me *hesed* and truth."

•The Talmud says (Avodah Zarah 5b) that doing acts of loving kindness rescues man from the clutches of his evil desires.

There is a story told (Avot Derabbi Natan chapter 3) about a saintly person who was habitually charitable. Once, he set out in a boat, and a storm developed and sank his boat in the sea. Rabbi Akiva witnessed this and came before the court to testify so that the man's wife could remarry.

Just as Rabbi Akiva was about to take the stand, *the man came back and stood before him.*

"Aren't you the man I saw whose boat overturned at sea last night?" The man nodded. "How did you get out alive? Who raised you out of the sea?"

"Let me tell you what happened", the man responded. "You see, when I sank to the depths I heard the noise of the waves of the sea. One wave said to the other, 'hurry, let us raise this man out of the sea for he practices charity every day of his life.'

You see, my charity that I gave and the *hesed* that I do — raised me up out of the sea. My charity saved my life indeed, as it says: "Charity rescues from death" (Prov. 10:2)"

Then R'Akiva spoke up an declared "Blessed be God, the God of Israel... "*

•The Book of Psalms guarantees that *hesed* delivers us from punishment. It says: (Psalms 41:2): "Happy is he that considers the poor, God will deliver him in the day of evil."

The Talmud (Ta-anit 24a) explains why the prayers of Ilfa were accepted so quickly. Ilfa (a colleague of Rav Yohanan who lived in Israel about 250 CE) had the beautiful custom of *feeding the hungry.* He used to bring wine for kiddush and havdalah for the people of his poverty-stricken village.

WITH YOUR OWN HANDS

The Talmud (Ta-anit 23b) explains why the prayers of Abba Hilkiyah's wife were accepted before his: She went out of her way to feed the poor herself — *with her own hands.*

Jewish tradition is of the opinion that it is much better for *hesed* to be performed by a person himself rather than delegating it to someone else. Even as the Torah describes Joseph as the second most powerful man in Egypt (and probably the world), it simultaneously mentions (Genesis 42:6) that Joseph was the "mashbir", the sustainer of all the people of the land.

Joseph made sure not to delegate the dispensing of grain to his commanders or servants. Joseph knew that, left in the hand of others, the act of giving out the food to the people who sorely need it might go awry. Perhaps others might not be as compassionate as he wanted. He thus left the tremendous responsibility of dispensing food to tens of thousands of *hungry families* to himself.

There is a Midrash that goes even further. It records the fact that each and every day of the famine, Joseph made sure not to eat even a morsel of food *until the last hungry person was fed.*

Later, when Joseph reveals himself to his brothers, he comforts them with words that sound as if he has been in the habit of saying them throughout the years of the famine. Joseph tells his brothers (Genesis 50:21): "And now, do not be afraid, I myself will sustain you and your children." Then the verse continues, "and he comforted them, and he spoke to their hearts." Joseph knew that people who have physical needs usually have emotional needs as well. They need to be consoled. Someone needs 'to speak to their hearts.' He also knew that this function, as with all *hesed,* should not be delegated to someone else.

The Talmud (Bava Metsiah 86b) asserts that every act of hospitality and *hesed* that Abraham did with his own hands, his descendants were rewarded for. In contrast, for every task that he delegated to his wife, and every time that he told his guests to 'help themselves', his descendants were punished. The sages felt it was very important to do *hesed* ourselves. Only if it is not possible, may we delegate it to others.

THE ANTITHESIS

According to Jewish tradition*, the people of Sodom had actually tortured and killed Lot's first daughter. One version has it that they burned her alive, another that they soaked her in honey and put her on a roof to be attacked by bees.

Why did the people of Sodom want to torture and kill an innocent girl? Because she violated their laws. *She went out and fed a poor man some bread.* She had compassion. She *fed the hungry.* For this, she was executed.

Perhaps it was this absence of compassion that sealed the fate of Sodom. Such a city, lacking *hesed,* and moreover, *opposing* it, could not be allowed to survive.

RABBI YEHEZKEL LANDAU: THE REWARDS OF FEEDING THE HUNGRY

There is a story told about Rabbi Yehezkel Landau, otherwise known as the *Noda Biyehuda.*

One day he was walking in the streets of Prague and he came upon a ten year old non-Jewish boy sitting on the street crying. Rabbi Landau asked the boy what was wrong. The boy told him that his father was a baker. Everyday, the boy would sell rolls and give the money to his stepmother. Today, he had been mugged and his rolls were stolen. Now, his family would have nothing to eat. He was afraid to face his stepmother with the truth.

Without batting an eyelash, Rabbi Landau reached into his pocket and gave the boy the money he would have earned. The boy just sat there, astonished.

Eight years later, Rabbi Landau answered a knock at his door.

A tall young man stood at the door. "I know that your Passover holiday ends on Monday. The non-Jewish bakers in this town have decided that they are going to pay the Jews back for killing Jesus. So, they are going to poison the bread. I am sworn to secrecy. So Rabbi, please don't let your people eat the bread. Do not let anyone know why or they will kill me."

Rabbi Landau looked at the young man incredulously. "Why? Why did you tell me?"

"Do you remember a little boy who sat on the street crying about eight years ago? Do you remember how you helped him? Well, I do. That little boy was me and I'll never forget you. You Jews are compassionate and good and I know that. This is my way of saying 'Thank you!'"

Rabbi Landau issued a decree that there was a mistake in the calendar and the Jews must celebrate another day of Passover and not eat bread yet.

The Prague bakers lost money (they couldn't sell the poisoned bread to anyone else). They complained to the local authorities that this Rabbi Landau had caused them monetary loss. An investigation ensued and the poisoned bread was discovered.

—26—

And Hesed For All

HESED IS PLURAL

The sages (Avot 1:2) tell us: "On three things the world stands: on Torah, on avodah, (service) and on gemilut hasadim (kindness)."

Throughout Jewish texts, acts of kindness are referred to as "gemilut hasidim" which is in the plural.

Perhaps this is to indicate that every act of kindness is, in reality, a two-fold act. As you do something for your neighbor, you are, indeed, doing something for yourself. As Shakespeare wrote in *The Merchant of Venice*, "the quality of mercy....is twice blessed: it blesses him that gives and him that takes."

Another commentary (Avot Al Banim, Avot 1) explains the plural form of the word differently: It is appropriate for all people to do acts of *hesed*. Whether you are rich or poor, old or young, man or woman, you are responsible to do *hesed*. Also, *hesed* should be done with your body (ie. physical acts) and your possessions, for both the living and the deceased. *Hesed* must be for all.

THE STORK

Nachmanides comments on the verses in Leviticus (11:13 and 19) that prohibit the eating of the stork. He states (quoting Hulin 63a), that the Hebrew name for the stork is *Hasidah*, because it acts with kindness, *hesed*, toward its friends. Yet, the birds listed by the Torah in this context were forbidden to eat because *of their cruelty*. Why is the stork among them? Our Sages point out that, although the stork does *hesed* for its friends, it is not kind to *all birds*. Since it does not do *hesed* for "strangers" as well, it is considered "unclean" and grouped into the category of cruel birds. The lesson is clear: *hesed* must be done for *everyone*, not just for our friends.

Proverbs (23:21) states: "We even have to help our enemies when they lack food or water" because, as it says in Malachi (2:10): "Have we not all one father? Has not one God created all of us?"

HESED FOR THE ELDERLY

General George S. Patton once said: "A lot of people die at forty, but they aren't buried until 30 years later".

In 1963, Myriam Mendilow was a highly respected teacher, in her early fifties, living in Jerusalem. Myriam was outraged when she would pass all the beggars, many of them elderly, on the streets of Jerusalem. Then, she would teach in school and hear her students ask her questions about the elderly such as: "Why does my grandmother just sit around?"

Myriam understood that both the children and the adults had a warped perception of what it is to be old. This misconception was tragic. It not only created hostility between the young and the old, it also gave the old people a sense of worthlessness. It robbed them of their self-esteem. Instead of feeling like people who have lived many years, people who have accomplished, who are loved and respected and wise, old people in Jerusalem felt foolish and miserable, many turning to the streets to beg for their daily substance.

Myriam was determined to change all this for both the young

and the old. One day, she walked into the Ministry of Labor and demanded they give her a teacher to teach bookbinding to elderly people.

She then set up a workshop in a small room, in a slum area called Musrara on the old border with Jordan. (This is where most of the old people lived, where rents were so low it was considered a slum).

Then, she went to the streets and prodded the beggars and berated them. She convinced them, one at a time, to join her *bookbinding workshop*. She went to old age homes and took people out of single rooms. These were people who spent the whole day staring out the window waiting for death. And then she put these people to work.

She then turned to the schools and convinced them to allow her Bookbinding Workshop to rebind all the books for the school children at a competitive price. She won the contract.

At this point in her new career, she was called "Hameshuga-at", the crazy woman. She didn't stop moving. She called her workshop *Lifeline*.

Myriam's *Lifeline Project* became very successful. Schools from all over Jerusalem gave her their books to rebind, not out of compassion, but because Lifeline provided the best quality service at the lowest price. The elders were paid a fair salary, *and they were given back their lives.*

She then took her students on tours of the workshop and showed them that old people can be very productive. She taught kids that they must treat the elderly with respect. She taught the elderly that they can feel a sense of self-respect, of self-esteem and self-worth.

Myriam was not satisfied. She expanded Lifeline to include a *ceramics workshop* where the elderly created unique jewelry, pottery, tile painting, leatherwork and ceramic combinations, mezuzot, menorot and other Judaica.

Then she created a *carton-making workshop* that built boxes for commercial businesses. Upstairs, she built a *Metal* Shop and a *Needlework* Shop. The elders design and create beautiful embroidery, crocheting, knitting, toys, sweaters, table clothes and more. In the *Weaving* Workshop the elders made Talitot and other fine items.

Many elderly people had other skills. So Myriam set up a *choir*, a *meals-on-wheels* program that services 200 people a week, a *Shoemaker's* Shop, a *Carpentry* Shop, a *Needlecraft* Shop for the disabled and a retail store she called *The Elder Craftsman* where Lifeline products are sold.

The Elder Craftsman has products which won awards again and again in fairs and exhibitions within Israel and outside the country—and that are now being sold in the U.S.A. At one time, over fifty percent of Lifeline's income came from the store's profits.

By 1988, Lifeline employed almost five hundred elderly people. Lifeline employees do not live on the premises. They come to work every day, as in any other business. It is not an old age home. There is no odor of medicine.

Lifeline employees include elderly people born in Algeria, Morocco, Tunisia, Libya, Iraq, Iran, Egypt, Greece, Italy, the Netherlands, France, England, Germany, Austria, Argentina, South Africa, and the U.S.A. Many are Holocaust survivors. There are Jews, Arab, and Christians all working side-by-side in a spirit of harmony and mutual cooperation.

Myriam Mendilow has taken depressed elderly people who felt despair, hopeless and helpless, and turned them into enthusiastic, happy, energetic, employees, who design and create items of beauty. Most of these people reduce their medication dramatically. They live longer, healthier, and more respectable lives.

Myriam Mendilow, a school teacher with a dream, but without any money, took "half-dead" people whom the world gave up on and gave them a chance to "come back to life." And they did. She has taken thousands of students (both young and old) on tours of the Lifeline facilities and inspired them to rethink their perception of the elderly. She has convinced others throughout the world to create their own versions of Lifeline. Her goal was to make dreamers and visionaries of all her students. More importantly, she wanted people to act on those dreams and visions. She taught the world a lesson about *hesed*, about caring for others and about human dignity. She taught the world that *hesed* should be for all people.

HESED TO THE DEAD
AND COMFORT TO THE MOURNERS

The Torah (Deut. 21:22) commands us: "You shall surely bury him". Jewish tradition urges people to attend funerals.* It is an act of *hesed* that expects no reciprocity — a "hesed shel emet" — the purest and truest kind of *hesed*.

The eulogy is considered an honor to the dead.** Even though it is to help and direct the living (as is the Kaddish), it is still considered *hesed* for the deceased.

Jewish tradition praises people who are sensitive to the feelings of others. It praises us when we love other people and treat them as we would like to be treated. The Talmud exclaims (Mo-ed Katan 25a): "Whoever sheds tears for a good man (having died) obtains forgiveness for all his sins." Another Talmudic dictum (Shabbat 105b) tells us: "If one sheds tears for a good man, God counts them and lays them up in his treasure house." Every tear, then, is important in the eyes of God, as we learn in Psalms (34:19): "God is near to them that are of a broken heart".***

HESED BY REJOICING WITH
THE BRIDE AND GROOM

The Rabbis consider the mitzvah of giving joy to the newlywed couple among the hundreds of Jewish customs that are essentially "*Hesed* Customs."****

Scripture (II Kings 9:36) tells us about the wicked Queen Jezebel, wife of Ahab, who convinced him to kill Navot, an innocent man, and to worship idols. According to Jewish tradition, she was ultimately punished by being devoured by dogs. Yet, when they wanted to bury her, only her skull and heels were found. The Rabbis say that these limbs were left intact because *she used her feet to dance and her head to nod in honor of brides.*

The Talmud (Berachot 6b) tells us, "whoever gladdens the bridegroom is privileged to acquire Torah, and it is considered as if he had sacrificed a thanksgiving offering in the Temple or as if he had rebuilt one of the ruins of Jerusalem."

"You Make a Difference to Me"

One day*, a New York City high school teacher called up each of her senior students, one by one, to the front of the class. She proceeded to tell them how important each of them was to her, and to the class.

Then, she handed each one a blue ribbon that said in gold letters: "*Who I Am Makes A Difference.*" She explained to the class how much she cares about and appreciates each student. This was her "acknowledgment ceremony", her way of showing *kindness to all* her students, regardless of their grades. It was her way of honoring and recognizing and making her students feel good about themselves.

The teacher then gave each student three more ribbons and told them each to hand them out to three people, and report back with the results. This class project would show what impact recognition would have on people.

One student was being counseled by a junior executive of a company. He thanked the man and told him how much he appreciated his help with his career planning. He told him "who you are makes a difference to me". Then he did something very special. He pinned one of his three ribbons on the junior executive's shirt. He gave the man his two remaining ribbons and asked him to help him by acknowledging and recognizing other people, giving them the ribbons and reporting back to him.

The junior executive had a meeting later that day with his boss. After their talk, he told the man (who was known for being grouchy) how much he appreciated him. He thanked him for the job and told him that he sincerely admired his creativity. The boss was very surprised to hear those words of recognition. He was touched. The junior executive took out one of his blue ribbons with the golden inscription of, "Who I Am Makes A Difference" and pinned it on the jacket of his boss.

Then he asked him to could give out the last ribbon. He explained to him about the class project. The boss agreed.

That night, the boss came home and told his fourteen-year old-son that an incredible thing happened to him at work.

He told him about the junior executive, and about how he felt when he put the ribbon on his jacket.

Then he said, "my days are really hectic and when I come home I don't pay a lot of attention to you. Sometimes I scream at you for not getting good enough grades in school and for your bedroom being a mess, but somehow, tonight, I just wanted to sit here and, well, just let you know that you do make a difference to me. Besides your mother, you are the most important person in my life. You're a great kid and I love you!"

The fourteen-year-old boy began to cry. His whole body shook. He just couldn't believe what he was hearing. He had been feeling a lot of anger, a lot of pain. He never heard his father use the words he just used. He looked up at his father and said through his tears, *"I was planning on committing suicide tomorrow, Dad, because I didn't think you loved me. Now I don't need to."*

This is the power of *hesed*. It is the power of acknowledging and recognizing the people around us. How important is it to just stop what we're doing, look around and say "thanks for being here for me". Could words of *hesed*, of loving-kindness and compassion, or thanks and appreciation, boomerang back to us? Can these words *actually save lives*?

The words we use can kill. Yet they can also create happiness, love and even sustain life itself. By "putting ourselves out" we create our own beautiful reality and live our dreams.

This boss almost lost his son forever. One act of *hesed* gave this boy enough confidence to stay alive. One kind word can begin to rebuild a relationship. One kind, loving statement can save a life.

The next chance you get, look around, extend yourself to the people beside you and watch the beautiful, reciprocal, boomeranging results.

LOST AT SEA

A story is told about a small fishing village in long-ago Holland. A fishing boat at sea capsized one night in a major storm. They sent out an SOS, and a team of volunteers launched their rowboat and fought their way through the wild waves. The villagers waited restlessly on the beach.

An hour later, the rescue boat reappeared through the fog and the cheering villagers ran to meet them. The exhausted rescuers fell on the sand and told them that they had to leave one man behind, since room ran out on their boat. They needed another volunteer to go after the lone survivor who was about to drown at sea.

A sixteen year old boy named Hans stepped forward, "I'll go." His mother grabbed him and pleaded, "you can't go. Your father died in a shipwreck ten years ago and your older brother, Paul, has been lost at sea for three weeks. Hans, you're all I have left."

Hans replied: "Please let me go. If every volunteer said 'let someone else go', no one would help anyone else." His mother gave him a kiss and let him go. Hans disappeared into the stormy night, as his mother cried from fear.

After an hour, the rescue boat appeared out of the fog and wind with Hans standing up in the bow. Hans couldn't contain himself.

He called out "MOM! WE FOUND THE LOST MAN. IT'S
MY OLDER BROTHER PAUL! MOM, I SAVED PAUL!"
We should do *hesed* without regard for whom it might help.
But, sometimes, it might "boomerang back" and actually help some-
one we love.

SHOULD I GET INVOLVED?
A man was walking down a dimly lit street when he suddenly
heard muffled screams coming from behind some bushes. The man
slowed down to listen, and almost panicked when he heard the
heavy grunting, the frantic scuffling, the tearing of fabric. He realized that he was hearing the unmistakeable sounds of a struggle: a
woman was obviously being attacked only a few yards away.

Here is how he described what he was thinking. *"Should I
get involved? I was frightened for my own safety, and cursed myself for having suddenly decided to take a new route home that
night. What if I became another statistic? Shouldn't I just run to
the nearest phone and call the police?"*

The woman's cries grew weaker. He knew he had to act
fast, but he couldn't decide if he had the courage to take action.
Finally he resolved to risk his life and help the woman. *"I am
not a brave man, nor am I athletic. I don't know where I found
the moral courage and physical strength - but once I had finally
resolved to help the girl, I became strangely transformed. I ran
behind the bushes and pulled the assailant off the woman. Grap-
pling, we fell to the ground, where we wrestled for a few minutes until the attacker jumped up and escaped. Panting hard, I
scrambled upright and approached the girl, who was crouched
behind a tree, sobbing. In the darkness, I could barely see her
outline, but I could certainly sense her trembling shock.*

*"Not wanting to frighten her further, I at first spoke to her
from a distance. "It's OK," I said soothingly. "The man ran away.
You're safe now."*

"There was a long pause and then I heard her words, uttered in wonder, in amazement.
"Dad, is that you?"
*And then, from behind the tree, stepped my youngest daughter, Katherine."**

JUST ONE LIFE

The following are excerpts from speeches I have given about an organization called *Just One Life*. My good friends, Rabbi Martin Katz, the Executive Vice President, and Jack Forgash, Founder and Chairman, operate *Just One Life* and they have allowed me to raise funds and speak publicly for them. No modern book on *hesed* can be complete without a description of organizations such as *Just One Life*, that enrich and enhance the lives of others on a daily basis.

Friday, April 19, 1991. A young couple, I'll call them Joseph and Mazal, were living in Jerusalem with their four year old son. Joseph lost his job and hadn't worked in months. After repeated attempts to find work, he was starting to lose hope. Teaching in school during the day and babysitting at night to help out, Mazal stood by her husband's side. But they just couldn't make ends meet. Joseph was overwhelmed by his debt, and was gradually losing his self esteem. A once somewhat successful photographer, he now felt like a total failure. To make matters worse, he had to serve in Israeli army reserve duty. He was leaving his family on Monday and would have to be away for three weeks.

It was a cold, wet, rainy Friday morning in Jerusalem when this little family was evicted from their apartment and thrown out on the street. Joseph held his young wife close to him. She cried to him. "What are we going to do now?" Joseph had nothing to say. "Where is our little boy going to sleep tonight? What is going to happen to us?"

She turned to him again and whispered, "I didn't want to upset you Joseph, I love you so much, but I need to tell you — *I'm expecting a baby!*"

Joseph was speechless.

Years ago, when Mazal told him these words for the first time, he was overjoyed. Now, the thought of another child *felt like a nightmare.* With no one to turn to and no one to call, they decided to knock on the door of a neighbor. The Jewish neighbor took the small family into his tiny, cramped apartment so they would not have to be on the street for Shabbat.

On Sunday, a friend suggested they call an organization called, *Just One Life.* Within hours, a *Just One Life* volunteer met with Joseph and Mazal. "We love our children," Mazal said. "Our baby is the joy of our lives. Yet we are desperate," she said. "We think we have decided to have an abortion, but we are very upset about it. Can you help us?"

Just One Life provided immediate funds to support the family. *Just One Life* had a special worker help them cope with their fear. *Just One Life* obtained government aid for them. They set them up with an apartment of their own.

Within two months, through its connections, *Just One Life* found Joseph a job. The counseling and emotional support and financial aid continued through Mazal's pregnancy.

Just One Life volunteers at her side, Mazal gave birth to a beautiful baby girl. Joseph now feels his family has a second chance. Thanks to *Just One Life,* their nightmare turned into a dream. Thanks to *Just One Life,* a young Jewish girl is now alive.

One of the most famous passages in the Torah occurs right in the beginning (Genesis 4:9-10): "And the Lord said to Kayin, 'where is Hevel your brother?' And he said, 'I don't know. Am I my brother's keeper?'"

The next verse is much less well-known, but, to me, one of the most powerful statements in the Bible. *"And He (God) said: 'What did you do? The voice of your brother's blood cries out to me from the ground!'"*

The Talmud (Sanhedrin 37a) explains why the witnesses at capital punishment cases must be admonished and thoroughly investigated. If an innocent man is put to death, his blood and the blood of his descendants, are the witness' responsibility. In the words of the Mishnah, "his (the innocent defendant's) blood and the blood of his descendants are dependent on him (the witness) until the end of the world. As we find with Kayin who murdered Hevel his brother, as it says, 'The blood(s) of your brother is crying out to me from the ground.' It doesn't say 'blood' (in singular form) but 'bloods' (in the plural). (This is to teach us that) his blood and *the blood of his descendants...*"

The Mishnah continues: "Therefore, man was created singly, to teach us that anyone who destroys a single soul from Israel *is as if he destroyed an entire world*, and anyone who saves *just one life* from Israel is regarded by scripture *as if he saved an entire world.*"

When we are faced with the opportunity to save a life, we must remember that every life is a world in and of itself. The voice of the blood of our brothers is crying out to us from the ground. The cries of pain, of unnecessary suffering and injustice are all around us, if we listen closely. Will we respond as Kayin did, "am I my brother's keeper?" Or will we respond with compassion and with action?

This year there will be almost 30,000 abortions in Israel. Since 1948, more than *half a million* Jewish children's lives were aborted. One of every four women in Israel aborts her child. Seventy five percent of those aborting are healthy, married women with children who *just can't afford to have a baby.*

Since 1988, *Just One Life* has given women a choice and *has saved* over 1,700 lives. That is, over 1,700 times a Jewish woman was able to say: "I know that without *Just One Life*, my baby would not have been born. They saved my baby."

I recently spoke to a *Just One Life* client, a Sephardic woman named Miriam. She was also once in a desperate situation. Yet, in

November she gave birth to two healthy twin girls. Dr. Mel Shay who is a *Just One Life* board member delivered Miriam's children. I spoke with her for a few minutes. She told me, "I am embarrassed that I have nothing I can return for their kindness. There are no words for me to thank *Just One Life*. These are beautiful, sincere people who helped my family in every way. They took care of everything for me. But most of all, they gave me hope."

"I was about to make a serious mistake," she confided in me. "Now I just look at my two babies and say, 'what would I have done if Just One Life hadn't been there for me?' Thank God for these people."

Unfortunately, there are so many worthy causes to donate to. There are so many *hesed* organizations and projects. Yet, how many causes do we know that take life about to be killed and save it? We lost one and a half million little innocent children in the holocaust. How many more can we afford to lose?

When a mature, healthy woman decides to end the tiny life that is just beginning inside her, before it has a chance, it is a horrible tragedy. When this woman really wants her baby and the only thing standing between life and death is money, what should our response be?

Just One Life turns nightmares into dreams. They turn misery into joy. *They literally turn death into life.*

—27—

Hesed by All People

HESED BY CHILDREN

Dr. Bernie Siegel, in his *Peace, Love and Healing* writes, "...I had a similar experience with a child. He was a beautiful young boy of two whom I had operated on. But he was now in the hospital to die; active therapy had been stopped. One day he said to his mother, 'I'm going to be a little bird soon and fly off. I wish you can come with me, but you can't', and over the weeks he continued to prepare his parents for his departure.

"Because I had been his surgeon I continued to visit him regularly, although there was no longer anything I could do for him as a physician. One morning when I went in, instead of the usual request for an ice pop from the refrigerator or some other errand I could run for him, he greeted me by pointing to a chair by his bed, indicating that I was to sit down and join him. He then had his mother put on a videocassette of the Muppets which we watched together for a few minutes. Soon I told him that I had to go, and he did something he had never done before: He pointed at his cheeks, meaning for me to kiss him on both sides. Which I did. I had never been given that privilege before, and when I left the room I felt highly honored by what he had allowed me to do so much so that it didn't occur to me until later that he had been saying good-bye. Fifteen minutes after I kissed him, he died."

Was this two year old boy thanking Dr. Siegel? Can it be that in some special, magical way this baby wanted to "give back" some of the love and kindness that Dr. Siegel gave to him? Can it be that Dr. Siegel's *hesed* would not go unnoticed even by a little boy on his death bed?

When I read this story I cried. Life is so short. There is no time for anger or intolerance. There is no time for greed. Our lives must be centered around love. This little boy taught me a lesson about the power of kindness, of compassion, of *hesed*. Just reading this story helped enrich my life.

"GIVE"

The following essay was written by Anne Frank, age twelve, in March, 1944— a few weeks before she was killed by the Nazis.

'Give'

"...We can start now, start slowly changing the world!
How lovely that everyone, great and small, can make their con-
tribution toward introducing justice straight-away!
Give of yourself, give as much as you can!
And you can always, always give something, even if it is only
kindness!
Give, give again and again, don't lose courage, keep it up and
go on giving!
No one has become poor from giving.
There is plenty of room for everyone in the world, enough
money, riches and beauty for all to share!

God has made enough for everyone!
Let us all begin then by sharing it fairly."

HESED BY PRISONERS

The Missouri Eastern Correctional Center is a state prison for convicted felons of serious crimes including armed robbery and first degree murder.

In February, 1988, a prisoner at this jail saw an article in *Parade Magazine* about Kimberly Martin, a ten-year-old girl with Leukemia. Kimberly's family couldn't afford to pay for her medical treatment and doctors gave this sweet little girl only a few days to live.

The prisoner was touched by the article. So he went around raising money from his fellow inmates to help Kimberly Martin. Within a few days the prisoners sent $25,580.27 to the Martin family to help pay for anything that could help keep her alive.

Kimberly went to the prison to thank them in person. The men continued to help her and she continued to visit, spending hours together playing ball and talking. Her birthday was declared by the men to be "Kimberly Martin Day".

Kimberly made many new friends. The prisoners saved her life. These convicted felons taught the world that people should never be labeled. A person can commit a terrible crime, but he can also do an act of altruism. "Kimberly Martin Day" teaches us never to write off anyone. We all have a chance to make a difference in the lives of others. Nothing can stop honest *hesed*. *Hesed* is for all. And, it can be done *by* all.

Epilogue

WALKING IN HIS WAYS

Epilogue

WALKING IN HIS WAYS

The Torah teaches us that man was created in God's image.
This obviously does not mean a physical image. God's image is
the divine spark of spirituality that each human being is blessed
with. The spark gives man the potential for unlimited spiritual and
creative success. This "divine image" separates man from beast. It is
the essential reason that man is the only animal in the world that
gets ashamed. When a human being makes a mistake he might feel
embarrassed, regretful.

When you look at the face of another human being, you are
looking into the eyes of divine spirit. When you help or connect
with the another person, *you are connecting yourself* with God.

The Mishnah (Avot 3:18) declares: "He (Rabbi Akiva) used
to say: Beloved is man, for he was created in the image of God."

All men were created in God's image. All men are brothers,
partners in the work of creation. Doing acts of *hesed* further unites
and promotes this spirituality in the world. To hurt another human

being is, in some way, to hurt the divine spark, the divine soul. It is to deplete the spirituality in the world.

The prophet, Malachi, put it very simply (2:10): "Have we not all one father? Has not one God created all of us?"

GOD'S IMAGE

Man was created in the image of God. The image of God can best be understood by reading how God describes himself in the Torah:

When God first appears to Moshe at the burning bush (Exodus 3:7-9), He gives Moshe very important information about His "image": "I have indeed seen the suffering of my people in Egypt. I have heard how they cry and I am aware of their pain. I have come down to rescue them... Right now, the cry of the Israelites is coming to me..."

God chose to first describe himself to Moshe as the God who hears and responds to the suffering of innocent human beings.

Later (Exodus 4:6-7), God again gives Moshe a full description of his thirteen most important attributes. He tells Moshe that if the Jewish people want to evoke his mercy, they should recite these thirteen attributes:

"The Lord! The Lord! A God compassionate and gracious, slow to anger, rich in steadfast kindness, extending kindness to the thousandth generation, forgetting iniquity, transgression and sin..."

Notice that in describing himself, God does not say that He is omnipotent or omniscient, nor does He remind Moshe that He created the world or that He is timeless or infinite. God defines the attributes that are most meaningful to humans. Jewish tradition (see Rambam et al) describes these attributes as "attributes of action". These attributes are *attributes of hesed.*

• Jewish tradition teaches us that God's foremost concern is *hesed.* The prophet, Hosea (6:6) quotes God: "Because *hesed* I wanted and not sacrifice."

•The Torah describes to us the creation of Woman (Genesis 2:22): "...and the rib which God had taken from the man, He made into a woman." The Sages (Berachot 61a) went so far as to say: "This teaches that God braided Eve's hair." Our Rabbis wanted us to imagine God as a loving parent, taking the time to braid Eve's hair. Then, when the Torah tells us to walk in God's ways, we know what to do, how to act. We can imagine that emulating God might include being *patient* and *forgiving*.

•Again and again in the Bible (see Psalms 78:38, Exodus 33:19, Deuteronomy 8:18) God is depicted as being "full of compassion, forgiving of iniquity and a God who does not destroy".

•Being created in the image of God obligates us to walk in God's ways. The Torah reminds us no less than eight separate times that we must emulate God and walk in His ways. (See Deuteronomy 8:6; 10:12; 11:22; 13:5; 19:9; 26:17; 28:9; 30:16)

•The Torah states: (Exodus 15:2): "This is my God, and I will glorify Him. Abba Shaul (Shabbat 133b) commented on this verse: "Emulate him. Just as God is compassionate and merciful, so too, you should be compassionate and merciful".*

•The Talmud** explains further:

"What is the meaning of (Deut. 13:5): "You shall walk after Hashem, your God"?... The meaning is that one should follow the attributes of the holy, One blessed be He.

As He clothed the naked (see Genesis 3:21 — 'and God made for Adam and for his wife coats of skin and clothed them'), so you clothe the naked.

As He visited the sick (see Genesis 18:1 — 'and God appeared to him by the oaks of Mamre') so you should visit the sick.

As He comforted the mourners (see Genesis 25:11 — 'and it came to pass, after the death of Abraham that God blessed Isaac his son') so you should comfort the mourners.

*As He buried the dead (See Deuteronomy 34:6 — 'and He buried him in the valley') so should you bury the dead. ***

GOD "CRIES" WHEN WE SUFFER

Rabbi Meir declared (Sanhedrin 46a): "At the time that a person suffers (for his sins), how does God express His anguish (so to speak) for the suffering of that person? God says, 'I am burdened... I am burdened...'"

In other words, God is "troubled" when human beings suffer.

Maimonides comments (commentary to the mishnah, Sanhedrin 46a):

"If God is saddened by the suffering of a convicted felon (or a wicked evildoer), how much more so, then, is God pained by the death of an innocent person!"

The point is clear: God is saddened, so to speak, when people are in pain. How can we expect to emulate God, while we ignore the suffering of others? No. To emulate God is to feel for others' pain, to be compassionate and sensitive to the feelings of other human beings, (no matter who they are or how evil you might think they are). Furthermore, it is to stand up and speak out against cruelty and injustice.

THE MAN OF HESED

Perhaps the best way to understand how to emulate God and walk in his ways is to emulate the only person described in the Torah as having accomplished this.

Abraham, our forefather, was the only biblical personality who deserved perhaps the highest and most prestigious compliment in history. The Torah tells us that Abraham walked in the *ways of God* (Genesis 18:19): "He would instruct his children and his household after him to keep the ways of God, to do righteousness and justice."

What is it that Abraham did to earn him this great compliment? Abraham understood and practiced the correct *blend* of *hesed*. To be sure, Jewish tradition actually calls Abraham "ish *hesed*", "man of *hesed*" (or "the *hesed* man"!). Abraham knew when it was time to be sympathetic and kind, and he also knew when it was time to stand up and speak out.

When three travelers passed his tent, he showed his unconditional hospitality as he ran out to greet them, comfort them, and feed them (Genesis 18). He identified with the suffering of others and responded constructively with immediate action. When his nephew, Lot, was held captive, he went after the aggressors and saved Lot.

When he heard that the evil city of Sodom was to be destroyed, he stood up and spoke out. He pleaded with God to spare the innocent (Genesis 18).

When he learned that King Avimelech's wives were stricken with infertility, he responded with empathy. He cried out to God and prayed for their health and relief (Genesis 20).

When his wife, Sarah, died, he eulogized her. But his grieving did not stop him from finding a suitable burial place (Genesis 23).

Having exemplified and personified the meaning of true *hesed*, Abraham was described as having walked in God's way. He is also the only person to whom God refers as "my beloved". If we want to fulfill our divine purpose as being created in the image of God; if we want to walk in God's ways; we need to look no further than Abraham.

A GOD WHO CARES

A well known Psalm (chapter 146) describes God through His actions : "He makes the heaven and earth, the sea and all that is in them... He keeps His promise faithfully and forever. He performs justice for the oppressed. He gives bread to the hungry. God releases the imprisoned. God gives sight to the blind. God straightens the bent. God loves the righteous. God protects strangers. He encourages the orphan and widow..."

God is not only our all-powerful, omnipotent Creator. He is a God who cares about and stands up for the suffering of the innocent. He stands up against cruelty and oppression. He keeps His promises and protects the less fortunate.

In the Shabbat morning prayer, Jews turn to God and say, "You save the poor man from the one stronger than he and the poor and needy from one who would rob him. You hear the cry of the impoverished. You are attentive to the scream of the weak; and You give salvation."

The prophet Jeremiah (9:12) declares: "Thus says the Lord, 'the wise man should not glory in his wisdom, nor should a mighty man glory in his might, nor should a wealthy man glory in his riches. But let him that glories, glory in this: that he understands and knows me, that I am the Lord who does *hesed*, justice and righteousness in the world. For in these things (*hesed*, justice, righteousness) I delight', says the Lord."

Perhaps the prophet is teaching us an important lesson about priorities. All a man's wisdom, all his might, all his wealth, accounts to nothing in the eyes of God. These blessings are means to an end. To the person who truly wants to understand and know God, they are to be used to pursue *hesed* (as well as justice and righteousness). Our mission in life is to use the blessings and skills that we have to do *hesed*.

We human beings, by acting as God does, with mercy and compassion, enrich our lives and live our spiritual purpose. It is not enough to be creative and strong. Man must rise above his animal-nature and emulate the ways of God: The ways of *hesed*, of empathy, the way of standing up and speaking out. *The choice is his. It is ours.*

Appendix

Hesed and the Jewish Holidays

—*28*—

Hesed and the Jewish Holidays

J ewish holidays offer us opportunities for rest and renewal. They provide us with quality time with ourselves, our families and our communities. The customs and celebrations of Jewish holidays were designed to add meaning and purpose to our lives.

The pressures of the fast-paced, work-oriented society in which we live have led to less time for relationships, for family, for rest and for *hesed*. Jewish holidays provide a temporary respite from our often monotonous, everyday life. They give us a time to catch our breath, to separate ourselves from the material focus of the year and to focus instead on introspective reflection, self-transformation and support of others.

Jewish holidays offer sanctuaries in time, safe havens in which we have support and encouragement to confront ourselves and the challenges of daily activities. The holidays give us the opportunity to reflect on who we are so that we may become more of who we may be. They provide a framework that can nourish and rejuvenate.

On Jewish holidays, our awareness of what we do, think and

feel is heightened. We are surrounded with opportunities for compassion and connection. We can passively sit back and let the holidays come and go, or just "happen to us". Or, we can become more active and "make the holidays happen". We can become engrossed in the holidays to the point where it they have lasting positive effects on the quality of our lives.

Each year, we celebrate the same holidays. We are faced with the same themes, read the same readings and prayers and practice the same customs and rituals. However, we are not the same. We see with different eyes and hear with different ears. Each holiday has the potential to connect us back to our core, to who we are as people. Each holiday can help clarify our path and our purpose, our views and our values, our lives and our love. It is through the practice of *hesed* that Jewish holidays can take on new meaning. It is through our outward focus, our selfless concern for others that Jewish holidays can transform us and enrich our lives forever.

We should not write about Jewish holidays without mentioning Shabbat. Shabbat is the queen mother of all Jewish holidays. Every Jewish holiday has some aspect of the Shabbat. During Passover we can relive its aspects of freedom. On Shavuot we celebrate the aspect of Torah and Divine laws. On Succot we detach from our mundane physical shelters and take refuge in God's protection. On the High Holidays we declare the sovereignty of God as our king and master of the world. Purim and Hanukah, too, commemorate God saving us from oppression and freeing us to serve him.

The Shabbat and the Jewish holidays can be experienced fully by delving into their essence and hearing their lessons. Yet, when we experience them with compassion for others, they can transform us, and we, by our reflections and our actions, can transform the world around us.

Every Jewish holiday has powerful themes and messages which we can use for our everyday life. We can experience the holiday, absorb its lesson, and then incorporate it into our habits, our attitudes, our very thinking.

For example, when we experience Yom Kippur deeply, then its message, the message of repentance and self-improvement can and should become part of our personality. Every day of the year has a little bit of "Yom Kippurness" within it. (i.e. everyday I can reflect on who I am and improve myself).

If every holiday has a lesson that can enrich our lives, it also provides us with unique and exciting opportunities for *hesed*. Every Jewish holiday is a time to greet people with a smile. It is a time to take notice of others and to try to help them in any way you can. Holidays afford us the opportunity to speak to friends and relatives in a kind and empathetic way. We can give charity, invite people to join us for holiday meals and spend time visiting the sick or the lonely.

In this section, we will briefly list the Jewish holidays, their themes and the special holiday readings, prayers and customs. We will also provide a random list of opportunities to enhance the holidays (and enrich our lives) with *hesed*.

—29—

Days of Awe

R osh Hashanah and Yom Kippur are often known as the *Days of Awe* or the *High Holidays*. These are days of repentance, of reflection, introspection and self-improvement. We pray for God's mercy, for his compassion, as we accept His judgment of our actions.

"Is This the Fast that I have Chosen?"

On the day that the Jewish people spend praying and fasting, on the holiest day of our year, when Jewish people beg God for mercy, our *haftarah* (reading from the prophets) is from the book of Isaiah. It reminds us of what our purpose in life should be. As follows:

> *...Day after day they seek me and desire to know my ways*
> *As if they are a nation that does righteousness...*
> *They desire that G-d should be near (them)*

"Why have we fasted" they say, and "you don't see?"
"Why do we afflict our souls and you don't notice?..."

... your fast is (replete) with quarrel, strife
and fighting with the fist of wickedness
You don't fast to make your voice heard on high

Is this the fast that I have chosen?
A day for a man to afflict his soul?...

Will you (really) call this a fast?
(Is this) an acceptable day to the Lord?

Is not the fast that I have chosen (as follows):
(1) to loosen the chains of wickedness
(2) to undo the bands of the yoke
(3) to let the oppressed go free
(4) and break all yokes of tyranny?
(5) to share your bread with the hungry
(6) to take the homeless poor into your home
(7) to clothe the naked wherever you see them
(8) and to never turn away from another human being
      (lit: "Your own flesh")?...
.... (9)   if you take away all tyranny from your midst
(10)   finger-pointing
(11)   and speaking iniquity (gossip)
(12)   if you draw out your soul to the hungry
(13)   and satisfy the afflicted soul
          (Isaiah, Chaps 57,58).

ASKING FOR HESED — OR PERFORMING HESED?

Rabbi Yisrael Salanter (1810-1883), was the founder of the musar movement, which emphasized techniques for spiritual, ethical, and character growth. After he served as the head of a yeshivah in Vilna, he founded a musar yeshivah in Kovno, then he moved to Germany and then to France to disseminate Judaism.

Rabbi Salanter, one of the most distinguished Rabbis of the nineteenth century, failed to appear one Yom Kippur eve to chant the sacred *Kal Nidre* Prayer. His congregation became concerned, for it was inconceivable that their saintly Rabbi would be late or absent on this very holy day. They sent out a search party to look for him. After much time, their Rabbi was found on the other side of town, in the barn of a Christian neighbor. On his way to the synagogue, Rabbi Salanter had come upon one of his neighbor's calves, lost and tangled in the brush. Seeing that the animal was in distress, he freed it and led it home through many fields and over many hills.

It is clear that Rabbi Salanter felt that it is more important to *show* compassion than to *ask for* compassion.

Rabbi Yisrael Salanter taught us an important lesson. The holidays are a time when many people are preoccupied with themselves: their hair, their clothing, their seating in the synagogue, their personal prayers. Yet, it is perhaps the most important time to focus instead on others, to seek out opportunities for *hesed* and to act on them.

Preceding Rosh Hashanah, and until Yom Kippur, it is customary to recite the *Selihot* prayers early in the morning. These are beautiful prayers and songs requesting God's mercy before the High Holidays. One day in 1993, during the month of Elul, I woke up at about 5:00 AM to go to the *Selihot* service at the synagogue. I had an important decision to make. My wife needed me to help her with our then three month-old infant, Ezra. Should I leave her, go out to the synagogue and "ask for *hesed*"? Or should I stay home and help her with the baby? Should I ask for *hesed* or practice it? I'm afraid I made the wrong decision.

I remember very vividly the morning of May 5, 1994. It was pouring rain outside. I was sitting in the train station and a blind man was exiting and needed someone to help him down the stairs. People are all rushing *up* the stairs to make the Manhattan-bound train. He asks for help to get *down* as people come up and other people, myself included are in the station, past the token-entry point waiting for one of the people coming up the stairs to help him down. Was anyone *obliged* to help this man? Did someone have to miss his or her train and be late for work, in order to help the poor blind man? How about the people sitting in the station? Does someone have to go out of the station, help him down and then come back in and pay another token (and possibly miss the train?)

What should I have done? What was the right thing to do?

As it happened, another experience of *irony*, I was sitting and writing a lecture about the importance of *hesed*. Instead of putting down my pen and pad and rushing over to this blind man's aid, I felt that I had "more important" things to do. I was preparing to teach a class on the value of showing compassion. As I look back on that rainy day in May, I try to remember that it is much more important to *practice hesed* than it is to write about it, to teach it or to talk about it.

I am sorry to say that in preparing this book there have been numerous times that I had an opportunity to do *hesed*, but instead I elected to continue to write about it. How many evenings could I have helped my wife bathe our children instead of working on this book? I can't even count them. As I sat on the train feverishly writing a chapter on "everyday kindness", I didn't even notice elderly women standing up. Did I stop what I was doing, get up and give them my seat? Did I practice what I preached? I am afraid to say that I did not.

The High Holidays season is a time for introspection and reflection. It is a time to find *hesed* opportunities and *"make hesed happen"*. More importantly, it is a time to come to terms with who we are as people, who we really want to be, and what we have to do to get there. Our High Holiday resolutions must include practicing more of what we believe in, living according to the principles we hold dear.

Our resolutions must include the determination to seek out opportunities for *hesed* *and to act on them.*

"FORGIVE ME"

It is customary on the eves of the High Holidays to forgive anyone who might have harmed you and to ask forgiveness from all those whom you might have harmed. Jewish tradition stresses repeatedly that one cannot begin asking God's forgiveness before he obtains forgiveness from other human beings.

HESED OPPORTUNITIES ON THE DAYS OF AWE

The High Holidays are an opportune time to give charity, to pledge to give charity and to volunteer and give of ourselves, our time, to help others. Many people send flowers, wine or other gifts to their family before the holidays. It is a special time to appreciate your loved ones, a time to thank God for blessing you with them, a time to say "I love you".

The High Holidays can refocus us to the core of our purpose in life: *hesed ve-emet* – kindness and truth. On Rosh Hashanah, as we listen to the shofar blasts, we can make a resolution to increase the *hesed* in our lives. As we say the *tashlich* prayer, we can think about the less fortunate.

"I KNOW HOW THEY FEEL"

One Friday night last summer my eight year old son, Hal, was complaining that we hadn't said *Kiddush* yet. "I'm starving!" he said. "Why can't we eat already? My stomach is empty!"

I took my son into the next room to talk privately and told him that it really was late and that I, too, was very hungry and that we were waiting for guests. Then I asked him to close his eyes and think about how his stomach felt. "It is paining me, dad. I didn't eat anything since lunch," he said. I said, "You and I both feel so hungry. Now let's remember how many poor children feel hungry every night. Let's think about them. Do we know how the homeless people feel when they beg for food? Let's try to feel their pain. Do you feel it? Do you feel how hungry they feel?"

"I feel it dad. I know how they feel," he answered. "Now" I said, "let's remember that inside our dining room is a full table of delicious hot food. Mommy made ten courses tonight for our family and our guests. We will be saying *Kiddush* and eating in just a few minutes. But the homeless and the poor will not. They will have to go to bed feeling as hungry as we feel right now!"

My son Hal opened his eyes and turned to me and said, "Okay dad. I can wait."

This Yom Kippur, as we feel the hunger pains, we can think about the millions of children who feel these pains each and every day, with little hope of eating the way we do. As we fast, we can remember to be compassionate and to empathize with the needy.

Think about who needs your help. Does everyone you know have a place to eat his holiday meals among family or friends? Are there any people you know who need help getting to the synagogue? Can you buy someone a holiday 'mahzor' (prayer book) and make sure that nobody is embarrassed this holiday without a book or place to pray? Can you help someone by teaching him or her how to read or what the prayers mean?

To find opportunities for *hesed*, just look around and notice what people need and then try to provide it. Many times it is just a warm hug or a bouquet of flowers with a note of appreciation.

—*30*—

Hesed and the Shalosh Regalim: Passover, Shavuot and Succot

The three Jewish *regalim* (Passover, Shavuot and Succot) are exciting and joyous times in the Jewish calendar. In all, they not only provide the opportunity to feel closer to God, but to our fellow man as well. The lesson of all three holidays is essentially the same: We are nothing without God's mercy, his compassion, his *hesed.*

On *Passover,* God's mercy led us out of Egypt. On *Shavuot,* his loving care provided us with the Torah. On *Succot,* his compassion protected us from the elements of a desert for forty years. Our role is to emulate God's compassion, to walk in His ways and to spread our love and kindness to everyone we touch.

Rabbi Yoseph Albo was a Fifteenth century philosopher who composed *Sefer Haikarim, The Book of Principles,* which provides a clear and comprehensive outline of Jewish thought. He succeeded in reducing all religious theology to three fundamental principles: God's existence, God's revelation and God's providence. The connection with the holidays is very logical. First you have to believe that God exists. This was proven to the world in Egypt, when God intervened into the natural order and freed the Jewish people. This is *Passover*. Next, during *Shavuot,* we commemorate and realize that God revealed himself to man through the giving of the Torah. He cares about our behavior and gave us a guide for life. Finally, on *Succot*, we rejoice with the realization that God's providence is never-ending. He is hidden, but active in our lives.

The last day of *Passover* (as well as *Succot*) is called *"Atseret"* by the Torah. The word *atseret* can mean *stoppage* as in a stoppage of work. It can also mean a kind of feast. According to Sforno, a well known medieval commentary, *Atseret* means a "gathering", or an "assembly".

Rabbi S.R. Hirsh comments that this 'Atseret' or gathering is, or should be, a *gathering of thoughts.* It should be a day in which people look back on the holiday in retrospect and ask themselves, "what did I take away from this holiday? How have I grown? What did I learn? How have I changed for the better?"

THE BOOK OF RUTH: GOING THE EXTRA MILE

Hesed is not doing what's expected or what's right. It is *lifnim meshurat hadin,* or *going the extra mile.* It is doing *more* than you're obligated to do. We learn this from the book of Ruth, which is customarily read on Shavuot.

First, a summary of the book:

There was a famine in the land of Israel. Elimelech takes his wife, Naomi, and his two sons to the land of Moav. His sons marry Moabite women. Elimelech dies right away. His two sons to die ten years later, childless.

Naomi then turns to her two daughters-in-law and tells them to return to their families and start new lives. She says she has decided to return to Israel and to her people. The first daughter-in-law, Orpah, does leave. Ruth, however, refuses to leave Naomi alone. Naomi (three separate times) urges Ruth to go back and build her life, to start over. Ruth gives her the now famous response: *"Do not insist that I leave you... For wherever you go I will go. And wherever you live I will live. Your people will be my people and your God my God. Where you will die, I will die and there I will be buried. So should God do to me and more, for only death will separate me from you."*

So Naomi returns to Israel with Ruth, her Moabite daughter-in-law. Noami is a penniless widow.

On the first day back, Ruth goes out to glean in the fields with the poor. She "happens" to find herself in the field of a wealthy landowner named Boaz, who "just happens" to be her deceased father-in-law's cousin. Boaz meets Ruth in the field and promises to protect her and feed her. She asks him an obvious question: "Why are you doing this for me? Why have you taken notice of me, seeing that I am a stranger?" (2:10).

Boaz answers her (2:11-12): "I have heard all that you have done for your mother-in-law since the death of your husband, and how you have left your parents and the land of your birth and come to a people who you never knew before (all for her sake). May God repay you for your actions (your altruism) and may your reward be full from God the Lord of Israel under whose wings you have come to take refuge".

Boaz then secretly told his workers to make sure enough corn falls (on purpose) so that Ruth can pick it up and take it home to her mother-in-law.

When Naomi found out what had happened, she told Ruth to meet Boaz privately to discuss with him the opportunity he has to marry her. Boaz tells Ruth that there is a closer relative than he and it would be more respectful, more honest to ask him if he would like to redeem the family name first. If he marries Ruth, he will support Naomi and inherit Elimelech's land.

"Ploni Almoni" is the man found to be the closest relative of Elimelech's family. He first wants to marry Ruth, but when he hears that she is a Moabite convert, he decides to back out. "Lest I harm my own inheritance... I cannot do it" (4:6).

Boaz, in front of the witnesses, declares the purchase of Elimelech's land, and acquires Ruth as his wife "to raise the name of the dead upon his inheritance, that the name of the dead be not cut off from among his brothers..." (4:10)

Ruth conceives and gives birth to Oved, the father of Yishay, the father of David. (4:17)

Now, if we look carefully at the Book of Ruth, we will notice three distinct protagonists or heroes, and four secondary characters. If we delve deeper we will find that the difference between the protagonists and the others is *the extent to which they practice acts of hesed.*

The protagonists practice *hesed.* As follows:

Ruth...

Naomi, the mother-in-law, pleads with Ruth, three distinct times, to leave her. She warns her that there is a stigma. The Jewish people did not marry Moabite women. She would be outcast, alienated and humiliated. She tells her that she is broke. She will live a life of poverty, a life of a beggar. *Yet, Ruth converts to Judaism, walks Naomi back to Judea, takes care of her, and spends her days gleaning the fields to provide for Naomi.* She brings her food every night, leaving Naomi home to spare her the embarrassment of going in the fields to glean with the poor.. She demonstrated her loyalty, her love, her kindness... her *hesed.*

Naomi...

... urges her daughters-in-law to leave her three times for *their own sake.* Though she would have no one to lean on, to support her, she was thinking of them, not herself.

... shows the strength of her values and personality by her silent response to the deaths of her husband and her two young sons.

Boaz...

... gives the poor more than he was required to. He was a man of *charity.* He tells his workers (2:15-16) "Let her glean among the sheaves, don't embarrass her, let some fall on purpose for her and leave them so she can take them and do not rebuke her, intimidate her or touch her."

... marries Ruth. The law of *Yibum* requires the brother of the deceased, childless man, to marry the widow. Boaz was just a *cousin* but he marries Ruth to show *hesed* to Naomi and Mahlon, his dead cousin. He knew that marrying Ruth, even at his late age, would help Naomi and Ruth emerge to live respectable, normal lives.

Unlike the three main characters, the secondary characters stop short of *hesed.* As follows...

Orpah...

... was not obliged to stay with Naomi. Orpah (the name, literally, means "the back of her neck") turns away and leaves.

The young man who worked for Boaz....

He did his job.

He did nothing wrong. He gave his required charity but his business was top priority over the beggars.

He felt that "business is business" and it was more important than the beggars or the homeless on the street.

Ploni Almoni...

... had the chance to marry Ruth.

Yet, "Ploni Almoni" (literally "somebody") decided not to take a chance. Did he have to perform *yibum?* After all, there was that stigma of marrying a Moabite. No. He had no obligation. So he didn't.

The irony is: The reason for the restriction upon the Moabites was that they refused to give the Jewish people bread and water when they left Egypt. They acted without *hesed.* The Torah was trying to teach us a lesson about the importance of *hesed.* So now the man (Ploni) acted without thinking about doing proper *hesed* for a young widow.

Another irony: The reason this man did not want to marry Ruth was to protect the name (and reputation) of his descendants. Ruth goes on to become the great-grandmother of *King David.* The Megillah *would not even tell us who this man was.* By *not* doing *hesed* he lost his opportunity to have a famous name for all time.

Elimelech...
The name implies *Big, Powerful, Leader.* We know there was a famine in the land. He was a wealthy man, a leader. Does he have to stay in Israel and help the people cope? No. Does he stay? No. He leaves.

THE WORD HESED
AS A HIDDEN STRUCTURE FOR RUTH
The word *hesed* appears in the book in three perhaps strategic places:
> In the beginning (1:8).
> In the middle (2:20).
> At the end (3:10).
The word *hesed* creates a structure for the book. Another hint about the underlying message. You must look carefully through or you'll miss it.

THE BOOK OF RUTH
AND THE HESED BOOMERANG

When we read the books of *Ketuvim*, the holy writings, we end many of them by *repeating* a key line in the book that might give us the true underlying message (and theme) of the book.

After reading *Ruth*, we repeat 2:12 (the words of Boaz to Ruth): "May the Lord recompense your deeds and may a full reward be given to you by the Lord God of Israel, under whose wings you have come to take refuge". The underlying message: God repays acts of *hesed*. Kindness and altruism *boomerang* back .

In the words of Rabbi Ze-era:

"This megilah has not come to teach us what is pure or impure, what is allowed or forbidden. Why then was it written? To teach us how great the reward is to the people who practice acts of *hesed*" (Ruth Rabah 2:15).

Rabbi Ze-era knew that people would read *Ruth*, think that it was placed in the canon of the Bible to teach us laws relating to Moabite women converts or laws concerning gifts to the poor or other such ideas. That is precisely why he spelled it out very clearly for us: This book teaches us that acts of *hesed* boomerang back to us.

SEE HOW GOD'S HIDDEN PROVIDENCE
REWARDS ACTS OF HESED

.... Ruth just "happens" to end up in the field of Boaz, her relative. It's called *"mikreh,"* a "coincidence", as if the author is being sarcastic! *"Mikreh!"* i.e. Do you *really think* this was a coincidence? *Coincidence is just God's way of remaining anonymous.*

.... "God *gave her* pregnancy" (4:13). This is the only time that the Bible uses this phrase, which implies God's gift or payback. (Of all the other barren women, Sarah, Rebecca, Rachel, Hannah, never does it say this phrase!)

.... Boaz tells Ruth (2:12): "God should repay you..." As we repeat at the end for emphasis.

.... The Midrash (*Ruth Rabah 7:6*) has God promising the boomerang effect of *hesed*: "Boaz did what he could, Ruth did what she could, Naomi did what she could, so too *I will do My share*".

RUTH AND SHAVUOT

Among the reasons given for reading Ruth on Shavuot: "Because this *megillah* is all *hesed*, and the Torah (which we received on Shavuot) is all *hesed*" (Lekah Tov, on Ruth).

We read the book of Ruth on Shavuot to remind us to use the Torah as a *bridge* to unite each other. It reminds us to use our Torah to *connect to each other* and to go "above and beyond the call of duty" with regard to our relationships with other human beings.

Rabbi Ze-era summarizes it all for us. The book of *Ruth* is *not* coming to tell us laws of Moabites or even of charity (gleaning in the field, leaving parts for strangers, orphans and widows) but to teach us how important the principle of *hesed* is, and how it naturally, mystically, but consistently boomerangs back to us!

HESED OPPORTUNITIES
ON THE SHALOSH REGALIM

The Jewish holidays of Passover, Shavuot and Succot are beautiful times to do *hesed*.

Every Passover, my grandmother, Virginia Sultan *(the woman on the cover of this book)*, makes it her business to deliver bottles of wine and jars of *haroset* to her children and grandchildren.

Is there someone you know who can't afford to buy all the matzah he/she needs? Can you deliver a "holiday package" of groceries to an elderly person? Can you visit the sick before the holidays and make them feel less lonely?

This holiday, can you try to greet everyone you meet with a

warm, sincere smile? Can you pledge money to charity? Can you invite guests for a festive holiday meal? On Passover, the seder is a beautiful opportunity for *hesed*. You can invite guests and listen to your children and talk to them. On Succot, your Succah can be overflowing with joy and songs and love. On Shavuot the family can get together to celebrate the giving of the Torah and the principles of *hesed* and of truth.

— 31 —

Hesed and Tu Bishvat

Tu Bishvat is...
.....the Jewish new year for the fruits and trees.
.....a time of thanks to God for the blessings of agriculture.
.....a time to reflect on the beauty all around us.

READINGS

It is customary to recite Psalm 104 (as well as other Psalms) which indicates how God's concern and care extends to all creatures and illustrates that God created the entire earth as a unity, in ecological balance.

SHEHEHEYANU

On *Tu Bishvat,* Jews take a fruit that they haven't eaten in a year, say the customary blessing of thanks and then add the blessing of *Sheheheyanu* which additionally thanks God for "keeping us alive, enabling us to reach this time." Jews eat fruits and nuts, sing celebrative songs and thank God for all the *hesed* that he bestows upon us.

HESED OPPORTUNITIES ON TU BISHVAT

The Midrash (Ecclesiastes Rabah 7:28) tells a moving story: In the hour that the Holy One, blessed be He, created the first person, He showed him the trees of the Garden of Eden and said to him: "See my works, how fine they are. Now, all that I have created, I created for your benefit. Think about this and do not corrupt or destroy my world. For, if you destroy it, there will be no one to restore it after you."

The message is clear: It is our responsibility to take care of the world. *Tu Bishvat* is a time to reflect on that and do things that show our concern for the ecological health of the environment. If *hesed* can be described as selfless, then wasting and destroying is just the opposite. If we truly care about other people, we can start showing it by taking care of the world we live in, the world that provides us with clean air to breathe, clean water to drink, healthy fruits and grains and vegetables, etc. When we treat the earth and the environment with respect, we are making a statement: We care about the people and the future of people in this world.

The Talmud (Taanit, 23a) expresses its concern for the world and its praise of people who care about it with a fascinating story:

The Sage Honi (known as "the circle maker") was walking along the road when he saw an old man planting a carob tree. Honi asked him, "how many years will it take for this tree to yield fruit?" The man answered that it would take about seventy years. Honi then asked him, "are you so healthy a man that you expect to live that length of time and eat of its fruit?" The man answered, "I found a fruitful world because my ancestors planned for me. So I will do the same for my children."

In 1993, over one thousand six hundred and seventy scientists (including one hundred and four Nobel Laureates) signed a *World scientist warning to humanity.* In the introduction it stated: "Human beings and the natural world are on a collision course. Human activities inflict harsh and often irreversible damage on the environment and critical resources. If not checked, many of our current practices put at serious risk the future that we wish for human society and the plant and animal kingdoms, and may so alter the living world that it will be unable to sustain life in the manner that we know. Fundamental changes are urgent if we are to avoid the collision our present course will bring about...

"We, the undersigned, senior members of the world's scientific community, hereby warn all humanity of what lies ahead. A great change in our stewardship of the Earth and the life on it is required if vast human misery is to be avoided."

The world's ecosystems are being threatened as never before. The messages of Tu Bishvat are crucial: Conserve! Recycle! Make a resolution today to stop polluting the air, the water or the Earth! Be thankful for God's blessings and fulfill your responsibility to take care of the world so that other human beings can be blessed in the future! It is a lesson of compassion, of concern, of care.

It is a lesson of *hesed.*

— 32 —

Hesed and Purim

After the Jewish people left Egypt, the Torah tells us, they were thoroughly exhausted. Almost immediately, they were attacked from behind by a nation known as Amalek.

There was no good reason for Amalek to attack the Jewish people. The Jews were a nation of freed slaves which finally thought it had found peace. Amalek, instead of fighting with the soldiers of Israel, decided to attack the feeble. They started their war by attempting to slaughter the women and children who were bringing up the rear. Amalek was indeed a cruel and evil group.

Thank God, Israel won the war with Amalek, but it was not an easy victory. God declared in the Torah that the Jewish people should never forget Amalek and what they have done. It is a specific commandment of the Torah to remember Amalek.

Why? It is not for the purpose of holding a grudge. It is because of what Amalek did: The cruelty of hurting defenseless women and children for no reason at all, is just untenable.

The evil of Amalek stands in contradistinction to the love and compassion of God; the love and compassion that the Jewish people are commanded to show for all human beings. What Amalek did should remind Jewish people for generations to come, that hurting defenseless and innocent people is a terrible crime. It is evil. It is the antithesis of the Torah's divine morality and it must never be repeated.

It is sad to say, that, some 3200 years after Amalek attacked Israel from behind, people are still persecuting and oppressing each other for no good reason. It is our duty to stand up and speak out against all forms of cruelty and oppression and to remember never to allow cruelty to go unnoticed.

Every year, on the Shabbat before the holiday of Purim, Jewish people read the part of the Torah that reminds them of the cruelty of Amalek. This day is called, "Shabbat Zachor", or the "Sabbath of Remembrance." It is important on this Shabbat for us to reflect on how much God despises cruelty and injustice.

Today, we do not know who is a descendant of the infamous Amalek. Yet, just a few days before the Purim holiday, on "Shabbat Zachor", Jews are reminded that the existence of Amalek in the world must be noticed and defended against.

THE BOOK OF ESTHER: SUMMARY

The Megillah of Esther tells the beautiful story of the event that took place during the reign of King Ahashverosh in the Persian kingdom. The king chooses Esther, a Jewish woman, to replace his wife. Esther was an orphan, brought up by her cousin Mordechai. She kept her family information secret.

During this time, Mordechai overheard two men who plotted to murder the king. He quickly sent word to Esther who told the king. The king's life was saved.

About five years later, Haman, a high-ranking official, sought to wipe out all the Jews from the entire Persian Empire. His main motive: Mordechai refused to bow down to him. He convinced the king to pass a royal edict that was sent out to all the provinces of the kingdom. He cast a lottery and picked the thirteenth day of the lunar month of Adar, for "all Jews, young and old, children and women" to be killed. Haman's exact words to the king were: "There is a certain people scattered abroad and dispersed among the people in all the provinces of your realm. Their laws are different from everyone else's. They do not observe the king's laws. Therefore, it does not benefit to tolerate them. So let it please the king to be recorded that they be destroyed..." (Esther 3:8).

Mordechai then convinced Esther to disclose her nationality and plead with the king to intercede on behalf of the Jewish people. Mordechai warns her: "For if you insist on being silent at a time like this, relief and deliverance will come to the Jews from some other place, while you and your family will perish. And who knows, if it was just for such a time as this that you attained the royal position!" (Esther 4:14).

Esther risks her life by approaching the king without being summoned first. She invites him and Haman for drinks, but does not yet divulge to the king the truth about her people.

One evening, the king has trouble sleeping. He has the royal diary read to him only to discover that years back, Mordechai, the Jew, had saved his life. Yet nothing was done to reward him.

Then, Haman approached the king and was about to ask permission to hang Mordechai in public. Before Haman had a chance to ask, the king asked him what the best way would be for the king to publicly honor a man. Haman imagined that it was he who the king wished to honor, so he gave the king an elaborate plan. Then, to Haman's dismay, the king told him to enact his own plan on Mordechai.

Haman had to reward Mordechai the Jew by dressing him in the king's royal robe and crown, putting him on the king's horse and parading him on horseback throughout the capital city. He had to proclaim before him to all those who witnessed, "this is what is done to the man whom the king wants to honor." Haman is publicly humiliated and Mordechai is shown tremendous honor and gratitude for saving the king's life (Esther 6:11).

Later that morning, the king and Haman come again for drinks with Esther. Esther finally tells the king of Haman's plan to destroy her people. She beseeches the king to spare the lives of the Jews. The king is furious with Haman and orders him killed. He grants Esther and Mordechai the right to send out another edict to allow the Jews to defend themselves (Esther 8:11).

On the very same day that the Jews were supposed to be exterminated, they defended themselves and were victorious. These days became a joyous holiday called "Purim", named after the lottery ("Pur" in Hebrew) that Haman had cast to pick a day to rid the entire Persian kingdom of all Jews. The Jews then accepted upon themselves to commemorate these days with feasts, gifts to the poor, the sending of food packages to their fellow Jews and thanksgiving to God. They shared their joy with their fellow man and with God. They chose to celebrate their victory appropriately with acts of *hesed*.

Even though the name of God is never mentioned in the entire Megillah, throughout the story the reader can notice the hidden hand of God. In our own lives today, we seldom see outright miracles. (When was the last time you saw a sea split?) However, if we look closely, we can notice the hidden hand of God in the seemingly monotonous or mundane events of our everyday lives. It is God who manipulates the events. He is the One Who causes the "coincidences". He sets the stage. We are left to decide if we are ready to notice God's ever present (albeit hidden) providence in our lives.

Just as in the Purim story, we are very often faced with difficult choices. Do we decide to take personal risks and get involved to help other people as Mordechai and Esther did? Do we stand up and speak out against cruelty and injustice? Do we stop to realize why God has put us in the specific positions and situations we are in?

In the Purim story, the Jews were almost exterminated. Their "crime" was: they were different. They had their own set of values.

Mordechai refused to bow down to Haman in the public square. For that crime, all Jewish men, women and children were to be killed.

The lessons for us are many. Do we tolerate other groups who have different values than our own or are we somewhat prejudiced? Perhaps Haman was the first anti-Semite, but he was definitely not the last. Intolerance naturally leads to hatred, which inevitably leads to violence and persecution. What might seem to be a harmless joke or comment, can ultimately lead to cruelty and injustice.

Mordechai understood the balance of *hesed.* He had the *kindness* to raise an orphan (Esther) in his house. Yet he also knew when to stand up and speak out for his people. Mordechai's kindness:

"Every day Mordechai walked in front of the courtyard to find out how Esther was..." (Esther 2:12).

Rabbi Yaakov Bar Aha (Esther Rabah 6:12) quotes God as saying to Mordechai: "You looked after the welfare of just one soul, to know how Esther was doing. You will merit to (lead the Jewish people) *and look after the welfare of the entire nation.*" As it says (Esther 10:3), "*He looked after the good of his people ...*"

The Sages (Bereshit Rabah 30:9) tell us why Mordechai was called "Ish Yehudi". Just like Yehudah (Jacob's son), Mordechai felt the responsibility to save his brothers.

Mordechai motivates Esther with harsh words (Esther 4:12):* "Because if you stay silent at this time..." Mordechai warns her that she must stand up and speak out against the impending destruction of the Jewish people. According to the Midrash (Esther Rabah 8:6), he threatened her: If you do not speak out in defense of your people, you will not be able to speak out in your own defense in the future.

If you have an opportunity to do good in your life, and you refuse to do it, you have no excuse.

The story of Purim, of the successful defense against wanton cruelty and injustice is centered around the decision of Esther and

Mordechai to stand up and speak out on behalf of the Jewish people.

HESED OPPORTUNITIES ON PURIM

Purim is a natural time for *hesed*. The laws of the holiday create a spirit of brotherhood and love. Purim is a time for Jews to unite and celebrate their existence. It is a day to give charity generously, to deliver gifts of (at least two different types of) food to your friends and relatives. Purim is a wonderful time to spend with family members who live too far away from each other to walk. Invite guests to your feast on Purim and celebrate together!

In the synagogue, Purim has an air of unity and excitement. It is a fun holiday. Contrary to popular belief, Purim is not a time to get drunk in a hedonistic, thoughtless way. It is a time to bring people to notice the poor, feed the hungry and spend quality time with your family and friends.

I have a friend who delivers a special book called *Random Acts of Kindness* to all her friends on Purim. Another friend of mine goes out and finds poor people and hands them stacks of money. This year, my wife made big jars of pickles, wrapped them beautifully and hand delivered them to twenty homes. My children go to a Purim party where they can win prizes and have a great time.

Enjoy the day. Teach your children to give and to enjoy the process of giving. Let them learn how to deliver gifts to others and give charity to the poor. Take them to visit a senior-citizen home and give out grape juice or treats. Show your children how much joy you can have in giving and doing acts of *hesed*. Teach your children how Purim became a magical day that can enhance and enrich the quality of our lives, a day that we won't quickly forget; a day that can transform us forever.

—33—

Hesed and Tisha Be-av

HISTORY

Tisha Be-av is the national Jewish day of mourning. We mourn for the destruction of the Jewish Temples and the dispersion of our people.

The following is a list of some of the events that occurred on Tisha Be-av.

(1) 1200 BCE: God decreed that Jews will stay in desert forty years (after the spies returned, and the people complained about what lay ahead).

(2) In 586 BCE: The first Temple was destroyed.

(3) In 70 CE: the second Temple was destroyed.

(4) 135 CE: the great city of "Betar" fell to the Romans and all the Jews were murdered.*

(5) 135 CE: Turanus Rufus, a Roman leader, as a final act of indignity, plowed up the area of the temple and its surroundings, and decreed to kill Rabban Gamliel.

(6) 1492: Spain- The Spanish inquisition by Ferdinand and

Isabella and their chief advisor Torquemada. The Jews
were faced with a choice: convert to Christianity or die.
(7) 1914: (World War I) Germany swept through Europe.
This led to Socialism, Bolshevism, the enlightenment, the
Iron Curtain. As a result of the Bolshevic Revolution, Jewish schools were closed, Jewish communities were poverty-
stricken, Jewish leaders were exiled and Jewish life was
almost entirely destroyed.
(8) 1938: Eichman's laws, "Who is a Jew", the "Nurem-
berg Laws" were decreed, giving rise to the Holocaust.*

MY BELOVED KNOCKS AT THE DOOR

As noted above, the first of the incidents which occurred on
Tisha Be-av took place in the desert. There, after the spies returned
from Canaan, the future Land of Israel, the Jewish people complained about their fate. The Person of *Hesed* does not live a life of
complaints. Rather, he, she, looks for opportunities to take an active role in the world.

After the Holocaust, Rabbi Dr. Joseph Soloveichik wrote an
essay called *Kol Dodi Dophek* , literally: *The Voice Of My Beloved
Knocks.* The title was inspired by the plot of King Solomon's *Song of
Songs.* In the essay, Rabbi Soloveichik discusses the problem of evil,
and of repentance. He also discusses the mission of the Jewish people.

As individuals, he says, each man must convert himself from a
man of *fate* into a man of *destiny.* He must turn a passive an influenced existence, into a life that is *active* and *influential.* His mission
is to turn a life full of compulsion, stress, anxiety, fear, anguish and
confusion into a life of "be fruitful and multiply and replenish the
earth and subdue it" (Genesis 1;28).

The same holds true for the Jewish nation as a whole. It must
go from a passive group of people who were acted upon into a
unified nation of actors that *create their own destiny.*

Kol Dodi Dophek. In the story of *Shir Hashirim (Song of*

Songs), the beloved is knocking on the door. The woman desperately wants her beloved to enter. She desperately wants to open the door yet for some reason she cannot. Instead, her mind tells her, "I just laid down, now I have to get up... now I have to put my robe back on. I now have to put my slippers on..." as she procrastinates. Her beloved still continues to knock and knock until *finally* she gets to the door, but tragically, it is too late. He already left. He's gone. So she runs out to try to find him, in vain. She cries and regrets not opening the door faster. He was knocking and knocking very patiently but she felt somewhat paralyzed. And now, in retrospect, in hindsight, she realizes and mourns her loss.

How many of us hear the knocking at our doors? What and who is knocking? It might be a loved one who needs help, yet we might just make believe the problem doesn't exist. We put him out of our minds and rationalize it away. "It's too difficult. It's not my responsibility. He'll be O.K. without me. He needs to solve his own problems...". But when we finally get to the door it's too late.

How many of us hear the knocking at the door? Perhaps there is an opportunity to enrich someone else's life in some small way, an opportunity for *hesed*. Perhaps an opportunity for love and intimacy is knocking? How many of us *listen for the knocks?* How many of us dash over to the door even with all the barriers and difficulties? How many of us can turn *fate* into *destiny?*

We often feel stressed or frustrated or out of control and under pressure from many different sides. Yet is it possible to listen for God's knocking at the door and then dash to the door and open it and let Him in? Is it possible to be the actor on the stage of life? Is it possible to change our mindset and believe that we're on this earth to *make* our *mark?*

We can make a difference in other people's lives. We can elevate ourselves from objects to subjects.

We just need to open the door when we hear the knocking, to invite opportunity in and dash off with it into the sunset! *Kol Dodi Dophek.*

"I shall pass this way but once;
Any good, therefore, that I can do
or any kindness that I can show to any human being,
Let me do it now.
Let me not defer nor neglect it,
For I shall not pass this way again..."

BASELESS HATRED

Our sages have taught us (Yoma 9a-b) that the First Temple was destroyed because we worshipped foreign gods, committed adultery and murdered.

During the period of the second Temple, however, we studied the Torah and kept the mitzvot. Why, then, was it destroyed? Because of *sin-at hinam*, baseless, causeless hatred. This, says the Talmud, teaches us that causeless hate is equal to murder, incest and idolatry.

BASELESS HATRED IN ACTION

The Talmud (Gittin 55b-56a) tells us that *Akamsa, u'bar kamsa, harub Yerushalayim*: because of a mixup between two men, one named Kamsa, and the other Bar Kamsa, Jerusalem was destroyed.

A certain man had invited his friend Kamsa to his feast. Instead, his attendant brought Bar Kamsa, his enemy. The man found Bar Kamsa at his table and told him, "what are you doing here? Get up and get out". Bar Kamsa quietly turned to the host and told him, "I am already here (don't embarrass me), let me stay and I will pay for whatever I eat and drink." The host responded, "No!" (I won't let you stay!) "I will pay you for half your banquet." The host responded, "No!" "I will pay you for your entire banquet." The host then took Bar Kamsa by the hand, stood him up and ejected him from the banquet, publicly humiliating him. The Rabbis seated at the table witnessed the exchange and did not rebuke the host or try to settle the situation peacefully.

Bar Kamsa then devised a sinister plan to destroy the Temple. He went to the Caesar in Rome and told him that the Jews have rebelled against him. "Send them an animal as a sacrifice in the Temple and see whether they offer it!" Caesar then took him up on his bet. He went and and sent a fine calf with Bar Kamsa back to Jerusalem. Bar Kamsa poked it in the lip (or the eye), causing a blemish in a place where it is considered a blemish for us, but where it is NOT considered a blemish for the Romans. (i.e. for offerings outside the Temple). The animal was thus unfit to be sacrificed in the Temple. The Rabbis contemplated offering it anyway for the sake of peace (with the Roman Government). Then R. Zechariah ben Abkulas (looked over his right shoulder and) said: "They will say that blemished animals can be offered on the Altar!" The Rabbis then considered killing Bar Kamsa so that he would not be able to tell the Caeser that his offering was refused. Yet R. Zechariah again replied, "They (the left wing) will say that for creating a blemish to a consecrated animal, one is put to death!"

As a consequence of this, the Temple was destroyed.

"Rabbi Yohanan said: 'The humility displayed by R. Zechariah destroyed our Temple, burned down our Sanctuary, and exiled us from our land.'"

What got us into trouble? The host didn't hear Bar Kamsa's cry. The Rabbis witnessed what happened and did nothing, twice. The Temple was destroyed because of an incident that must have exemplified what was going on at the time.

Obviously this Bar Kamsa had to be a horrible, vicious, sinister man, a man who could not forget his anger, who would take a long journey to Rome and plot to destroy our people, just for his own personal revenge, to satisfy his own anger. Why would God care about the feelings of such a despicable, cruel person? Perhaps because he is still a person. He was in pain, (before he took revenge), he let out a cry. And NO ONE would hear.

It is as if God said, "I have had enough."

THE LETTER OF THE LAW

The Talmud (Bava Metsia 30b), in another place, gives a seemingly different reason for the destruction of the second Temple.

Rabbi Yohanan said, "Jerusalem was destroyed only because (its inhabitants) decided cases according to Torah law". Should they have instead decided cases according to the law of tyranny? Rather, say the following: Jerusalem was destroyed because they limited their decisions to the letter of the law of the Torah, and did not perform actions that would have gone beyond the letter of the law (lifneem meshurat hadin).

Hesed makes the world go 'round. It is the cement of human society. Without *hesed*, society disintegrates. Standing upon the letter of the law alone *leads to ruin*. Jerusalem's destruction was not retributive punishment. It was a natural *consequence*. A wholly legalistic society, one that does not practice acts of kindness, cannot exist.

The rejection of *hesed*, of "going above and beyond the letter of the law for others", is characterized by some (Pirkei Avot 5:10) as the trait of Sodom! Those who say "what's mine is mine, and what is yours is yours", in many cases would be excellent judges. Yet in situations where there is a need for their help, chances are, these people would refuse. They are thus associated with Sodom. What would happen if everyone felt "what's mine is mine"? What would happen to charity? To mercy? To compassion? Legalistic, uncharitable people who seem to be obsessed with their private concerns and property create barriers between fellow human beings. *These barriers make society crumble.*

The people of Sodom probably respected the law. They probably valued personal property. Yet perhaps, over time, their compassion and concern for others became extinct. Sodom represented a legalistic, uncharitable society, a society where *hesed* didn't exist. In the end, Sodom disintegrated as well.

Perhaps the attitude of standing on legalese allowed for the "baseless and unwarranted hatred toward others" which ultimately led to the destruction of the Jerusalem in 70 CE. Where does hatred start? It starts with intolerance. Intolerance begins with closing my ears, my mind, my heart, to your pain, your needs, your feelings. Why do I do that? Perhaps because I have decided to be strict and follow the letter of the law and not go beyond it.

Hesed, on the other hand, opens us up, it opens our hearts, our veins, our arteries and our minds. It keeps us from hatred. It keeps society functioning.

Nachmanides (Commentary on the Torah, Deut 6:18) tells us that "it is impossible for the Torah to mention all aspects of man's conduct with his neighbors and friends, all the various transactions of societies and countries... so after the Torah mentions many of them, ... it states in a general way that, in all matters, one should do what is good and right. As the Torah tells us, 'And you shall do what is good and right in the eyes on God'. This includes compromising with people and going above and beyond the letter of the law."

The Talmud is replete with instances which encourage people to go above and beyond the letter of the law for other people.

One such case (Bava Metsia 30b) involves Rabbi Yishmael who was an old man and a great Rabbi. As such, he was not obliged to help the porter whom he met on the road. A porter was trying to load some wood on his donkey. The Rabbi wasn't strong enough to help him, (and neither was he obligated to), yet he went above and beyond the letter of the law, and *bought* the wood from him. Then he pronounced the wood as "ownerless", so he wouldn't have to load it. Yet this porter was very clever. Realizing that the wood was now ownerless, he quickly grabbed it and took possession of it for himself. He then tried to load it again. So Rabbi Yishmael *paid him for the wood again*!

Another well-known incident related in the Talmud (Bava Metsia 83a) involved Rabbah Bar Bar Hana, who had a keg of wine.

The porters whom he hired to move the keg not only did not get the job done, but acted negligently and broke the keg. He thus did not owe them their fee, and he then took their coats as payment for the wine. They approached Rav and told him what had transpired. Rav turned to Rabbah Bar Bar Hana and said: "Give them back their coats!" He asked him, "Is that the law"? Rav answered him "Yes! As it is written (Proverbs 2:20) 'in order that you go on the path of good people'." Rav was thus instructing him to go above and beyond the letter of the law.

The porters then turned to Rav and said: "We are poor people and we labored the entire day. We are hungry and we have nothing to eat." Rav turned again to Rabbah Bar Bar Hana and said "Pay them their fee!" Again he asked, "Rav, Is that the law?" The answer was: "Yes. As the verse continues (ibid) 'and keep the ways of righteous people'." Obviously, to Rav, the way of the righteous is the way of *hesed.*

"WHERE ARE YOU?"

On Tisha Be-av we read the book of *Eichah.* Our Sages have mentioned that the letters of the word "eichah" can form a different word: "ayekah", which means "where are you?" God had asked Adam that question, after Adam ate from the tree. Did God not know where Adam was? Perhaps He meant it *morally. "Where do you stand?"* This question is for all of us. Where do we stand on *hesed?* Can we incorporate the lessons of Tisha Be-av into our lives? When our stomachs ache from hunger and we start feeling tired, grouchy, and irritable, we can think about why the Temple was destroyed and how we can transform our lives by enriching the lives of others. Tisha Be-av should not just come and go without affecting us with its lessons. On this day we have an opportunity to increase our love for others, to practice more acts of kindness, more acts of *hesed.*

THE HOLY TEMPLE

The Midrash (on Deut. 33:12) asks an interesting question: Why was the Holy Temple put in the portion of the tribe of Benyamin? The answer: because he was the only brother who was not involved in the sale of Joseph.

The Temple's function was to serve as a place where people can come and pray to God for mercy. God wanted "His house" to be in the portion of those who themselves were merciful. The message is simple: To deserve God's *mercy* we must act *mercifully*.

TWO BROTHERS ON THE HILL

There is a Midrash about two brothers on a hill. One had a wife and children, the other was single. They reaped and split their grain equally. The brother with the wife and children thought to himself, "my poor brother is lonely. He needs the grain more than I do". The single brother thought to himself, "my brother has a wife and kids to support, he needs the grain more than I do". So each night each of them would take stalks of grain and put it by the other's house. In the morning, they would notice that their piles were the same size again. They each thought it was some kind of miracle. One night they bumped into each other, realized what had been happening and embraced. *That is the exact spot where the Holy Temple was built.*

What is the message of this Midrash? Perhaps it is: The place where we can build our temple so we can approach God, should be the place *where compassion and true love was practiced.* Before we approach God to grant us our requests and desires, we first have to *give* to others. Before we ask for God's love, we first have to show that we can love each other.

HESED IS GOD'S FIRST PRIORITY

Imagine if we could know what God's first priority is for

mankind. Well, the Prophet Michah (6:6-8) tells us what God really wants: *"I'll tell you, man, what is good and what does God require of you? To practice justice and fair-play, to love hesed and to walk humbly with your God".*

Notice that the prophet doesn't say "doing *hesed*", but "Loving *hesed*". If we are approached to help someone and we do, we just "did *hesed*". When we go out and *seek* areas in which we might be of assistance, then we show that we "love *hesed*". Michah is saying that God really wants us to be proactive about *hesed*. Just as we would seek out something we love to do, so too we should seek out *hesed* opportunities.

The prophet Hosea (6:6) further describes God's preference: "For I desire kindness and not sacrifice". The Midrash (Yalkut, Hosea) explains: "God declared: 'The kindness you extend to each other is more precious to me than all the sacrifices offered by King Solomon.'" (I Kings, 3:41 states: "Solomon brought a thousand burnt offerings").

The sages (Avot De Rabi Natan 4:5) relate that once Rabbi Yohanan ben Zakkai and Rabbi Yehoshua were leaving Jerusalem and saw the Holy Temple in ruins. Rabbi Yehoshua cried, "woe is to us, for it is destroyed. This was the (only) place for the atonement of our sins." Rabbi Yohanan ben Zakkai comforted him: "My son, do not upset yourself. We have another path to atonement just as effective as the Holy Temple! It is acts of loving kindness. As the verse says (Hosea 6:6): 'Because I desire kindness and not sacrifice.'"

Perhaps the most emphatic statement was offered by the Mishnah (Yerushalmi, Peah 1:1): "Charity and acts of *hesed* are equal in importance to all the rest of the mitzvot of the Torah".

HESED OPPORTUNITIES ON TISHA BE-AV

There are many good opportunities to practice acts of kindness on Tisha Be-av. It is a day to give charity, or to invite people to your home to "break the fast". It is a good day to visit the sick or the lonely. When we integrate the lessons of Tisha Be-av into our lives, we can focus on other people. Is there someone you need to forgive? Is there someone you know who needs a friend? The list goes on and on.

—*34*—

Hesed and Hanukah

The eight days of Hanukah begin on the twenty-fifth day of the month of Kislev. We light the candles of the menorah in commemoration of the Jews' victory over their Greek adversaries, in about the year 165 BCE.

After the Greek ruler, Antiochus, created laws that forbade the study and practice of Judaism, the Jews, led by Judah Macabee and his brothers, revolted and were victorious. The Greek idols that were placed in the sanctuary were removed, the altar was reconsecrated, and Jewish practices were reinstituted.

If God had not shown us his *hesed* by allowing the Jews to win the first war for religious freedom, the war against the Greeks, it is very conceivable that there would be no Jewish people today. As a result of the victory, the kingdom of Israel was restored for more than 200 years, until the destruction of the temple by the Romans in 70 CE. More importantly, Judaism and monotheism stayed alive. The entire period of the Mishnah, the Talmud as well as almost every major world religion (Christianity and Islam are offshoots of Judaism) had a chance to exist.

At the time of Passover the Jews were enslaved. On Purim, we were threatened with annihilation by Haman. During the time of the Macabees, however, the Jews lived in their own land. They were not faced with a physical extermination. But they were face with a spiritual one. The Greeks were not looking to kill all the Jews. They were committed instead to force the Jews to abandon the Torah and become integrated into Greek culture, Greek religion, Greek life. The Greeks sought a melting pot and a unity of all people. They wanted the Jews to forego the Torah and mitzvot, to give up their "chosen-ness" and forget about their mission in life: to be a light among nations.

Determined to erase Judaism and monotheism from the world, the Greeks forbade the Jews from keeping kosher, from studying Torah, from circumcision, from keeping Shabbat and holidays. They broke down the walls of Jerusalem and raised statues of the Greek gods in public squares. They broke into the holy temple, entered the sanctuary and ravaged it, tearing it apart with axes. Then they poured pigs blood over the scrolls of scripture and set them aflame. The Greeks raised a huge statue of Zeus, ordered pigs to be slaughtered on the altar and forced Jews to eat them. Any resistance was met with death. Women who were caught circumcising their newborns were hanged together with their babies in the public square. Syrian troops marched from town to town burning Jewish books, killing Jews who disobeyed. The Greeks were very determined to erase our spirituality; to make us forget what made us unique, what gave our lives meaning.

When the Maccabees regained control of the sanctuary, they rededicated it. This was called *hanukat hamizbeyah*. The name "Hanukah" was derived from that rededication. The word is also the etymological source of the word for education, "hinuch". Hanukah is a time for learning, for education.

JUDAISM'S TRIUMPH AND
CONTRIBUTION TO SOCIETY

Thanks to the miracle and victory of Hanukah, Judaism was able to contribute a great deal to society. Below is a list of just twenty eight of these contributions (in no particular order).

1. *Monotheism.* The belief in one God who is "The last word".
2. *Circumcision.*
3. Washing, and the importance of good *hygiene.*
4. *Compassion for people.* Judaism commands not to stand idly by while your neighbor needs help or is suffering. "Love your friend as you love yourself" is a command of the Torah. Reason alone does not bring man to morality. The ancient Greeks, with all their reason and wisdom would leave deformed and ugly children on mountain tops to die. Greek writers said that the Jews were barbarians for keeping their children alive. The Greeks only kept aesthetically pleasing ones alive. Judaism says all human beings were created in God's image.
5. *Compassion for animals.*
6. *Concern for ecology* (the shemitah year is a good example of this. Jews must leave the land fallow, *they must let it rest.* It is a sin to *waste* time, land, air, resources....).
7. *Emphasis on health* (the body is holy and must be taken care of...).
8. *Respect for parents* (and parenthood).
9. *Discipline* (Judaism introduced a host of mitzvot that are between man and God. There are mitzvot called *hukim,* that could not be a result of rational thinking or basic human logic. Discipline is to keep mitzvot in the face of unbelievable obstacles and odds).
10. *The concept that learning is considered worship!* (Jews, known for millennia as *people of the book,* are commanded

by the Torah to study).

11. *Spirituality* (prayer, meditation, mysticism).

12. *Happiness and joy are not merely positive virtues, but mitzvot.* (Judaism allows Jews to rest and to feast on the Sabbath and Jewish holidays, which make up a full one sixth of the year).

13. *Appreciation.* For example, Judaism demands that we make blessings of thanks before and after we enjoy food.

14. *New concepts of respect* . In the Torah, *women* could inherit land. In the Torah, *slaves* had to be respected as human beings and taken care of like family. In the Torah, even kings had to have respect for others and were responsible for their actions. They had positive commandments to fulfill and they were punishable just as other people were.

15. *It is a positive commandment to have children.*

16. *Laws of war* (even in wartime, Jews had to act decently and ethically).

17. *Bitul Torah — wasting time.* Time is God's most precious gift to us. To squander it, is a sin. It literally means *annulling the Torah.*

18. *The concept of the Yetser Harah: The Bad Inclination*
The Torah introduced the concept of psychological health by stating courageously that bad thoughts and desires are normal.

It taught the world about moral health, that life is a constant "raging" battle with the *Yetser Harah*. Most people believe that nature and people are good, and evil comes from external forces: Racism, sexism, economic inequality etc. The most defining characteristic of the truly religious person is the understanding that life is and should be a raging battle with his nature. The greatest moral progress comes from self-transcendence; from inner restraint.

19. *The concept of Kedushah: Holiness.*
How does a secular person translate this? How does he trans-

late "unholy"? Vulgar? Profane? These words are almost never used. The world seems to be deaf to the proliferation of vulgarity: Lust, sex, greed, foul language, obscene gestures etc. Can some behaviors, while not being immoral still be wrong because they are unholy? The religious Jew says "yes". His life is filled with holiness of (and purity of) time, place, body, language, eyes etc (Good examples would be chastity, modesty etc.).

20. *The concept of Lashon Hara: Gossip and slander.*
The secular world seems to have no concept of this evil. People devote lifetimes and livelihoods to its proliferation (columnists, radio talk show hosts, politicians, comedians etc...).

21. *The mindset of issur and mutar: Prohibited and permitted actions.*
The mindset of a religious Jew is "Can I do this?" Actions, thoughts and speech is either right or wrong. There's no neutral. Life is like a down escalator. If you're not improving, you're going down. Judaism teaches man to have a "halachic mentality", it teaches us to ask ourselves *"but is it permitted?"*.
In the secular world this concept also seems not to exist. There seems to be no moral code that outweighs people's own feelings. When people are asked "why don't you steal (assuming you would not be caught)?" they usually reply "because I feel it's wrong." The Jew can reply "because I believe in a God Who commands me not to". The latter response can lead to true, divine morality. It begins with a mindset of *assur* and *mutar*, what is prohibited and what is permitted.

22. *The concept of Teshuvah: repentance* (admission of guilt, regret of the past, and acceptance of a new beginning).

23. *The concept of daily tahanun (confession): admission of guilt.*

24. *The concept of Mikveh:* Sexual and marital constraint, purity and holiness.

25. The Ten Commandments.
26. The Prophets, The Psalms and other Holy Writings.
27. The laws of justice, morality and charity.
28. The principles of hesed.

There have been many thinkers with a lot to say about Judaism, and the "chosen-ness" of the Jewish people. Let us begin with Mark Twain, and his famous essay, "Concerning the Jews".

"Concerning The Jews"
By Mark Twain

If the statistics are right, the Jews constitute but one percent of the human race. It suggests a nebulous dim puff of star dust lost in the blaze of the Milky Way. Properly, the Jew ought hardly to be heard of; but he is heard of, has always been heard of. He is as prominent on the planet as any other people and his commercial importance is extravagantly out of proportion to the smallness of his bulk. His contributions to the world's list of great names in literature, science, art, music, finance, medicine, and abstruse learning are also way out of proportion to the weakness of his numbers. He has made a marvelous fight in this world, in all the ages; and has done it with his hands tied behind him. He could be vain of himself, and be excused for it. The Egyptian, the Babylonian, and the Persian, rose, filled the planet with sound and splendor, then faded to dream-stuff and passed away; the Greek and the Roman followed and made a vast noise, and they are gone; other peoples have sprung up and held their torch high for a time, but it burned out, and they sit in twilight now, or have vanished. The Jew saw them all, beat them all, and is now what he always was, exhibiting no decadence, no infirmities of age, no weakening of his parts, no slowing of his energies, no dulling of his alert and aggressive mind. All things are mortal but the Jew; all other forces pass, but he remains. What is the secret of his immortality?

There were many others great thinkers who are worthy enough to quote.

• Aristotle's successor at the Lyceum, Theophrastus, called the Jews: *"A nation of philosophers."*

• Numenius, a Syrian philosopher of the second century and a forerunner of the neo-Platonic school, regarded Moses as *"the first and greatest of the philosophers".*

• Christian historian Eusebius (circa 300CE) said of the Jews: *"For of all mankind these (the Jews) were the first and sole people who, from the very first foundation of social life, devoted their thought to rational speculation...".*

• Turning to modern times, Harvard graduate John Adams, the second president of the United States, expressed the conviction of many 18th century American educators: *"The Jews have done more to civilize men than any other nation. They are the most glorious nation that ever inhabited the earth. The Romans and their Empire were but a bauble in comparison to the Jews. They have given religion to three-quarters of the Globe and have influenced the affairs of mankind more, and more happily than any other nation, ancient or modern".*

• British Historian and statesman Thomas B. Macaulay also admired the Jews: *"In the infancy of civilization, when our island was as savage as New Guinea, when letters and arts were still unknown in Athens, when scarcely a thatched hut stood on what was afterwards the site of Rome, this condemned people had their fenced cities and cedar palaces, their splendid temple, ... their schools of sacred learning, their great statesmen and soldiers, their natural philosophers, their historians and poets."*

• Friedrich Neitzsche (wrongly viewed as an anti-Semite) had this to say in *The Joyful Wisdom: "Wherever the Jews have attained to influence, they have taught to analyze more subtly, to argue more acutely, to write more clearly and purely: it has always been their problem to bring people 'to raison.'"*

• Rabbi Abraham Isaac Kook, in his seminal work, Orot, writes: *"Israel alone affirms the undiluted monotheism that enhances our inner character, that motivates the Jewish culture's magnificent resurgence."*

It is no wonder that Hanukah does not have a *seudat mitzvah*, a holiday meal (even though Purim does). The threat of Hanukah was spiritual annihilation. It makes sense that we should celebrate it with lights and special prayers, just as on the holiday of Purim we were physically saved, so we sit down to eat a festive holiday meal and even have a drink!

The Jewish people have a mission and purpose in life. The Torah requires the Jewish people to become a "light among nations". On Hanukah, as the lights on the Menorah sparkle, we should think about what our responsibility it is to fulfill this mission. If not for the events and holiday of Hanukah, there might not have been a Jewish people (or a Christian, or Muslim one either for that matter) today. As we celebrate Hanukah, let us keep in mind what our role is in the world.

OUR MISSION

Before lighting the menorah, we make sure that it is placed in a place where as many people as possible can see it. The special mitzvah of *pirsum hanes* or the publicizing of the miracle; is accomplished when the menorah lights are displayed at the front window of the house so that all who pass by can see them.

The menorah can symbolize our capacity to shine out into the places of darkness. The lights of the menorah remind us of our mission in life: To radiate our kindness and our truth out into the world. *The menorah should remind us of our work and inspire us to rededicate ourselves to our life purpose.*

Each night, as we add a new and additional light, we are reminded that we should take life step by step. We gradually increase the light as we should gradually increase our practice of *hesed.* Each day we can decide to add more *hesed* to our lives. Each day we can grow and improve ourselves over the day before. A former student of mine, *Esther Dayan Arking,* used to say, "life is like a down escalator." This means, unless you are improving yourself, unless you are stepping up, life will pull you down. Life is like a car with only two gears: forward and reverse. If you do not make an effort to go forward, you will reverse.

HESED OPPORTUNITIES ON HANUKAH

Hanukah is a beautiful time for *hesed.* It is a time to exemplify what it means to be Jewish; a time to proudly light the menorah and then to publicly demonstrate *hesed,* kindness and consideration for all human beings. Hanukah is a time to show the world why there is good reason for Jewish survival and Jewish choseness. The Jewish people has brought the world the Torah and will continue to promote compassion and ethics; it will continue to pursue truth and peace.

In many homes, parents buy Hanukah presents for their children and for each other. It is a good time for families to sit together, to tell stories, to sing songs and to talk to each other. Hanukah is a time to rededicate ourselves to our families and to our principles. It is a time to teach our children Torah and instill in them the appreciation and thanks to God for Judaism. In many circles, before Hanukah, people drop off a box of candles and a menorah at the homes of the needy.

Hanukah is an opportune time for charity. It is a time to look around and notice if anyone around you needs any help. Every holiday is a good time for hospitality. Is there someone you know who would like to be invited for a Hanukah meal? Do you know anyone who would enjoy lighting the menorah with your family? Are there sick people or lonely people who would appreciate a visit on Hanukah? I remember having Hanukah parties in the senior citizens center when I was a high school student. We would sing and dance with the elderly and make them feel loved. Hanukah was always a special time of bright lights, of delicious potato pancakes and of *hesed*. It should be a festive time, but also a time for rededication to our principles and our mission in life.

Finally, Hanukah should be a time to stand up and speak out against the injustice and cruelty that we witness. It is a time to do what we can to stop the persecution of religions all over the world. It is a time to protest the imprisonment of people just because of their race or their creed. To truly appreciate the lessons of Hanukah is to fight to make the world free, to fight to make the world a better, more forgiving, more tolerant place. If we close our eyes to the suffering and torture of others, we missed the message of the holiday.

We Jews who have lived through persecution after persecution should remember to feel the pain of others who suffer a similar fate. As of this writing, there are more than twenty seven million people who are registered as "persons of concern" by the office of the United Nations High Commissioner for refugees. These people were forced to flee their homes to escape human rights abuses and armed conflict. There are several million people who are registered by Amnesty International as "prisoners of conscience". These people are being held in prison for *no crime.* They have not used nor advocated violence. Their crimes are only ones of "conscience": political beliefs, ethnic origin, sex, language, or color. These people are being persecuted each and every day. It is our job to find out about these human rights abuses and to do what we can to help stop them. Hanukah is an appropriate time to voice our outrage at these terrible acts, it is a time to sympathize with others who share a fate we Jews had to face again and again for more than two thousand years.

This year, on Hanukah, please let the dual-nature of *hesed* permeate your day. Kindness and compassion can be a major part of the holiday. Standing up and speaking out against apathy and cruelty can also enrich your life and the lives of those around you. It can make the world a better place to live in. It can make Hanukah an unforgettable experience.

Torah Publications Cited in this Book

As you will notice in reading this book, hundreds of Torah sources are quoted. This includes the *Humash* (the five books of the Torah), the *Neviim* (the prophets), the *Ketuvim* (Writings), the Talmud, the Midrash, the Shulhan Aruch, and more. We have spent much effort to cite the sources, usually in parentheses, directly in the text (and at times, when notes are more lengthy, in *For Further Study.*) It is our hope that interested readers will delve further into the Torah sources which interest them, and study the material more deeply.

Editor's Note Regarding Transliteration...

In transliterating Hebrew words into English, we have used a basic Sephardic system. Therefore, the letter ת is transliterated as a *t (Shabbat).* We have chosen to use the letter *h* for the hebrew letter ח *(hesed)* and the letters *ch* for the hebrew letter כ *(beracha).* For ease in reading, we have chosen not to distinguish between an א and an ע, and for the same reason, we have transliterated צ as *ts (mitsvah).* Also, we have avoided using the pronunciation of any single *edah* of Sephardic Jews, and therefore transliterated the hebrew ב as *v (avodah).*

FOR FURTHER STUDY

Introduction
P. 19   *Avot, 1:3, said by Antignos Ish Socho: *Al tihyu ka-avadim hamshameshim et harav al menat lekabel peras.*

Prologue
P. 24   *For a definition of *hesed*, see Rambam's *Guide to the Perplexed*, 3:53.
P. 25   *The Talmud relates (Sotah 9:15) that when Ben Azzai died, "diligent scholars passed from the earth." Also, when scholars of later generations wanted to show their own scholarship, they would say, "behold I am like Ben Azzai" (Kiddushin 20a, Eruvin 29a).
P. 25   **We have explained Ben Azzai's opinion according to the opinion of Korban Ha-edah on Yerushalmi, Nedarim, 9:4.

Chapter 1, The Physical Impact of Hesed
P. 30   *For a discussion of acts of compassion and the way they return to us and even save lives, see "The Symptomology and Management of Active Grief," *American Journal of Psychiatry*, 101 (1944), PP 141-148.
P. 30   **Superjoy*, by Dr. Paul Pearsall. With permission of Doubleday, A Division of Bantam Doubleday Dell.
P. 31   *Dr. Dean Ornish, *Reversing Heart Disease*, 1990, Random House, Inc, 1984, P. 215, with permission.
P. 31   **Ibid.

Chapter 3, Hesed as a Healthy Response to Suffering
P. 36   *Hans Selye, *The Stress of Life*, McGraw Hill, 1978.
P. 42   *Haberman, Clyde *The Story of Nachson Waxman*, reprinted with permission of The New York Times Company, Copyright 1994.

Chapter 4, The Liberating Effect of Giving
P.43   *Irving Bunim, Ethics From Sinai, Vol I, P. 261, on Avot, 3:8.
P. 45-46 *Frankel, Dr. Victor, *Man's Search for Meaning*, with permission of the Publisher, Beacon Press.

Chapter 6, Hesed Is Forever
P. 49   *Based upon *Pirkei de Ribbi Eliezer*, Ch. 34.
P. 50   *Siegel, Bernie, *Peace, Love and Healing*, with permission of the publisher, Harper Collins Publishers, Inc.
P. 51   *Siegel, Bernie, *Peace, Love and Healing*, with permission of the Publisher, Harper Collins Publishers, Inc.

Chapter 7, Are we Giving or Receiving?
P. 58   *For more information about Chai Lifeline's Camp Simcha (which has performed over 37,000 separate social services for children and their families over the past decade and sent almost 1,500 children to Camp Simcha) please write: Chai Lifeline, 48 West 25th Street, New York, NY 10010; (212) 255-1160; Attn: Rabbi Simcha Scholar, Director; Email: Info@Chailifeline.org

Chapter 9, When Will We Wake Up?
P. 71   *These statistics are from *On an Average Day in America*, quoted in *Living, Loving and Learning*, by Bernie Siegel.

Chapter 11, "I Went Back to Bed"
P. 80   *Rosenthal, AM, *The Double Crime*, The New York Times Company, copyright 1996, with permission.

Chapter 12, The Cursed Earth
P. 82   *See the Maharsha on Sanhedrin 37b, and the Artscroll commentary, Mesorah Publications.

Chapter 13, Outrage
P. 84   *Weisel, Elie, *Night*, published by Farrar, Strauss and

Giroux, Inc.

P. 86   *The Elie Wiesel Foundation for Humanity sponsors educational projects, human rights essay contests as well as worldwide conferences on human rights and tolerance. Elie Wiesel has been awarded 73 honorary degrees from Universities in the U.S., Canada, France, Israel, Finland, and Argentina, among others.

Chapter 14, Abraham's Response to the Suffering of Others
P. 94   *Betsah 32b, Yevamot 79a, Ketuvot 8b.
P. 94   **See also Gittin 61a, Rabbi Moses Cordovero, Tomer Devorah, chap. 3.
P. 94   ***Rambam, Mishneh Torah, Hilchot Issurei Bi-ah, 19:17
P. 94   ****Rosenthal, A.M., January 17, 1955, A27 of The New York Times, with permission of the New York Times Company copyright 1997.
P. 95   *Rosenthal, A.M., April 25, 1997, A27, of The New York Times, with permission of The New York Times Company, copyright 1997.

Chapter 15, A Seasoned *Hesed* Professional
P. 100   *Source: Olam Hesed Yibaneh, P. 128.

Chapter 16, Why Moshe?
P. 104   *The Mishnah (Avot 2:6) put it very simply...*and in a place where there are no men, strive to be a man.*

Chapter 17, The Choice is Ours
P. 105   *Mishneh Torah, Laws of Shabbat, 2:3.

Chapter 18, Everyday Kindness
P. 120   *Isaiah the prophet expressed the rewards of *hesed* in a number of different ways:
   32:17: *And the work of charity shall be peace and the effect of charity shall be quietness and confidence forever.*

56:1-2: *Thus says the Lord, 'Keep my judgments and do charity, for my salvation is near to come, and my charity will be revealed. Happy is the man who does this and the man who holds on to this and keeps his hands from doing evil.'*
33:15-16: *He who walks in charity and speaks uprightly...shall dwell on high... i.e. hesed exalts the soul...*

Chapter 19, Taking Notice of Others
P. 128 *For further study on this: Please see the Talmud Yerushalmi. 1:2, and the Pnei Yehoshua on Berachot 9b.
P. 131 *Midrash Tanhuma, Mishpatim.
P. 132 *Buscaglia, Leo Ph.D., *Living, Loving and Learning*, (p. 33) copyright 1982, by Leo F. Buscaglia, with permission of the publisher, Stack, Inc.

Chapter 20 Smile and Watch the World Smile Back
P. 142 *Diamond, Harvey and Marilyn, *Fit for Life*, Warner Books, NY, 1987, P. 19-22.

Chapter 21, *Hesed* with our Speech
P. 150 *See Genesis 40:14, where Joseph asks the *sar hamashkim* (officer of drinks) to intercede for him, and calls it *hesed.*
P. 151 *Pesikta 42:3, Agadat Bereshit 28:1.
P. 152 * Taanit, 23a.
P. 152 **Regarding praying for others, the Hesed Boomerang Principle clearly applies. The Talmud (Bava Kama 92a) declares: "Whoever prays for mercy for his friend, while he himself is in need of the very same thing (that he is praying for his friend to get), will be blessed by being answered first." It cites the book of Job (42:10), when it says that God blessed Job only after he prayed for his friends.
P. 152 ***Bava Batra 9a, 10a and 88b.
P. 154 **Are you Going to Help Me?* from *Chicken Soup for the Soul,* copyright 1983 reprinted with permission of Health communications, Inc, 3001 S.W. 15th Street, Deerfield Beach, FL 33442-8190.

Introduction Part Four

P. 160 *For more on this concept, see page 273 and following.

Chapter 22, Charity

P. 167 *This verse is included in the Sephardic text of the *Birkat Hamazon, Grace After Meals.*

P. 167 **See Rashi on Pesahim 8a.

P. 168 *Pesahim 50b, Berachot 17a and Bava Batra 9a.

P. 168 **Gitin 7a, Ketuvot 67b, Ta-anit 20a

P. 169 * Shulhan Aruch, Yoreh Deah 244:6-13. See also Rambam, Mishneh Torah Hilchot Matanat Laevyonim.

P. 169 **Ketuvot 67b, Kiddushin 67b.

P. 170 *See Sefer Hahinuch Mitsvah 66 and Ketuvot 66b.

P. 174 *See also Devarim Rabah, 33:1.

P. 174 **Bragg, Rick, *She Opened the World for Others and Now the World has Opened for Her,* reprinted with permission of the New York Times Company, copyright 1996.

P. 176 *McCarthy, Oseola, *Simle wisdom For Rich Living,* reprinted with permission of Longstreet Press, Inc.

P. 177 *Bragg, Rick, *She Opened the World for Others and Now the World has Opened for Her,* reprinted with permission of the New York Times Company, copyright 1996.

P. 177 **A closing note on the subject of charity: Rabbi Dostai ben Rabbi Yannai declared in the Talmud (Bava Batra 10a): "Look at the difference between the ways of God, and the ways of man. How does man act? If a person brings a large present to a king, it may be accepted, and it may not be accepted. Even if it is accepted, it is still uncertain as to whether or not the man will be accepted into the king's chamber. Not so by God. If a person gives just a small coin to a pauper, he is deemed worthy to be received by the Divine Presence... "

In fact, the Talmud (Sukkah 49b) attributes Rabbi Elazar ben Pedat with the categorical, unequivocal teaching: "The performance of charity is greater than sacrifices."

Chapter 23, Hospitality
P. 179 *Olam Hesed Yibaneh, P. 153, based on the Maharam Shif, (Ayin, Tet, Taf, I: 132).
P. 182 *Hospitality How- To is based upon Olam Hesed Yibaneh, pp. 143, 214-215, 263-267.
P. 182 **The sages comment (Sotah 38b): A neck had to be broken because of miserliness of spirit.

Chapter 24, Visiting the Sick
P. 195 *Yoreh De-ah 335.
P. 198 *The Les Brown Story is from Hanson, Mark V. and Canfield, Jack, Chicken Soup for the Soul, 2nd Helping, copyright Aprill 1995, reprinted with permission of Health Communications, Inc, 3001 S.W. 15th St., Deerfield Beach, Fl 33442-8190.

Chapter 25, Feeding the Hungry
P. 201 *Genesis Rabah on Gen. 24:17.
P. 211 *Midrash Tanhuma (Kedoshim) notes that one who is condemned to die is delivered from his fate by doing acts of hesed.
P. 213 *Pirkei de Ribbi Eliezer 25, Zohar Vayera 106b.

Chapter 26, And Hesed for All
P. 219 *See Mo-ed Katan 27b, Ketuvot 17a and Shulhan Aruch, Yoreh De-ah, chapter 361.
P. 219 **See Sanhedrin, 46a-47a.
P. 219 ***See Page 236 for more about how God is "anguished" when people suffer.
P. 219 **** See Pirkei De Ribbi Eliezer chapter 16 and Ahavat hesed page 216.
P. 220 *Hanson, Mark V. and Canfield, Jack, "You make a Difference to Me", from Chicken Soup for the Soul, copyright 1993, with permission of Health Communications, Inc., 3201 S.W. 15th St., Deerfield Beach, FL 33442-8190.

P. 224 *This story is from *Small Miracles,* by Yitta Halberstam and Judith Leventhal, copyright 1997, reprinted with permission of the publisher, Adams Media Corp., Adams Publishing.

Epilogue, Walking in His Ways

P. 235 *The book of Psalms (25:10) clearly defines the "ways of God." It states: "All the ways of God are *hesed* and truth."

P. 235 **Sotah 14a, Ketuvot 111b, Midrash Levit. Rabah 25:3.

P. 235 *** The Midrash rewards acts of *hesed with all the blessings promised in the Torah.* When the Torah (Deut. 28:22) says, "and all these blessings shall come upon you and overtake you if you will listen to the voice of God", the Midrash (Tanna Deveh Eliyahu chapter 26) comments: "When will all these blessing come upon you? If you will obey God and walk in His ways, the ways of heaven."

What are the "ways of heaven"? The sages give us three explantions (Tana Deveh Eliyahu, 26):

1) As He is merciful, as He has compassion even on the wicked and receives them when they repent whole heartedly, and as He feeds and sustains all creatures – so shall you be merciful to one another, support one another, be gracious to one another.

2) Another explanation: What are the "ways of heaven"? – He is gracious and gives His bounty as a free gift both to those who know Him and to those who do not. So shall you give free gifts to one another.

3) Yet another explanation: What are the "ways of heaven"? – He dispenses *hesed* in abundance, and inclines His acts toward *hesed*; So shall you favor one another, grant charity to one another and incline toward goodness..."

There are many Midrashim and sayings of our Rabbis (see Genesis Rabah 8:15; Kohelet Rabah 7:7) that provide even more detailed analysis and descriptions of God's ways as the ways of *hesed.*

Chapter 33, Hesed and Tisha Be-av

P. 268 *For more information *on this,* see Rambam, Hilchot Ta-aniyot, 5:3.

P. 269 *Tisha B'av, Mesorah Publications, pp157-159.

About the Author

Jack Doueck is a principal of Stillwater Capital Partners, LLC, a successful money management company. Additionally, Jack currently serves on the Board of Directors of several companies and charitable organizations. He graduated Valedictorian and Summa cum Laude, from Yeshiva University in 1985 and has completed all course work for a Masters degree in Philosophy at the Bernard Revel Graduate School.

For more than a decade, Jack has volunteered for, or spoken on behalf of, numerous charitable organizations, including: Sephardic Bikur Holim, Success Track, Magen David Yeshiva, Bnei Shaare Zion, Young Shaare Zion, The Sephardic Educational Center, Magen David of West Deal, Lenox Hill Hospital, Just One Life, Hatzoloh of Flatbush, The Jerusalem Center For Research, The Sephardic Scholarship Fund, National Children's Leukemia Foundation, Ride For Freedom, Count Me In: For Children with Down's Syndrom, Tzivos Hashem, American Friends of Olam Hachesed and Yeshiva University.

Since 1985, Jack has taught Torah classes in New York and New Jersey on a variety of topics such as Jewish Philosophy, compassion, ethics, leadership, holiday inspiration, prayer, repentance, Bible, Maimonides, and Talmud. He is a regular speaker known to both educate as well as motivate the audience to "make a change". An active member of the Jewish community, Jack has also helped run numerous youth and adult educational seminars for many Jewish organizations.

Jack is currently writing a number of other books including: *A Life of Kindness: A Tribute to Joseph D. Beyda.*

Jack lives in New York with his wife, Jamie, and their four children.

Questions and comments are welcome. Please send all correspondence to:

Jack Doueck
c/o Stillwater Capital Partners LLC
1333 Broadway – Third Floor
New York, New York 10018
Tel. (212) 629-7866 Fax (212)967-7990
Email at JDoueck@erols.com